Prophet Against Prophet

Above all else, the . . . prophet was an adventurer with God, a pioneer blazing trails on as yet unexplored frontiers. Only rarely could the questions confronting him be settled by appeal to well-established precedents. . . . Although he was the heir of a rich past, he used its achievements not as the rule of progress, but as a guide to progress. As servant of the living God, whose lordship embraces the future as well as the past, he appealed all questions to the bar of the Judge to whom no time is a stranger and from whose control no time is exempt. . . . One searches the ancient past in vain for a real parallel. . . . He was truly God's representative of his time and place, for the problems with which he struggled were the monumental, yet practical, problems – political, social, economic, religious – of his own day and circumstances. . . . The great prophet confronts us with the demand to purge ourselves of all purposes that compete with God's in the arena of decision.

C. Everett Tilson, *Decision for Destiny*

Prophet Against Prophet

The Role of the Micaiah Narrative (I Kings 22) in the Development of Early Prophetic Tradition

by

Simon J. De Vries

William B. Eerdmans Publishing Company
Grand Rapids, Michigan

255 Jefferson Ave. SE, Grand Rapids, Mich. 49503

Printed in the United States of America

Library of Congress Catalog in Publication Data

De Vries, Simon John.
Prophet against prophet.

Includes indexes.
1. Prophets. 2. Bible. O.T. 1 Kings XXII—
Criticism, interpretation, etc. 3. Bible.
O.T. Former prophets—Criticism, interpretation,
etc. I. Title.
BS1198.D43 222'.53'06 78-2590
ISBN 0-8028-1743-2

To Everett

Preface

THIS IS NOT THE FIRST BOOK WITH THE TITLE "PROPHET AGAINST Prophet," nor is it the first book to study prophetic conflict. What is different about it is its endeavor to trace this conflict to its roots and demonstrate that this conflict was a cause and no mere symptom of Israel's ultimate breakdown. For the documentary record of that breakdown we turn to the closing chapters of II Kings, where the deuteronomistic historian recounts the sad events that led to the ruin of king, temple, city and nation. We turn also to the classical prophetic collection, specifically to Hosea, Amos, Micah, Isaiah, Zephaniah, Habakkuk, Jeremiah and Ezekiel, where we encounter many grim predictions delivered against king and against people, accompanied here and there by stern denunciations of the "false prophets" who deluded them. These contemporary sources, of unique value in their own right, reveal Israel/Judah *in extremis*. The last hour has come, the patient is dying. But how can we interpret the nation's final agony unless we understand the causes that have led to this sorry state?

James A. Crenshaw's recent book, *Prophetic Conflict* (1971), is thorough in its own way but does little more than others of its kind in tracing origins. Like others, it takes notice of I Kings 13 and 22, identifying them as instances of emerging conflict within the early prophetic schools, without scrutinizing these passages closely in their own right or examining their place within the entire collection of early narratives about the prophets. So similarly books like Alfred Jepsen's *Nabi* (1934) and Johannes Lindblom's *Prophecy in Ancient Israel* (1962), which discuss early prophetism from a phenomenological rather than a theological, tradition-historical point of view. Such treatments have their value but make little progress in identifying the sources of prophetic conflict. Biblical scholarship has until now little sensed the significance of an insight of the early rabbis. In naming the books from Joshua through Kings *nᵉbîʾîm riʾšōnîm,* "Former Prophets," they were pointing to the essential character of these books. It may be that they considered these books prophetic because they supposed their putative authors, Joshua,

Samuel, and others unnamed, to be prophets themselves, or it may be that they considered them prophetic because they contained stories about the prophets. But this is where prophecy actually began, and the rabbis may have understood that these books are equal to the "Latter Prophets" in sharing a prophetic ideology and affiliation.

Christian exegetes may still be suffering from an unknowing bias in their habit of regarding the classical prophetic collection as the norm, raising this up as a standard by which to consign the "histories," along with the Pentateuchal laws, to the category of subnormal preparation. This is a serious error. The period of national breakdown in Israel/Judah — from the eighth to the sixth century B.C., when Assyrian and neo-Babylonian imperialism gradually crushed this tiny nation's political structure and disrupted its public life — was certainly nonnormative in the sense that it was a period of crisis and alarm. Therefore the prophecy of this period must be regarded as nonnormative. It was forced to assume an exaggerated form because the times were "out of joint," even as the prophets themselves strove to explicate radical loyalty to the principles of essential Yahwism. What we must see is that these same principles had guided the prophets before the time of crisis. Our study of the writings which the pre-classical prophets have left, now taken up as "historical" materials within the Former Prophets collection, shows how the seeds of ruin were already then being sown. It is the incipient conflict of this period, still a time of relative harmony, that provides the key to the debilitating conflicts of the coming age of national destruction. We shall see that the conflict was not only between prophet and prophet but, more fundamentally, between prophet and king.

Many cherish the notion that Israel's prophets were irrepressible rebels, intractable haters of the institution, iconoclastic despisers of tradition. But our prophet narratives can show that, far from glorying in autonomy, Israel's prophets aspired to be living exemplifications of a radical theonomy, subjecting themselves to God's rule and demanding that all others — especially kings anointed to perform his purpose — do likewise.

Another gross error is that all claims to prophecy are equal. Although we are instructed by the New Testament to "test the spirits," a widespread assumption in our day is that there is no test. The only standard is perhaps being true to oneself, but we have already stated that this is not how the prophets understood prophecy. If appeal should be made to the phenomenon of prophet against prophet within the life of ancient Israel, it needs to be emphasized that the Old Testament emphatically refuses to place all who claim prophecy on an equal plane. The name "false prophet" itself presupposes a standard for judging. One will not deny that the so-called false prophets felt equally inspired and were equally sincere. Yet some prophets were wrong and others were right.

Though many contemporaries allowed themselves to be deluded by those who were wrong, the community of faith that produced the Old Testament Scripture were able to say, sooner or later, which was which. They had tests. Some of these tests have been discussed in previous treatments of prophetic conflict, but a clear advantage of the present study is that it traces the underlying ideology of prophetism in its development from its formation. We can now know that the pre-classical prophets were constantly testing one another for the true spirit of prophecy. The tests they chose remained as the tests of prophecy to Israel's age of final crisis, and they offer themselves as our tests for today.

We need to re-examine the view that the recording of objective history was the object of the documents that arose during the time of Israel's nationhood, before the exile. These include the narratives about the prophets, the so-called prophet legends. The recording of objective history was certainly not the goal of the "Former Prophets" as a whole and it was certainly not the purpose of the Pentateuch, "the Five Books of Moses." Very little that is now contained in the extensive literature from Genesis to II Kings was written except to render a theological judgment on, and bear the witness of faith to, Israel's existence in peculiar partnership with God. Some may perhaps point to sporadic annalistic materials drawn from the official court records, but even these were colored by a minimal theological bias of their own, and in the Deuteronomist's grand combination were arranged to support his strikingly God-centered interpretation of Israel's history. Much the same can be said about the documents that were expressly created to propagandize certain political innovations, specifically the throne-succession narrative legitimizing Solomon in II Samuel 9–I Kings 2 and the Jehu accession narrative of II Kings 9–10, which interpreted the political changes they were designed to support on the theory of divine choice, participation and approval.

Certainly this is emphatically true also with respect to the stories about the prophets who lived in the pre-classical age. These stories can be called "historical" only to the extent that they illustrate the various ways in which the principle of prophetic superintendency over political choices affecting Israel's history came to manifestation. We are well cautioned, then, not to employ these stories as ready data for a disinterested historical reconstruction. True, they are important for history, but not in a naive and literalistic sense. They must be weighed not so much for what they *tell* — since what they tell is often imaginative and highly schematic — as for what they intend to *say*. They say that God is sovereignly present in human events, using his prophets to bring mankind to responsible, obedient action. The prophet legends are intended to serve as witnesses to Yahweh's rule over every aspect of Israel's public life, bringing blessing to those obeying it and sorrow on those who oppose it or seek to subvert it. The great books of the classical prophets show us that the prophets challenged the political leaders, and how. We need the pre-classical narratives to show us why.

As will be seen, the present book goes far beyond an examination of I Kings 22, proposing for the first time a complete pattern of subgenres for all the prophet legends. It seeks also to trace the development of the entire prophetic tradition prior to the work of the "writing" prophets, and to describe the literary processes by which these traditions became part of Scripture. Our analysis of redaction history aims to avoid the superficiality and schematization of much previous work, presupposing our own careful treatment of relevant textual, literary critical, form-critical, and tradition-historical questions arising out of the Micaiah materials. This book could, perhaps, have been shorter if it had been content to treat the Micaiah story from only one point of view; but each question has led to others, and these in turn to still others. We have not allowed any to stand unaddressed, without a serious attempt to answer it. We are confident, thus, that our end result will bear testimony to the validity of our comprehensive method.

After the present book had already gone to the publisher, two closely related works became accessible, and because each would otherwise have deserved to have been taken into serious discussion at appropriate points in our book, it is necessary to make a brief comment about each of them. The first is by Hans-Christoph Schmitt: *Elisa; traditionsgeschichtliche Untersuchungen zur vorklassischen nordisraelitischen Prophetie* (Gütersloh, 1972), which discusses I Kings 20 and 22 along with its treatment of the Elisha cycle. Schmitt has nothing new to say about the Micaiah pericope (pp. 42ff.), accepting Würthwein's literary analysis while assigning early materials in the two passages mentioned and in II Kings 3:4ff. and II Kings 6:24ff. to the first half of the eighth century B.C. This assessment reflects the general trend of Schmitt's treatment. Among the prophetic narratives only the Jehu accession history is seen as part of the original deuteronomistic composition, while literary expansions to the Micaiah and Elisha stories are seen to continue into the postexilic period. Schmitt's neglect of genre analysis has inevitably produced an idiosyncratic historical reconstruction. The writer naively assumes that the earliest form of each story was that of an historical report, later modified as *Sage*, with the viewpoint of the prophets interjected only at a stage of literary redaction. This is, in fact, the least likely stage of all at which the prophets would have influenced the development of this distinctive narrative material. Generally injudicious and often superficial, Schmitt's work exhibits the kind of hypercriticism that superior scholarship has largely outgrown.

Far different in scope and conception is Harald Schweizer's detailed study of three Elisha pericopes, *Elischa in den Kriegen; literaturwissen-*

schaftliche Untersuchung von 2 Kön 3; 6,8-23; 6,24-7,20 (Munich, 1974), applying the methods of W. Richter. This treatment is concerned only peripherally with redactional processes and the identification of literary documents, and pays but scant attention to questions of genre and the dynamics of tradition development. Its interest is directed toward the "kleine Einheiten," with close scrutiny of syntactical and formulaic patterns. Seeing the text exclusively in terms of its linguistic structure, Schweizer's book seldom gets around to questions of aesthetic effect, kerygmatic impact and theological relevance. That is to say, the individual words (and word-patterns) are stressed at the expense of *the word*; one comes to understand the function of linguistic collocations, but ends up knowing little more about what the text means. Clearly, Schweizer's methodology needs to be brought into better balance if such material is to come to greater clarity. It may be added that Schweizer's remarks respecting I Kings 22 (pp. 32-38) scarcely justify his claim that this pericope shows dependence on II Kings 3.

* * *

Stimulating me in the early phases of this research was a series of discussions in the Form-Criticism Seminar of the Eastern Great Lakes Region, Society of Biblical Literature. My students Gary Bekofske and Leslie Peine assisted in various phases of data gathering. My esteemed fellow scholar, W. Eugene March, contributed the careful gaze of a sympathetic but forthright criticism. Encouraging me along the way has been my wife Betty. This book cannot go before the public without an expression of my warm appreciation to these and to all by whose teaching and research I have learned the greatness and the uniqueness of Israel's prophets.

Contents

Abbreviations and Symbols

1. Books, sets, series, and journals

ANEP	*The Ancient Near East in Pictures Relating to the Old Testament,* ed. by J. B. Pritchard; Princeton, 1954, 2nd ed. 1969
ANET	*Ancient Near Eastern Texts Relating to the Old Testament,* ed. by J. B. Pritchard; Princeton, 3rd ed. 1969
ATANT	Abhandlungen zur Theologie des Alten und Neuen Testaments
BeO	*Bibbia e Oriente*
Bib	*Biblica*
BJRL	*Bulletin of the John Rylands University Library of Manchester*
BKAT	Biblischer Kommentar: Altes Testament
BotAT	Die Botschaft des Alten Testaments
BWANT	Beiträge zur Wissenschaft vom Alten und Neuen Testament
BZAW	Beiheft zur Zeitschrift für die Altestamentliche Wissenschaft
EHAT	Exegetisches Handbuch zum Alten Testament
EvT	*Evangelische Theologie*
ExB	The Expositor's Bible
FRLANT	Forschungen zur Religion und Literatur des Alten und Neuen Testaments
HKAT	Handkommentar zum Alten Testament
ICC	International Critical Commentary
IDB	*The Interpreter's Dictionary of the Bible,* ed. by G. A. Buttrick *et al.;* New York-Nashville, 1962
JBL	*Journal of Biblical Literature*
JTS	*Journal of Theological Studies*
KBANT	Kommentare und Beiträge zum Alten und Neuen Testament
KEHAT	Kurzgefasstes Exegetisches Handbuch zum Alten Testament
KHCAT	Kurzer Hand-Commentar zum Alten Testament
KKAT	Kurzgefasster Kommentar zu den Heiligen Schriften Alten und Neuen Testamentes
KV	Korte Verklaring
OTL	Old Testament Library
OTS	*Oudtestamentische Studien*
PEQ	*Palestine Exploration Quarterly*
SCS	*Septuagint and Cognate Studies*

SVT	Supplements to *Vetus Testamentum*
TLZ	*Theologische Literaturzeitung*
VT	*Vetus Testamentum*
WMANT	Wissenschaftliche Monographien zum Alten und Neuen Testament
YTT	*Yesterday, Today and Tomorrow,* by Simon J. De Vries; Grand Rapids and London, 1975
ZAW	*Zeitschrift für die Alttestamentliche Wissenschaft*
ZTK	*Zeitschrift für Theologie und Kirche*

2. General

acc.	accusative case
Chron.	Chronicles
ET	English translation
Heb.	Hebrew
hiph.	hiphil
impf.	imperfect
LXX	the Greek Septuagint ([A] Codex Alexandrinus; [B] Codex Vaticanus; [L] Lucianic recension; miniscule designations as in the standard editions)
mss.	manuscripts
MT	Masoretic Text
N.F.	neue Folge
niph.	niphal
OG	Old Greek (= the Alexandrian LXX)
om	omit(s)
par	parallel
pass.	passive
pi.	piel
pl.	plural
pu.	pual
ser.	series
Syr	Syriac version
Syr^{h}	Syro-Hexaplar
Tg	Targum
tr	transpose(s)
Vg	Vulgate
VSS	(ancient) versions
1, 2 Aqht	the Aqhat mythological texts as in Cyrus Gordon, *Ugaritic Manual*
1cs	first personal common-gender singular
2ms	second personal masculine singular
3ms	third personal masculine singular

3. Biblical books (Hebrew order)

Gen., Exod., Num., Deut., Josh., Judg., I Sam., II Sam., I Kings, II Kings, Isa., Jer., Ezek., Hos., Joel, Amos, Mic., Hab., Zeph., Zech., Ps., Prov., Job, Ruth, Dan., Neh., I Chron., II Chron.
In the LXX I Sam. through II Kings = I-IV Reigns.

4. Special symbols

=	is equivalent to
≠	is not equivalent to
+	adds, addition(s)
>	becomes, is changed to
Θ	Theodotion
ab, αβ, אב	As indicated by Masoretic accentuation, verses in the Hebrew Bible are divided into two halves, a and b, each of which may be subdivided into halves α and β, each of which may be further subdivided into halves א and ב.

Transliteration of Hebrew Script

(Daghesh and raphē are not represented)

1. Consonants: א ', ב b, ג g, ד d, ה h, ו w, ז z, ח ḥ, ט ṭ, י y, כ ך k, ל l, מ ם m, נ ן n, ס s, ע ', פ ף p, צ ץ ṣ, ק q, ר r, שׂ ś, שׁ š, ת t
2. Pointed vowels: ָ (long qāmeṣ) ā, ַ (pathaḥ) a, ֶ (seghol) e, ֵ (ṣērē) ē, ִ (ḥireq) i (short) ī (long), ֹ (ḥōlem) ō, ָ (qāmeṣ ḥatuph) o, ֻ (qibbuṣ) u
3. Vowels represented by points and vowel letters: ה ָ â, א ָ ā', י ֵ ê, א ֵ ē', ה ֵ ēh, י ִ î, וֹ ô, הֹ ōh, וּ û
4. Diphthongs: ו ָ āw, י ָ āy, ו י ֵ êw, יו. îw
5. Sh[e]was: ְ (silent) = nothing, ְ (mobile) [e], ֳ [o], ֲ [a], ֱ [e]

List of Tables

INTRODUCTION

The Basis of Prophetic Conflict

ALTHOUGH COMPARATIVE STUDIES IN ANCIENT NEAR EASTERN literature have brought to light a number of striking parallels to Israelite prophetism, some important differences remain. Among these appears to be the tradition of ideological conflict between contending groups of prophets, or of one individual standing against the many. Since it may be viewed as more or less inevitable that prophetism, like other religious phenomena, should incline toward domestication, the challenge of an individual or minority against the "establishment," civil or ecclesiastical, must inevitably be the manifestation of an acutely sensitive conscience, combined at times with a strong feeling of authority and independence, in the former, or of a remarkable tolerance, restraint or weakness in the latter. In ancient Israel, where both sides took seriously the anterior claims of a single, transcendent authority, the voice of challenge could be heard more clearly (or at least survive more easily) than in some other spiritual climes. But as it did so, conflicting claims as to who possessed the genuine word of God inevitably intensified anxiety and encouraged vacillation among all who were willing to respect the divine will as supreme.[1]

Lying outside the canonical collection of prophetic books are two narratives that feature the motif of conflict between an individual prophet of Yahweh and a king supported by prophets, also speaking for Yahweh. These are I Kings 13 and I Kings 22. It is only in the latter, however, that this motif is structurally central; only here is the king accompanied by an organized group of well-sayers, a prophet guild recognizable as precursors of the controversial *Heilspropheten* (salvation prophets) who misled the kingdom of Judah in its final hour of fateful decision. It is inevitable, therefore, that studies of Hebrew prophecy and prophetism, especially those that deal with prophetic conflict,[2] should make much of Micaiah and the anonymous Judahite of I Kings 13 — obvious models for someone like Jeremiah, eventually the most fiercely independent of all the canonical prophets. Yet the literary development of these two model chapters has never been satisfactorily clarified.[3] In spite of assurances on the part of many critics that each is a substantial unity, inconsistencies and complexities abound. And as these continue unexplained, the origins of certain essential aspects of Israelite prophetism remain in unresolved obscurity.

The present study deals explicitly with I Kings 22, which has a virtual word-for-word parallel in II Chronicles 18.[4] Until now, little has been done by way of applying emerging techniques such as form and tradition criticism to the analysis of this chapter. Insights drawn from the writer's recent book. *Yesterday, Today and Tomorrow,*[5] which details the peculiar importance of the time-designatives *bayyôm hahû'* ("on that day") and *hayyôm* ("today") as functional elements within the structure of many early types of biblical narrative, may now be applied to the isolation and reconstruction of two independent original stories within this chapter, leading in turn to a better understanding of the dynamics of prophetic conflict within a broader context.[6]

NOTES TO INTRODUCTION

1. Old Testament scholars are now aware that the nearest affinities of Israelite prophetism are with Amorite, not Canaanite, antecedents; cf. the definitive study by Friedrich Ellermeier, *Prophetie in Mari und Israel* (Herzberg, 1968), where the extensive literature on this problem is listed. As Ellermeier has argued (see especially pp. 165-223), Mari prophetism shares several striking elements with Israelite prophetism, such as a numinous, indisputable authority, a structure as message from the deity to a particular individual (supporting the argument of C. Westermann, *Grundformen prophetischer Rede* [Munich, 1960; 2nd ed. 1964; ET, *Basic Forms of Prophetic Speech,* Philadelphia, 1967], who gives priority to the oracle against an individual over against the oracle to the nation), the juxtaposition of oracles of blessing alongside oracles of judgment (showing that Westermann is in error in attempting to derive the Israelite salvation oracle from the judgment oracle), a concern with historical decision-making, and even a willingness, however reluctant, to challenge the policies of the king. Nevertheless one is impressed by two unresolved and essential differences: (1) although Mari prophetism issues at times from laymen, and hence is not exclusively cultic, it never ventures to challenge the cultic establishment and is very frequently concerned with securing regal patronage for the cult; (2) since it is promulgated by a variety of deities, the regal addressee is understandably left in frequent doubt and anxiety over its fulfillment. In Israel, prophetism is more emphatically independent of the cultic institution than of the regal institution. Its authority is supreme and unchallenged wherever Yahweh is recognized as the sole source of transcendent revelation. In the final analysis, we have to say that its attribution to a single, sovereign deity is the essential and distinctive mark of biblical prophetism over against all other varieties. The important difference is theological, not phenomenological.

2. Regularly, where books on prophetism deal with origins, these two narratives

come under discussion, though seldom with fresh, independent textual analysis. J. Lindblom, *Prophecy in Ancient Israel* (Philadelphia, 1962), which may be taken as one of the most helpful and incisive books among a vast literature on the Hebrew prophets, deals with the Micaiah narrative in fewer than six pages (210-15). Even those studies that are directly concerned with the theme of prophetic conflict and the problem of "false" prophecy (cf. G. von Rad, "Die falschen Propheten," *ZAW* 51 [1933], 109-120, now in *Gesammelte Studien zum Alten Testament,* II [Munich, 1973], pp. 212-223; G. Quell, *Wahre und falschen Propheten* [Beiträge zur Förderung Christlicher Theologie 46/1; Gütersloh, 1952]; Jörg Jeremias, *Kultprophetie und Gerichtsverkündigung in der späten Königszeit Israels* [WMANT 35; Neukirchen-Vluyn, 1970]; J. A. Crenshaw, *Prophetic Conflict; Its Effect upon Israelite Religion* [BZAW 124; Berlin-New York, 1971)]; F. L. Hossfeld–I. Meyer, *Prophet gegen Prophet; eine Analyse der alttestamentlichen Texte zum Thema: Wahre und falsche Propheten* [Biblische Beiträge 9, Fribourg, 1973]) deal cursorily with these passages, if at all.

3. On I Kings 13, see our discussion in Chapter Five. Recent studies are M. A. Klopfenstein, "I Könige 13," in ΠΑΡΡΗΣΙΑ (Festschrift K. Barth, Zurich, 1966), pp. 639-672; A. Jepsen, "Gottesmann und Prophet, Anmerkungen zum Kapitel 1 Könige 13," in *Probleme biblischer Theologie* (Festschrift G. von Rad; Munich, 1971), pp. 171-182. See also Werner E. Lemke's essay on I Kings 13 in *Magnalia Dei; the Mighty Acts of God,* ed. by Lemke and Frank M. Cross (Festschrift G. E. Wright; Garden City, N.Y., 1976).

4. This study received an initial impetus from a series of consultations sponsored by the Form-Criticism Seminar of the Eastern Great Lakes Region, Society of Biblical Literature. The writer acknowledges special indebtedness to preliminary papers offered by Professors Ronald Hals (Columbus), Jared Jackson (Pittsburgh), and Conrad L'Heureux (Dayton).

5. *Yesterday, Today and Tomorrow; Time and History in the Old Testament* (Grand Rapids and London, 1975; hereinafter cited as *YTT*).

6. Cf. *ibid.,* pp. 112f., 292-95.

CHAPTER ONE

The Present State of the Question

1. QUESTIONS OF DATE, PROVENANCE, AND REDACTION

IN LIEU OF AN EXHAUSTIVE TABULATION OF PUBLISHED TREATMENTS,[1] we present a synopsis of the main lines of investigation followed in the history of the interpretation of I Kings 22, starting with the closing decades of the previous century, when historical criticism first came to be seriously applied. In addition to his valuable text-critical observations, Julius Wellhausen's major contribution to the analysis of I Kings 22 was his claim that vss. 1-38, along with chap. 20, II Kings 3, II Kings 6:24–7:20, and II Kings 9–10, does not belong to the Elijah cycle but was composed by an early "Ephraimite" writer sympathetic to Jehoshaphat and antagonistic to the house of Ahab; apart from glosses in vss. 28b, 30, and 38, the present pericope is a literary unity.[2] This is essentially the view defended by S. R. Driver, Carl Steuernagel, Oesterley and Robinson, and Norman Snaith.[3] Steuernagel infers, however, that this pericope, sympathetic to Ahab and part of a very early "history of Ahab," could not have been part of the early text of the deuteronomistic history because of vs. 40, which speaks of a peaceable death for Ahab. Oesterley and Robinson agree in identifying the original source as a special document, an "acts of Ahab," dating from the end of the ninth century B.C., but emphasize that this document has been considerably worked over by later hands. Hugo Gressmann, assuming the literary unity of this pericope, makes a pioneering form-critical identification of the genre, ascribing to this narrative a generalizing designation, *Sage*; Gressmann remains mainly absorbed in the *religionsgeschichtliche* analysis that dominated all his research.[4]

There has been some discussion of this chapter's redactional history. While Martin Noth identifies the Deuteronomist as the redactor responsible for the present position of this pericope,[5] R. H. Pfeiffer agrees with Steuernagel that the Micaiah narrative, along with I Kings 20, could have come into the book only as an addition by a second deuteronomistic redactor, *ca.* 550 B.C.[6] Alfred Jepsen's elaborate theory of redaction, identifying traces of no fewer than eight separate levels of composition in I Kings 22, assigns vss. 1-38a to a special *Nabiquelle* (prophet source) and vs. 38b to the Deuteronomist.[7] J. Maxwell Miller has recently found support for double redaction in this chapter: the narrative, not in the original deuteronomistic history because of vs. 40, was in his opinion first constructed by a circle of northern prophets and later touched up by a group of Judeans.[8] J. Fichtner follows the more usual redactional theory in identifying the Deuteronomist as the one who placed this pericope, originally having nothing whatever to do with Ahab, in its present position.[9]

Through the years various writers have recognized that the "king of Israel" involved in this narrative need not in fact be the historical Ahab,[10] and that therefore the time period reflected could have been considerably later than that of the Omride dynasty. Making much of the fact that vs. 40 implies Ahab's peaceable death, Gustav Hölscher denied that the king in question could have been Ahab; because of the prominent role assigned to Jehoshaphat he joined others in designating Judah as the place of origin for this narrative.[11] Noting that I Kings 22 and II Kings 3 both glorify Jehoshaphat as the ideal pious king, Jepsen's extensive treatment of the entire prophetic tradition in his book, *Nabi*, confidently identified Judah as the place, and the seventh century B.C. as the time of composition.[12] Otto Plöger admitted that I Kings 22 shows Judean redaction, but argued that it originated in Ephraimite tradition.[13] C. F. Whitley has made the argument that I Kings 22 originally had to do with the death of Joram, reported from another source in II Kings 9, and has been misplaced by the Deuteronomist, along with the reports of various events belonging to the Jehu dynasty, in the narrative cycle concerning events of the Omride period.[14] Miller has a similar but somewhat more detailed theory, to the effect that, whereas II Kings 13:19, 25 intend the battle of I Kings 22 to be understood as one of Jehoash's three victories over the Arameans, along with the two mentioned in I Kings 20, I Kings 22 was actually composed in the reign of Jehoahaz, confusing two separate battles in which Joram (not Ahab) was involved, i.e., a victory toward the end of his reign and the fateful conflict in which he was assassinated by Jehu.[15]

Although a minority of the writers mentioned have been willing to acknowledge that prophets were peripherally involved in the composition or redaction of I Kings 22, Jepsen's work *Nabi* has exerted influence in persuading many recent critics that this chapter is dominated by prophetic rather than by political concerns. Jepsen has argued that our narrative is a *Nabigeschichte* programmatically critical of the established guilds of prophets (*die Nabitum*), and that its narrative setting in Ahab's reign is a fictional guise for a late polemic on the part of the independent lay prophets (*Landnabis*) against the court prophets (*Hofnabis*) of

Jerusalem.[16] While refusing to accept Jepsen's theory for the composition of this chapter, Otto Eissfeldt has agreed with him in emphasizing that this chapter basically employs a prophet narrative, not a battle report; assuming the unity of the entire pericope, vss. 1-38 (except for redactional glosses), Eissfeldt emphasizes the historicity of its account of Ahab's death and argues that its intent is to praise Ahab's virtues while blaming him only for his opposition to Yahweh's word.[17] Fichtner likewise considers our account to be purely prophetic in character rather than the record of a battle, using this as an argument against historicity.[18] J. A. Montgomery and H. S. Gehman take the side of Eissfeldt: hesitating whether to call this pericope a prophetical or a political narrative, they accept its essential literary unity while arguing for its historical verisimilitude.[19]

2. SUSPICIONS OF PREDEUTERONOMISTIC CONFLATION

All the critics mentioned to this point have assumed that I Kings 22: 1-38 is of one piece literarily, apart from widely agreed-upon minor glosses. In recent years this virtual unanimity has been only slightly dented by the suspicions of John Gray and Georg Fohrer. Gray, in his commentary on Kings, seems to recognize two separate sources, viz., a highly reliable historical narrative drawn from what he calls "a dynastic history or perhaps even a biography of Ahab," and the Micaiah story, which had an independent origin in prophetic circles and was subsequently worked over by a Judean editor.[20] Fohrer, similarly emphasizing that the Ramoth-Gilead incident must have been drawn from a highly reliable ninth-century Ahab tradition, acknowledges that I Kings 22 also incorporates an originally separate prophet legend.[21] Gray and Fohrer have thus attempted to reconcile the persistent claim for what seems to be a political-military document with a growing awareness of elements from narratives circulating in prophetic circles — without, however, endeavoring a new and independent literary-critical investigation into the text.

Here we recall that in 1892 Friedrich Schwally argued that I Kings 22 has to be composite.[22] Schwally saw a number of severe conflicts within this pericope, caused in his opinion by extensive redactional rewriting and partly by the incorporation of originally independent materials. He pointed out that vss. 10-13 appear to belong to a different literary source than vss. 5ff.; also that vss. 19-23, featuring a developed angelology, give evidence for being postexilic and hence a very late intrusion.[23] Schwally received some slight support from Paul Volz,[24] but generally his analysis has been set aside as hypercritical. It has remained for a very recent writer, Ernst Würthwein, to subject our pericope to a fully independent, far-reaching critical analysis, resulting in the isolation of two separate documentary sources combined with each other in a complex pattern of redaction.[25]

Würthwein agrees with the consensus that vss. 1-2a, 28b, 35bβ, 38 are secondary, but takes exception to the assumption of compositional unity in the remaining verses. He challenges the view that we are dealing here with a reliable historical account. Würthwein argues that vss. 2b-4, 29-37 constitute a Judahite "*Sage*" with "*märchenhafte*" motifs, characterizing the king of Israel as hateful and despicable, a model "deceived deceiver." This "*Sage*"[26] made no mention of prophets, who appear in the text only as a result of the redactional interweaving of the *Sage* with the remaining material. This last is a highly complex controversy narrative built up in successive levels of compositional restructuring. First was the original prophet story, concerned with a process of testing whether Micaiah's words were true by having him put in prison (vss. 5-9, 13-17 (18?), 26-28); next was a redactional rewriting sponsored by a group of *Heilspropheten,* introducing Zedekiah as the true prophet because he in fact possessed the Spirit (vss. 10-12, 24-25); the final stage was a counterredaction made by the *Unheilspropheten* (judgment prophets), admitting that the *Heilspropheten* may have been led by the Spirit but claiming that this was in fact a "lying spirit" (vss. 19-22). In this involved process Micaiah emerges as a type rather than as a believable person. The narrative is now designed as pure propaganda, reflecting the ideological controversy in which the *Unheilspropheten,* claiming admission into the secret council of God (cf. Jer. 23:22; Isa. 6:1ff.; Amos 3:7; Ezek. 1:1ff.), profess a higher authority than any authority attested merely by possession of the spirit of Yahweh, the claim of the *Heilspropheten*.

Horst Seebass, for one, does not seem to have been convinced of the validity of Würthwein's ingenious analysis and reconstruction. In a recent text-critical treatment defending the originality of vs. 38 and arguing that vs. 35 at first contained no mention of the king's death, Seebass expresses dissatisfaction with the separation of original prophet material from the historical narrative, mainly on the ground that without the latter, the former would possess no meaningful internal development.[27]

3. SUMMARY

We may summarize the issues raised by past and current scholarship regarding the interpretation of I Kings 22 by making the following list of unresolved questions:

(1) Is this pericope in fact a substantial literary unity, with only minor inconsistencies explicable on the assumption that they arose in oral

transmission, or does it presuppose the redactional combination and expansion of diverse literary materials?

(2) Is its narration of a political-military event factual and reliable? In particular: were the kings involved in this tragic event the historical Ahab and Jehoshaphat, and was there an alliance in which the Judean army joined the army of Israel in a battle against the Syrians at Ramoth-Gilead, resulting in the mortal wounding of the king of Israel?

(3) If the narrative is a unity, what are its genre, structure, and *Sitz im Leben?* Or if it is composite, what are the respective genres, structures, and *Sitze im Leben* defining each constituent element?

(4) Where was the narrative and/or its constituent elements preserved, by whom, and for what purpose? What ideologies and tendencies are reflected in the elements interjected by the respective tradents?

(5) What is its redaction history as a literary composition? Specifically: was it touched up and put in its present place before, during, or subsequent to the definitive deuteronomistic redaction?

(6) To this list we may add the problem of the text, to which every other issue ultimately returns. Recent manuscript discoveries have completely reopened the question of the relative merits of the Masoretic Text (MT) over against the various recensions of the Greek Septuagint (LXX), here as in many other pericopes.

Through a fresh, patient and detailed treatment we intend to suggest answers to the above questions, more satisfying we hope than have emerged thus far. From this we expect ultimately to find definitive clues to what was truly special and unique in the prophetic movement in Israel. But before we reach this goal it will be necessary to go far beyond an examination of I Kings 22 in itself. To evaluate its structure, ideology and provenance, we shall have to endeavor what has never seriously been tried before — an identification of all the subgenres of prophetic narrative. We cannot be content with assigning the Micaiah narrative to some vague process of oral development, hence our study of redactional history must be a thorough one. We ask the reader patiently to follow us through this discussion, promising that no idle question will be raised and no unexamined answer offered.

NOTES TO CHAPTER ONE

1. Alongside numerous treatments in works of general introduction and special studies concerning the prophetic movement as a whole, the following commentaries, added to those reserved for special comment in our discussion,

deserve to be mentioned: O. Thenius, *Die Bücher der Könige erklärt* (KEHAT; Leipzig, 1873); A. Klostermann, *Die Bücher Samuelis und der Könige* (KKAT; Munich, 1887); F. W. Farrar, *The First Book of Kings* (ExB; 1893); J. Skinner, *I and II Kings* (Century Bible; London, 1893); I. Benzinger, *Die Bücher der Könige erklärt* (KHCAT; Freiburg i. B., 1899); R. Kittel, *Die Bücher der Könige* (HKAT; Göttingen, 1900); A. Šanda, *Die Bücher der Könige* (2 vols.; EHAT; Münster i. W., 1911-12); C. van Gelderen, *De Boeken van Koningen* (3 vols.; KV; Kampen, 1936-1947; J. Mauchline, "I and II Kings," *Peake's Commentary* (London, 1962), pp. 338-356. To this list should be added pertinent titles dealing with Chronicles, the parallel passage. For a comprehensive survey of recent research on the books of Kings, see E. Jenni's article in *Theologische Rundschau* N.F. 27 (1961), 142ff.

2. *Die Composition des Hexateuchs und der historischen Bücher des Alten Testaments* (4th ed., Berlin, 1963), pp. 283-87.

3. S. R. Driver, *Introduction to the Literature of the Old Testament* (8th ed., New York, 1898), p. 195; C. Steuernagel, *Lehrbuch der Einleitung in das Alte Testament* (Tübingen, 1912), pp. 362f., cf. pp. 372f.; W. O. E. Oesterley and Th. H. Robinson, *An Introduction to the Books of the Old Testament* (London, 1934), pp. 97f.; N. Snaith, Commentary on Kings in *The Interpreter's Bible* (New York-Nashville, 1962), p. 13.

4. *Die Schriften des Alten Testaments in Auswahl,* II, i (2nd ed., Göttingen, 1921), pp. 279f. Gressmann is not disturbed by contradictions in the prophets' oracles because, like those of Delphi, the prophetic oracles are seen by him as deliberately designed to be ambiguous.

5. *Überlieferungsgeschichtliche Studien; Die sammelnden und bearbeitenden Geschichtswerke im Alten Testament* (2nd ed., Tübingen, 1957), p. 80.

6. *Introduction to the Old Testament* (New York, 1941), p. 409. Pfeiffer identifies these chapters as "extracts from the history of Israel's kings."

7. *Die Quellen des Königsbuches* (2nd ed., Halle, 1956). Vss. 40-42, 45, 48-50 belong to a "Synchronistische Chronik" and vss. 39, 43-44, 46-47 to a first redactor, author of a so-called "Priesterliche Geschichtswerk."

8. "The Elisha Cycle and the Accounts of the Omride Wars," *JBL* 85 (1966), 441-454; cf. also "The Fall of the House of Ahab," *VT* 17 (1967), 307-324.

9. *Das Erste Buch von der Könige* (BotAT 12/1; Stuttgart, 1964), pp. 297f. The Deuteronomist, assuming the anonymous king to be Ahab because he is presented as a contemporary of Jehoshaphat, has arranged all his material to build suspense toward chap. 22's report of Ahab's death (cf. 19:16; 20:42; 21:19). But see our interpretation of the Deuteronomist's intent at the end of Chapter Seven.

10. Cf. M. Noth, *The History of Israel* (rev. ET, London, 1960), p. 243.

11. "Das Buch der Könige, seine Quellen und seine Redaktion," *Eucharisterion Hermann Gunkel zum 60. Geburtstag* (FRLANT 19; Göttingen, 1923), I, pp. 158-213.

12. *Nabi; soziologische Studien zur alttestamentliche Literatur und Religionsgeschichte* (Munich, 1934), p. 89. Cf. *Archiv für Orientforschung* 14 (1942), 154ff.

13. *Die Prophetengeschichten der Samuel- und Königsbücher* (diss., Greifswald, 1937), pp. 33f.

14. "The Deuteronomic Presentation of the House of Omri," *VT* 2 (1952),

137-152. Though Whitley fails to offer a special analysis of I Kings 22, he ventures the following conclusion: "The biblical account of the death of Ahab is a compilation from sources dealing with the facts concerning the alliance of Jehoshaphat and Joram against Moab, from a similar alliance of Joram with Ahaziah against the Syrians at Ramoth-Gilead, and from the circumstances of Joram's death" (149).

15. "The Elisha Cycle," *loc. cit.*

16. Jepsen includes II Kings 3 in this assessment.

17. *Einleitung in das Alten Testament* (2nd ed., Tübingen, 1956), p. 349. Eissfeldt argues for the existence of a predeuteronomistic history of the kings combining materials from the continuing L, J and E strands of the Hexateuch (pp. 353, 357ff.); similarly Benzinger, Hölscher, Smend.

18. *Op. cit.,* pp. 325-27. The narrative is solely concerned with the conflict between two opposing prophetic words.

19. *A Critical and Exegetical Commentary on The Books of Kings* (ICC; Edinburgh, 1951), pp. 41, 336.

20. *I and II Kings; A Commentary* (OTL; Philadelphia, 1963), pp. 371f., 394f.; cf. 2nd rev. ed., 1970, pp. 416f., 444f.

21. *Introduction to the Old Testament* (ET Nashville-New York, 1968), p. 232 (cf. p. 229). Fohrer repeats verbatim Eissfeldt's claim that the Ahab tradition "honors the greatness of this clever, ambitious, magnanimous, and courageous king."

22. "Zur Geschichte der historischen Bücher," *ZAW* 12 (1892), 159-161.

23. The scene in the heavenly court is compared with that of Job, but it is mainly because the *ṣ^ebā' haššāmayim* is identified as the object of blameworthy idolatry in Deuteronomy that Schwally labels this intrusion as postexilic.

24. *Der Geist Gottes und die verwandten Erscheinungen im Alten Testament und im anschliessenden Judentum* (Tübingen, 1910), p. 20. A recent treatment identifying as a late intrusion the section that Schwally and Volz suspected (vss. 19-23) is Hossfeld-Meyer, *Prophet gegen Prophet,* pp. 27-35.

25. "Zur Komposition von I Reg. 22:1-38," in F. Maass, ed., *Das ferne und nahe Wort* (Festschrift L. Rost; BZAW 105; Berlin, 1967), pp. 245-254.

26. On the problem of appropriately translating the German term *Sage,* see now P. Gisbert in *VT* 24 (1974), 411-420. Cf. our discussion of genre identifications in Chapter Five.

27. "Zur 1 Reg. xxii 35-38," *VT* 21 (1971), 380-82. See our remarks in Chapter Two, n. 23 and n. 28, and in Chapter Three, n. 1.

CHAPTER TWO

The Text

WHEN COMING TO TERMS WITH THE TEXT OF I KINGS 22:1-38, WE encounter the special opportunity and responsibility offered by a virtual word-for-word parallel in II Chron. 18:1-34. The Chronicles text follows Kings except at the beginning and end. It is characteristically interpretive and paraphrastic, but offers here and there a better reading, particularly where its Septuagintal rendering diverges from the MT perpetuation of a corruption in the Hebrew text of Kings.[1]

The MT of Kings in general manifests a more sober tendency than do the expansive Palestinian and Antiochian texts presupposed in our most primitive witnesses to the LXX.[2] It so happens that I Kings 22 falls just at the beginning of a *Kaige* section in the Vaticanus (LXX[B]) text;[3] this section continues to the end of II Kings,[4] featuring in our pericope some Hebraizing readings characteristic of the *Kaige* recension, such as ἀνήρ for distributive אִישׁ in vs. 10,[5] καί γε for וְגַם in vs. 22,[6] and ταμεῖον τοῦ ταμείου for חֶדֶר בְּחֶדֶר in vs. 25.[7] Yet some old Greek (OG) readings (representing the LXX of Alexandria) do remain in the [B] text of this chapter, most remarkably ἕκαστος for distributive אִישׁ in vss. 17 and 36 (1st).[8] Meanwhile, the proto-Lucianic revision [(L)],[9] representing the Antiochian text and witnessed especially in Theodoret and in the miniscules boc$_2$e$_2$, often diverges from the OG as much as, or more than, *Kaige*.

1. INNER-SEPTUAGINTAL ANALYSIS

Inasmuch as we possess no consistently primitive LXX for I Kings 22, it is necessary to introduce our discussion of the text by a careful comparison of [B] with [L], the two relatively oldest Septuagintal witnesses available to us. We list the readings in which these two recensions differ significantly from each other in this pericope, evaluating them according to the following categories of comparison:

I. ᴮ more closely represents OG.

A. ᴮ = OG: 2 ᴮ καὶ ἐγενήθη; ᴸ καὶ ἐγένετο.[10] 6 ᴮ καὶ εἶπαν; ᴸ καὶ εἶπον.[11] 9 ᴮ τάχος; ᴸ τὸ τ.[12] 10 ᴮ ἐκάθηντο ἀνὴρ ἐπὶ τοῦ θρόνου αὐτοῦ; ᴸ acc.;[13] cf. 19.

B. ᴮ is idiomatic or reflects a separate tradition, while ᴸ in whole or part approaches MT; 3 *passim* ᴮ ῥεμμὰθ γ.; oc₂ ῥαμωθ. 3 ᴮ λαβεῖν; ᴸ τοῦ μὴ λ. 4 ᴮ μεθ' ἡμῶν; ᴸ μετ' ἐμοῦ. 5 ᴮ ἐπερωτήσατε δή; ᴸ ἐπερωτήσωμεν.[14] 8, 9 ᴮ 'Ιεμιά/άς; ᴸ (ν)αμάλει. 11 ᴮ Χαανά; ᴸ Χαναάν. 16 ᴮ ὅπως λαλήσης; ᴸ ὁ. λαλήσεις.[15] 17 ᴮ ὡς ποίμνιον ᾧ; ᴸ ὡς πρόβατα οἷς. 19 ᴮ θεὸν 'Ισραήλ; ᴸ κύριον τὸν θ. 'Ι.[16] 22 ᴮ πάντων τῶν προφητῶν αὐτοῦ; ᴸ π. αὐτοῦ τ. π. τούτων. 24 ᴮ ποῖον πνεῦμα κυρίου τὸ λαλῆσαν ἐν σοί; ᴸ π. π. κ. ἀπέστη ἀπ' ἐμοῦ τοῦ λαλῆσαι ε. σ. 25 ᴮ τῇ ἡμέρᾳ ἐκείνῃ; ᴸ ἐν τ. ἡ. ἐ. 26 ᴮ Σεμήρ; ᴸ Εμμηρ. 27 ᴮ εἰπόν; ᴸ εἶπε(ν). 34 ᴮ εὐστόχως; ᴸ ἀφελῶς. 35 ᴮ αἷμα ἐκ τῆς πληγῆς; ᴸ αἱ. τ. π. 37 ᴮ εἰς τὴν Σαμάρειαν; ᴸ εἰς Σ. 38 ᴮ καὶ ἀπένιψαν; ᴸ κ. ἔνιψαν. ᴮ καὶ ἐξέλιξαν; ᴸ κ. ἔλειξαν. ᴮ αἱ ὕες καὶ οἱ κύνες; ᴸ οἱ κ.

C. ᴮ ≠ MT, while ᴸ is atticizing: 13 ᴮ λαλοῦσιν πάντες οἱ προφῆται; ᴸ π. οἱ π. λ. ᴮ γίνου δὴ καὶ σὺ εἰς λόγους σου; ᴸ γ. δ. κ. σ. ἐν λόγοις σου. 27 ᴮ θέσθαι τοῦτον; ᴸ τοῦ θ. αὐτόν.

D. ᴮ = MT, but ᴸ is atticizing: 4 ᴮ ἀναβήσῃ; ᴸ εἰ ἀ. 10, 12 ᴮ ἐπροφήτευον; ᴸ προεφ. 11 ᴮ ἕως συντελεσθῇ; ᴸ ἑ. ἂν σ. 14 ᴮ ἃ ἂν εἴπῃ; ᴸ ἃ ἐὰν εἰ. 15 ᴮ εἰς χεῖρα; ᴸ ἐν χεῖρι. 17 ᴮ τὸν πάντα 'Ισραήλ; ᴸ π. τ. 'Ι. 18 ᴮ οὐ προφητεύει οὗτός μοι; ᴸ ὅτι οὐ π. οὗ. ἐμοί. 20 ᴮ καὶ ἀναβήσεται καὶ πεσεῖται ἐν 'Ρ. Γ. ᴸ κ. ἀ. εἰς 'Ρ. Γ. κ. π. ἐκεί. 23 ᴮ πάντων τῶν προφητῶν σου; ᴸ π. σου τ. π. 32 ᴮ πολεμῆσαι; ᴸ τοῦ π. 34 ᴮ τέτρωμαι; ᴸ τετραυμάτισμαι.

E. ᴮ ≠ MT, while ᴸ is interpretive and/or theologizing: 8 ᴮ εἷς ἐστὶν ἀνήρ; ᴸ εἷς ἐ. ὧδε. 24 ᴮ τὸ λαλῆσαν ἐν σοι; ᴸ τοῦ λαλῆσαι ε. σ. 25 ᴮ ταμεῖον τοῦ ταμείου; ᴸ τ. ἐκ ταμιείου. 34 ᴮ τὸ τόξον; ᴸ τ. τ. αὐτοῦ. 38 ᴮ τὸ αἷμα; ᴸ τ. αἱ. ἀπὸ τοῦ ἅρματος. ᴮ ἐλούσαντο ἐν τῷ αἵματι; ᴸ ἐ. ἐ. τ. αἱ. αὐτοῦ.

F. ᴮ = MT, but ᴸ is interpretive: 2, 5, 10, 37 ᴸ + 'Αχααβ. 4, 6, 7, 10 (16), 29, 30, 31 ᴸ + article. 6 ᴸ + 'Ισραήλ. 15 ᴸ + ὁ Μιχαίας. ᴸ + αὐτῷ. 16 ᴸ + ἔτι. 17 ᴮ οἶκον αὐτοῦ; ᴸ ἑαυτοῦ οἰ. 19 ᴮ ἄκουε; ᴸ ἀκοῦσον. 30 ᴮ καὶ συνεκαλύψατο; ᴸ κ. συνκαλύψομαι. 32 ᴸ + καὶ κύριος ἔσωσεν αὐτόν. 34 ᴸ + ὁ βασιλεύς. 35 ᴸ + τῆς τροπώσεως. ᴸ + ὁ βασιλεύς.

G. ᴮ = MT, but ᴸ is euphemizing: 35 ᴮ καὶ ἀπεχύννετο; ᴸ κ. ἐξεπορεύετο.

H. ᴮ = MT, but ᴸ is corrupt: 20 ᴸ + καὶ εἶπεν οὐ δυνήσει καὶ εἶπεν ἐν σοι. 22 ᴮ καὶ εἶπεν 'Απατήσεις καί γε δυνήσει; ᴸ κ. ἀπατήσω αὐτὸν κ. εἶπεν δ.

II. ᴸ more closely represents OG.

A. ᴸ = OG, ᴮ = MT: 4 ᴸ καθὼς συ οὕτως καὶ ἐγώ; ᴮ καθὼς ἐγώ κ.

σ. οὐ. [L] καὶ καθὼς ὁ λαός σου οὕτως καὶ ὁ λαός μου; [B] καθὼς ὁ λ. μου ὁ λ. σου. [L] καὶ καθὼς οἱ ἵπποι σου οἱ ἵπποι μου; [B] καθὼς οἱ ἵ. μου οἱ ἵ. σου.[17] 10 [L] ἕκαστος; [B] ἀνήρ. 34 [L] τὴν χεῖρά σου; [B] τὰς χεῖράς σου. 38 [L] κατὰ τὸ ῥῆμα κυρίου; [B] κ. τ. ῥ. κ. ὃ ἐλάλησεν.

B. [L] is idiomatic, while [B] is literalistic: 3 [L] ἡμῶν ἐστι; [B] ἡμῖν. 6 [L] ὅτι; [B] καί. 18 [L] εἶπον σοι; [B] εἶπα πρὸς σέ. [L] ἀλλ' ἢ κακά; [B] διότι ἀ. ἢ. κ. 19 [L] τὸν λόγον κυρίου; [B] ῥῆμα κ. 25 [L] καὶ εἰσελεύσῃ; [B] ὅταν εἰσέλθῃς. 31 [L] μὴ συνάψητε πολέμον πρός; [B] μὴ πολεμεῖτε. [L] ἢ μέγα(ν); [B] καὶ μέγαν. [L] πρὸς τὸν βασιλέα 'Ισραήλ; [B] τ. β. 'Ι. 36 [L] καὶ εἶπεν; [B] λέγων.

C. [L] = MT, but [B] is corrupt: 13 [L] στόματι ἕνι; [B] ἐν σ. ἐπί. 16 [L] ποσάκις; [B] πεντάκις.

D. [B] has a peculiar *Kaige* reading: 19 [L] ἐξ ἀριστερῶν αὐτοῦ; [B] ἐ. εὐωνύμων αὐ.[18]

III. Uncertain.

A. Both [B] and [L] are corrupt: 10 [B] ἐν ταῖς πύλαις; [L] ὅδῳ πύλης. 17 [B] οὐ κύριος τούτοις θεός; [L] εἰ κύριως(ος) αὐτοὶ πρὸς θεόν.

B. [B] = MT, but [L] is interpretive and/or theologizing: 5 [B] ἐπερωτήσατε δὴ σήμερον; [L] ἐ. δ. 10 [B] καὶ ὁ βασιλεὺς 'Ισραὴλ καὶ 'Ιωσαφατ βασιλεὺς 'Ιούδα; [L] κ. 'Ι. β. 'Ι. κ. ὁ β. 'Ι. 20 [B] καὶ εἶπεν κύριος; [L] κ. εἶ. 23 [B] ἔδωκεν; [L] δέδωκεν. 27 [B] καὶ ἐσθίειν αὐτόν; [L] κ. ἐσθιέτω καὶ πινέτω. 33 [B] καὶ ἀπέστρεψαν; [L] κ. ἀπεστράφησαν. 38 [B] ἐπὶ τὴν κρήνην; [L] ἐν τῇ κρήνῃ.

C. Others: 8 [B] καλά; [L] ἄγαθα. 16 [B] ἐξορκίζω; [L] ὀρκίζω. 31 [B] δυσίν; [L] δύο. 34 [B] ἐπέτεινεν; [L] ἐνέτεινεν. 36 [B] δύνοντος; [L] δύναντος.

Summary. Where LXX[B] and [L], the two oldest witnesses in I Kings 22, differ from each other, it is evident that [B] preserves OG more often than does [L]. Most of the [L] divergences appear, however, at the stage of late normalization to classical Greek models. Enough survives of genuine early readings to serve as a partial control to [B], which has suffered various corruptions and at several points has been normalized to a Hebrew text (proto-MT) later than the *Vorlage* of the Alexandrian LXX.

2. INTER-VERSIONAL ANALYSIS

With these recensional differences in mind, we may now review in detail the evidence for a probable original Hebrew text in I Kings 22:1-38, mentioning only those readings that are potentially important foı criticism and interpretation.

4ff. (Chron. 3ff.) LXX[B] in Kings exhibits a tendency toward superfluous explication, adding the subject βασιλεὺς 'Ισραήλ in vs. 4 (perhaps in the *Vorlage* of OG, whence adopted by MT Chron.; the latter further embellishes the regal names and titles in this verse), ὁ βασιλεύς as subject in the second clause of vs. 6, πρὸς βασιλέα 'Ισραήλ and τὸν κύριον in vs. 7, οὗτός in vs. 18, Μειχαίας in vs. 19, βασιλέα 'Ισραήλ after "Ahab" in vs. 20, and μετ' αὐτοῦ in vs. 29. So also αὐτῷ in ᴸ of vs. 15. Although β. 'Ιούδα following 'Ιωσαφάτ agrees with MT in vss. 2, 10, and 29, here the king so designated appears in combination with "the king of Israel"; LXX allows 'Ιωσαφάτ to stand alone in vss. 8, 32 (2nd) (*sic* MT), but in vss. 5, 8, 18, 30, and 32 (1st) it adds β. 'Ιούδα.

4-5 (3-4) In the question of the king of Israel in vs. 4 and in Jehoshaphat's reply of vs. 5, LXXᴮ reads pl. for MT sing. (μεθ' ἡμῶν for אתי, ἐπερωτήσατε for דרש), but MT, antecedently more likely and supported by ᴸ, is demanded by vs. 6.

The LXX transposition of "to (the) battle" and "(to) Ramoth-Gilead" suggests that למלחמה, wanting in Chron., may have been added through normalization from vss. 6, 15 (possibly influenced by II Kings 3:7). Chron., reading במלחמה at the end of the verse, has a garbled *Vorlage*. אל מלך ישראל, wanting in LXX and paraphrastically represented in Chron., is a normalization from II Kings 3:7.

כסוסי כסוסיך, read by LXXᴮ but wanting in Chron., is a normalization from II Kings 3:7. Chron.'s reading, ועמך *(wᵉ'immᵉkā)* עמי *('ammî)* וכעמך במלחמה, while involving conflation, indicates that LXXᴸ Kings has an order (2ms/1cs) more original than that of MT Kings.[19]

Although Tg supports MT דבר in vs. 5, retaining it also in Chron. and in vs. 8, where MT omits it, its omission by LXX makes its originality highly suspect.

6 (5) The LXX reading, assuming Heb. *wᵉnātōn yittēn,* may result from a conflation of MT ויתן (so Chron.) and the MT reading in vs. 15, ונתן.

LXX πάντας here and in vs. 13 is tendentious, consistent with its omission of עוד in vss. 7-8. It may have been influenced by MT, vs. 23.

The singularistic readings in MT, האלך, אחדל, and עלה, are supported by LXX Kings, Chron., though MT Chron. reads the first as pl., as in Chron., vs. 14. Whereas the parallel forms in vs. 15 (14) may have been influenced by the singulars in vs. 6 (5), the sporadic plurals in MT (הנלך and נחדל in Kings; הנלך, עלו, והצליחו, and בידכם in Chron.), unsupported by LXX even in Chron., probably result from late textual normalization to vs. 10, which appears to be placing the two kings on a co-ordinate basis.

Tg and a number of Heb. mss. support the entire Greek tradition in reading an original יהוה in place of the pre-Masoretic scribal alteration to אדני.

7-8 (6-7) LXX, Lat, Vg omit MT Kings and Chron. עוד, tendentiously avoiding the implication that the four hundred were also prophets of Yahweh. Consistently, LXX reads אחד foremost in vs. 8, thereby emphasizing Micaiah's singularity. Though MT is supported only by Syr^h in vs. 8 (a correction to MT), the antecedent likelihood is that the Greek tradition has eliminated a suspicious but original theological implication. MT יתנבא (LXX^B λαλεῖ; Thdt λεγεῖ) is a normalization from vs. 18 (cf. Chron.).

10 (9) MT's apparently over-full reading, בגדים בגרן פתח שער שמרון, has been eased by Chron.'s additional ישבים before בגרן. LXX^B ἐν ταῖς πύλαις Σ. may represent both פתח and שער; ^{L} is closer to the original. The LXX omission of בגרן can best be explained as a haplography from בגדים.[20]

12 (11) Although the Heb. idiom *nātan b^{e}yad,* without object, is rendered literally by LXX in vss. 6, 15, in vs. 12 LXX creates an object by splitting up the construct phrase, ביד המלך, reading εἰς χεῖράς σου καὶ τὸν βασιλέα Συρίας. Literary-critical considerations (see below) open up the possibility that MT has normalized an original LXX.[21]

13 (12) LXX reads a דברו that is more probable than MT דברי (so Rehm, Allen), but ^{B} is corrupt. *Qere* and Chron. read דבריך as singular, in agreement with the sing. verb, but LXX has pl. for the noun and verb. The *Kethibh* is original but represents a redactional reading. Chron. (LXX pl.) כאחד מהם for MT Kings כדבר אחד מהם involves haplography.

14 (13) LXX reads יאמר as past and harmonistically reads אתו as pl. in agreement with vss. 17, 19ff.

Chron. is theologically tendentious in rendering the second יהוה as אלהים, avoiding the implication that Yahweh himself might be responsible for Micaiah's lie.

15 (14) Chron. has niph. pass. of נתן, omitting the divine name as subject, thus avoiding the ascription of an impious act to Yahweh. The second MT אליו, missing in Chron. and not read by LXX, is an obvious addition.

17 (16) A dittography after ויאמר has produced LXX οὐχ οὕτως,[22] read as if from Heb. ל(א)כן, as in vs. 19. The LXX intends it as Micaiah's protest against what is said in vs. 16.

The LXX renderings for MT לא אדנים לאלה involve double readings (see above). ^{L} reads לו, "if."

19 (18) In attempting to improve a somewhat ambiguous Heb. text, LXX translates לכן as in vs. 17,[23] interjecting οὐχ ἐγώ (Heb. לא אני?) before, and a second οὐχ οὕτως following, "hear the word of Y." Unless it

reflects corruption in its *Vorlage,* LXX must be understood as a frenetic effort to depict Micaiah's protest of innocence: "Not so! Not I! Hear the word of Yahweh! Not so! I saw. . . ."[24] This is in line with the omission of עוד in 7-8. LXX's interpretive tendency is further revealed in its substitution of θεὸν 'Ισραήλ for an undoubtedly original יהוה. Likewise interpretive are Chron.'s שמעו for שמע and עמדים for עמד.

20 (19) Chron. and Vg follow LXX Kings' interpretive identification of Ahab. MT Chron.'s insertion of אמר after the second זה (not supported by LXX but read by Tg) wrongly places the entire final clause in Yahweh's mouth. Chron.'s ככה *bis* for Kings' בכה *bis* is a normalization to later usage. MT and LXX^{B} Kings "in Ramoth-G." is explicative of a probably original שם (LXX^{L} ἐκεῖ).

21 (20) LXX Kings πνεῦμα for MT Kings הרוח (so Chron.) is a theologizing normalization to πνεῦμα ψευδές in vss. 22-23. In Chron., vs. 21, לרוח is interpretive.

23 (22) Contrary to Chron., Kings has כל before נביאיך (so vss. 10, 22; cf. LXX's additions in vss. 6, 13, where כל is wanting in MT). Literary-critical considerations (see below) allow the possibility that MT Kings is original while Chron. is normalizing.

24 (23) Zedekiah's troublesome question (אי זה does not elsewhere appear with a verb) has been variously emended in Chron. and the VSS. Chron. adds an interpretive הדרך. Omitting עבר, LXX^{B} in Kings follows a theologically more acceptable reading, but MT is supported by ^{L}. LXX Chron. likewise omits עבר, but thereafter seems hopelessly garbled. The disagreement between these alternative readings suggests that they are all emendations of an anomalous, offensive, but probably original MT.[25]

26-27 (25-26) In MT Kings the king's commands for Micaiah's arrest occur in the singular; LXX, influenced by Chron.'s interpretive plurals and by the plurals in the quotation of vs. 27, has wrongly pluralized קח and והשיבהו in vs. 26, while retaining the sing. in vs. 27. Since LXX retains the *waw* in ואמרת for the preceding phrase, it is clear that the Heb. reading is original. Accordingly, the singulars in vs. 26 must likewise be original.

Although MT כה אמר המלך represents the proper form in an instruction to a messenger, the early LXX witnesses omit it; the normalization of the Heb. text is more probable than an arbitrary omission on the part of the Greek.

MT Kings עד באי בשלום has been normalized in LXX and Chron. to the שוב of vs. 28 (cf. 17).

28 (27) MT vs. 28b (= Θ), omitted in LXX Kings (cf. LXX Chron.), is an evident gloss from Mic. 1:2.

30 (29) The unusual infinitive constructions, which do not seem to involve textual corruption, have been rendered idiomatically in early LXX, Syr, Tg; although LXX Chron. reads התחפש as an imperative addressed to Jehoshaphat, the 2ms independent personal pronoun, emphatically forward in vs. aβ, together with vs. b, makes clear that the 1st person is intended. LXX τὸν ἱματισμόν μου is an interpretive misreading.

31 (30) Kings' "thirty-two" following אשר לו is syntactically awkward; its omission in Chron. marks it as a probable gloss (cf. I Kings 20:1, 16).

32 (31) MT ויסרו has been emended in LXX according to Chron.'s ויסבו; LXX^{L} also follows Chron. in reading the first part of its theologizing addition regarding Jehoshaphat's cry (superfluous in view of vs. 33).

34 (33) Although pl. ידיך in the Bomberg text (so LXX^{B}, Chron.) is attested with הפך in II Kings 9:23, LXX^{L}'s and ben Asher's sing. is supported by LXX Chron. and *Qere* Chron. The pronominal suffix to לרכב may be interpretive; cf. Chron. LXX ἐκ τοῦ πολεμοῦ for MT מן המחנה is influenced by המלחמה at the beginning of vs. 35.[26]

35-36 (34-35) Paraphrastic and interpretive alternatives to MT ותעלה המלחמה in Chron. and the VSS confirm its priority.[27] Kings' היה מעמד במרכבה is more commensurate with the trend of the narrative (see below) than Chron.'s מעמיד, "kept standing," "caused himself to stand," a reading carried further by LXX Kings, Chron., ἦν ἑστηκὼς ἐπὶ τοῦ ἁ.

The remainder of the verse has been preserved in two LXX variants (^{L} omits part of the second). Since MT Kings seems to be structurally meaningful, there is no reason to suspect that it has been expanded, and accordingly Chron. is to be seen as a summarizing paraphrase. Since Chron. completes this verse (and its entire narrative) with an adaptation of the temporal notice in Kings vs. 36, its omission of reference to the king's blood cannot be taken as evidence that this was missing in the original text of Kings. But inasmuch as the Heb. text of Kings is preserved in LXX variants and the reference to the king's blood follows the mention of his death, it must be seen as a likely gloss coming in as a late reflection from vs. 38, itself a gloss to the original Heb. narrative.[28]

The LXX, with most VSS, reads MT ויעבר as ויעמד and הרנה as *hārōneh,* "the herald," no doubt to avoid the seemingly anomalous disagreement in gender;[29] whereas MT is meaningful in suggesting a spontaneous cry of panic suitable to the situation, the Greek assumes a formal announcement in hellenistic fashion, scarcely possible in a situation of defeat, panic and confusion. MT במחנה, missing in LXX, is an interpretive addition.

37 The Heb. intends this verse as a resumptive summary. Understanding this, LXX substitutes ὅτι for the copula and offers a perfect in

place of the aorist of vs. 35, thus showing that it read ומת המלך in vs. 35. LXX καὶ ἦλθον is interpretive of a difficult but original MT ויבוא.

38 LXX contains interpretive expansions; its special fascination with the king's blood reflects the same tendency responsible for the addition in vs. 35bβ. LXX[L] reflects the original Heb. *Vorlage* in omitting MT/LXX[B] "which he had spoken."

3. RESULT

The result of this analysis is a considerable paring-down from the sum total of all readings. In no instance is a plus offered by LXX or Chron. to be adopted, while all but one or two of the pluses in MT Kings are to be sacrificed, evidence for their removal being offered by LXX Kings in vss. 4, 5, 10, 15, 27, 28, 31, and 36, by Chron. in vss. 4, 15, and 34, and by LXX Chron. in vs. 34. On the other hand, where readings have been altered from one text to another, it is almost always MT Kings that carries the day. MT Kings is to be preferred in vss. 4, 6, 7, 8, 14, 17, 19, 20, 21, 23, 24, 26, 27, 30, 32, 34, 35, 37, 38, whereas LXX Kings is to be preferred only in vss. 8, 12, 13, and 15, and Chron. (supported by LXX[L] Kings) is to be preferred in one reading in vs. 4. From this it can be seen that the proto-Masoretic text of Kings, so far as we can reconstruct it, clearly establishes its priority over its rivals; the essential utility of the LXX arises in the task of identifying additions to the Heb. text. The original that commends itself is, therefore, a text that lacks all the LXX and Chron. pluses and virtually all the pluses of the MT.

In summation, we list the following MT readings (omitting the pointing) as additions (+) or alterations (> or tr): 4 + למלחמה. + אל מלך ישראל. + כסוסי כסוסיך. tr 2ms/1cs. 5 + דבר. 6 יהוה > אדני. 7 מאתו > מאותו. 8 ידבר > יתנבא. 12 בידך גם מלך ארם > ביד המלך. 13 דברו > דברי. 15 + אליו. האלך > הנלך. אחדל > נחדל. 24 אתך > אותך. 27 + כה אמר המלך. 28 + ויאמר שמעו עמים כלם. 31 + שלשם ושנים. 34 לרכב > לרכבו. 36 + במחנה. 38 + אשר דבר.

Here follows a translation of the probable original that results from our foregoing text-critical analysis:

1 So they remained for three years: no warfare between Aram and Israel.
2 And it happened in the third year that Jehoshaphat king of Judah went down to the king of Israel.
3 And the king of Israel said to his servants, "Do you know that Ramoth-Gilead belongs to us, yet we refrain from seizing it from the hand of the king of Aram?"
4 And he said to Jehoshaphat, "Wilt thou[30] go with me to Ramoth-Gilead?" And Jehoshaphat said, "As thou shalt act, so shall I; as thy army shall act, so shall my army."
5 And Jehoshaphat said to the king of Israel, "Inquire

thou first of Yahweh." 6 So the king of Israel assembled the prophets — about four hundred persons — and said to them, "Shall I go up to Ramoth-Gilead to fight or shall I desist?" And they said, "Go thou up, and Yahweh will deliver it to the king's hand." 7 But Jehoshaphat said, "Is there not one other prophet here, so that we may inquire from him?" 8 And the king of Israel said to Jehoshaphat, "There is yet a certain man from whom one may inquire of Yahweh, but I reject him because he does not announce good concerning me but evil: Micaiah son of Imlah." And Jehoshaphat said, "Let not the king say that!" 9 And the king of Israel summoned a certain officer and said, "Quickly, Micaiah son of Imlah!" 10 Now the king of Israel and Jehoshaphat king of Judah were sitting each upon his throne, clad in robes, in the open space at the doorway of the gate of Samaria, while all the prophets were prophesying before them. 11 And Zedekiah son of Kenaanah made himself iron horns and said, "Thus says Yahweh, 'By these shalt thou push Aram to their destruction.' " 12 And all the prophets prophesied the same, saying, "Go thou up to Ramoth-Gilead and succeed, and Yahweh shall deliver into thy hand even the king of Aram." 13 And the messenger who went to summon Micaiah said to him, "Look now, the prophets have spoken good to the king with one mouth. Let thy words be like the word of one of them: so speak thou good!" 14 And Micaiah said, "By Yahweh's life, I swear that whatever Yahweh shall say to me, that is what I will speak!" 15 And he came to the king; and the king said to him, "Micaiah, shall I go up to Ramoth-Gilead to fight or shall I desist?" And he said, "Go thou up and succeed, and Yahweh shall deliver it into the king's hand." 16 And the king said to him, "How often must I adjure thee that thou art not to speak to me in Yahweh's name except in truth?" 17 Then he said,

I saw all Israel
  scattered on the mountains,
  like sheep for whom there is no shepherd.
And Yahweh said,
  They have no masters,
  they shall each return home in safety.

18 And the king of Israel said to Jehoshaphat, "Did I not say to thee that he does not prophesy good concerning me but only evil?" 19 And he said, "Therefore hear thou the word of Yahweh! I saw Yahweh sitting on his throne, with all the host of heaven standing beside him, to his right and to his left. 20 And Yahweh said, 'Who shall deceive Ahab, so that he will go up and fall at Ramoth-Gilead?' And one said this and another said that. 21 Then the Spirit came forth and stood before Yahweh; and he said, 'I will deceive him.' And Yahweh said to him, 'How?' 22 And he said, 'I will go forth and become a lying spirit in the mouth of all his prophets.' And he said, 'Thou shalt deceive him; indeed, thou shalt succeed! Go and do it!' 23 So now, look! Yahweh has appointed a lying spirit in the mouth of all these thy prophets; thus Yahweh has spoken evil against thee." 24 And Zedekiah son of Kenaanah approached and

struck Micaiah on his cheek, and said, "In what manner did Yahweh's spirit pass from me to speak with thee?" 25 And Micaiah said, "Behold, thou shalt be an observer of it on that day, when thou shalt enter an inner chamber to hide!" 26 And the king of Israel said, "Take thou Micaiah and bring him back to Amon, the city governor, and to Joash the king's son. 27 And thou shalt say, 'Keep this person in jail and feed him with scant bread and scant water until I come in safety.' " 28 And Micaiah said, "If thou indeed return in safety, Yahweh has not spoken through me." 29 Then the king of Israel and Jehoshaphat king of Judah went up to Ramoth-Gilead. 30 And the king of Israel said to Jehoshaphat, "With respect to girding for combat and entering into battle: dress thou thyself in thy robes." But the king of Israel girded himself for combat and so went into battle. 31 And the king of Aram ordered his chariot commanders, "Fight not with the small or the great, but expressly with the king of Israel." 32 And it happened that, when the chariot commanders saw Jehoshaphat, they said, "Surely, he is the king of Israel!" So they turned to fight against him, and Jehoshaphat cried out. 33 And it happened that, when the chariot commanders saw that he was not the king of Israel, they turned away from him. 34 But someone drew the bow at a chance and struck the king of Israel between the scale armor and the breastplate. And he said to the charioteer, "Turn thou thy hand and bring me away from the battle line, for I have been wounded!" 35 So the battle intensified that day, while the king remained propped up in the chariot facing toward Aram. But he died at evening, and the blood from his wound seeped into the bottom of the chariot. 36 And the alarm spread just as the sun went down, "Each man to his city, and each man to his land!" 37 So the king died. And he came to Samaria, and they buried the king in Samaria. 38 And they washed the chariot at the pool of Samaria, and the dogs licked his blood and the harlots washed in it, according to the word of Yahweh.

NOTES TO CHAPTER TWO

1. Cf. M. Rehm, *Textkritische Untersuchungen zu den Parallelstellen der Samuel-Königsbücher und der Chronik* (Münster i.W., 1937); W. E. Lemke, *Synoptic Studies in the Chronicler's History* (diss., Harvard, 1964); L. C. Allen, *The Greek Chronicles; The Relation of the LXX of I and II Chronicles to the Massoretic Text* (2 vols.; SVT 25, 27; Leiden, 1974).

2. Cf. F. M. Cross, "The History of the Biblical Text in the Light of Discoveries in the Judaean Desert," *Harvard Theological Review* 57 (1964), 281-299; *idem*, "The Evolution of a Theory of Local Texts," *SCS* 2 (1972), 108-126.

3. Citations of this and other LXX readings are from A. E. Brooke, N. McLean, and H. St. John Thackeray, *The Old Testament in Greek* (London, 1930).

4. Though this division has been recognized since Thackeray's *The Septuagint and Jewish Worship* (London, 1920), the identification, dating and characterization of the *Kaige* recension has followed from D. Barthélemy's pioneering work, *Les Devanciers d'Aquila* (SVT 10; Leiden, 1963). Cf. Emanuel Tov, "The State of the Question: Problems and Proposed Solutions," *SCS* 2 (1972), pp. 3-15.

5. Cf. Barthélemy, *op. cit.*, pp. 48-54.

6. Cf. *ibid.*, pp. 31-47.

7. Cf. T. Muruoka, *SCS* 2 (1972), p. 97. Old Greek (= the putative original LXX) is in III Reigns 21:30.

8. A plausible explanation for the mixed character of the Greek text in I Kings 22:1-40 is offered by James D. Shenkel, *Chronology and Recensional Development in the Greek Text of Kings* (Harvard Semitic Monographs 1; Cambridge, Mass., 1968), pp. 62-64.

9. See Barthélemy's arguments for designating this as a revision rather than as a recension in the full meaning of that word: *SCS* 2 (1972), pp. 65ff.

10. Though καὶ ἐγενήθη has been edited out of parts of the OG sections in [B] I-IV Reigns, it continues to predominate in I Reigns 1–7, 14–20, 24–30, where [L] has καὶ ἐγένετο. *Kaige* preserves this form in the [B] text of IV Reigns 17:3; 22:3; 24:1; 25:1, 25, 27, as well as here.

11. The 1st aorist form prevails in OG sections of I-IV Reigns and is read by LXX Chron.

12. Τάχος, only here, is idiomatic for MT מהרה, while [L], attested in third century B.C. papyri, is probably dialectical. Cf. Shenkel, *Chronology*, p. 115, for *Kaige*'s preference for ταχύνειν in place of OG σπεύδειν; neither [L] nor [B] represents OG in this reading.

13. From III Reigns 2:19 to 22:19 a scribe has emended [L] to read acc.

14. [L] reads Heb. דרש נא as דרשנו.

15. [L] reflects Chron.

16. [L] = Chron.

17. See below, p. 14 n. 19.

18. [L] = Chron. The three passages where this [B] reading is found (II Reigns 16:6; III Reigns 22:19; IV Reigns 11:11) are all in the *Kaige* section.

19. It is necessary to resolve the striking differences between the various versions of I Kings 22:4bβ (= II Chron. 18:3b) in comparison with II Kings 3:7bβ. The major discrepancies lie in two particulars: (1) the respective order of the 1cs and 2ms pronominal suffixes in the sequence of comparisons; (2) the omission of the third comparison in Chron., with attendant corruption. Inasmuch as the establishment of the original reading has importance for our ensuing literary analysis, some effort must be made to account for the development of these divergences.

Although Chron. displays obvious corruption in revising the Kings gloss למלחמה to במלחמה, and placing it at the end of the verse following a misread and superfluous ועמך, it is not probable that its lack of the third comparison is to be blamed to accident or intentional omission; it seems reasonable to suppose that its Kings *Vorlage* lacked it also. Since it is unlikely that the order of the pronominal suffixes in MT Chron. would have been influenced by the 2ms/1cs order of any Greek text, in particular that of LXX^{L} in Kings, the fact that its second comparison follows the 2ms/1cs order is evidence that its Kings *Vorlage* already had it. Although LXX^{Bec2} in Chron. revises this item to fit the order of MT Kings (1cs/2ms), all other mss. cited in the Cambridge Septuagint support MT Chron. As a matter of fact, LXX^{be2}, so much like MT that they read καὶ before μετὰ σοῦ, read the 2ms/1cs order in the second comparison as well as in the first, suggesting that the original Heb. text in Chron. was entirely like that of the original Heb. text in Kings, with the 2ms/1cs order in the first as well as in the second comparison, while lacking the third.

The transmission of the original Heb. text in Kings came under strong influence from the similar reading in II Kings 3:7bβ, which was in all likelihood originally the same as that of our present MT: כמוני כמוך כעמי כעמך כסוסי כסוסיך. The fact that Jehoshaphat is speaking here as well as in I Kings 22 provided an irresistible temptation to translational and transcriptional emendation in the latter.

The Lucianic text worked from I Kings 22 to II Kings 3. But in the former passage it does not systematically represent the OG. From the absence of οὕτως in the third Lucianic comparison in I Kings 22, we may infer that OG here had no more than καθὼς σὺ οὕτως καὶ ἐγώ, καὶ καθὼς ὁ λαός σου οὕτως καὶ ὁ λαός μου, idiomatically but faithfully rendering the old Heb. text. Very probably after the emergence of the OG translation, the latter was emended according to MT II Kings 3, adding the third comparison and transposing the order to 1cs/2ms. The LXX^{L} text of I Kings 22 accepted this addition from II Kings 3 but retained both the style and the order (2ms/1cs) of the OG. LXX^{L} in II Kings 3 was on its part so strongly influenced by its rendering in I Kings 22 that it carried the 2ms/1cs order to this new text, meanwhile prefixing καὶ εἶπεν to the citation in order to make Joram the speaker, thus keeping Jehoshaphat in a place of subordination by having him ask the question leading to Joram's authoritative decision at the end of vs. 8.

I Kings 22 MT eventually transposed the 2ms/1cs order to agree with that of II Kings 3, thus creating complete harmony. The *Kaige* recensionist, who apparently was introducing the final phase of his revision of Kings at I Kings 22, could not entirely free himself from the style of OG, but did reverse the 2ms/1cs order, still retained in LXX^{L}, to suit a Heb. text now identical with, or very similar to, the MT. Awkwardly, LXX^{B}, which here represents *Kaige,* transposes LXX^{L}'s καθὼς συ οὕτως καὶ ἐγώ to καθὼς ἐγώ καὶ συ οὕτως. This relatively late text drops the second οὕτως and the connective καὶ in the third comparison.

LXX^{L} in II Kings 3 is conflate in the first comparison, inserting ὅμοιός σοι ὅμοιος ἐμοί directly after the proto-Lucianic reading ὡς ἂν σὺ καὶ ἐγώ. It borrowed this from the *Kaige* text $^{(B)}$ in II Kings 3, which reads ὅμοιός μοι ὅμοιός σοι in the first comparison, then reverts to the ὡς-style of LXX^{L} in the second and third comparisons. LXX^{B} naturally insists on retaining MT's 1cs/2ms order.

20. Although the OT nowhere else specifically associates a *gōren* with a *ša'ar* (gate), Jer. 15:7 with *wā'ezrem b^{e}mizreh b^{e}ša'^{a}rê hā'āreṣ*, "And I will winnow them with a winnowing fan in the gates of the land," strikingly suggests that threshing (and winnowing) was often done at village or town gateways; cf. G. Dalman, *Arbeit und Sitte in Palästina,* III (Gütersloh, 1933), 67ff., especially pp. 70-74, "Im Altertum."

The great majority of passages with *gōren* associate this term with threshing or winnowing (Num. 15:20; 18:27, 30; Deut. 15:4; 16:13; I Sam. 23:1; II Sam. 24:16, 18, 21, 24 (= I Chron. 21:15ff.); II Kings 6:27; Jer. 51:33; Hos. 9:1f.;

13:3; Joel 2:24; Mic. 4:12; Job 39:12; Ruth 3:2f., 6, 14; II Chron. 3:1), though the term as such may designate merely the bare or empty space with a rock or earth floor (cf. Judg. 6:37-40) where these activities were carried out. Judg. 6:37 cannot be specifically associated with agricultural activity; the *gōren* of Nakon in II Sam. 6:6 (= *gōren kîdōn* in I Chron. 13:9) may have cultic associations, while *gōren hā'āṭād* in Gen. 50:10f. is identified as a place of public mourning.

Since *gōren* is a familiar Heb. word, its omission in the LXX can hardly be motivated by any translational difficulty. This might be used as an argument for a Heb. dittography from בגדים, were it not for (1) the unusualness of reading that the *gōren* in question is located at the gate of a famous city and (2) a striking parallel from Ugaritic literature (cf. John Gray, *PEQ* 85 [1953], 118-123; *idem, Kings* [OTL; 2nd ed. 1970], p. 450) putting these two terms in parallelism. The text in question, 2 Aqht V, 3-8 (cf. par 1 Aqht I, 19-25), reads as follows:

(3) whn šb['] (4) bymm.	And behold, on the seventh day —
apnk.dnil.mt (5) rpi.	straightway Daniel the Rapha-man,
a[p]hn.ģzr.mt.hrnm[y]	for[th]with Ghazir the Harnam[iyy]-man,
(6) ytšu.yṯb.bap ṯgr.	is upright, sitting before the gate,
(7) tḥt adrm.dbgrn.	beneath a mighty tree on the threshing floor,
(8) ydn dn.almnt.	judging the cause of the widow,
yṯpṭ.ṯpṭ.ytm	adjudicating the case of the fatherless.

(H. L. Ginsberg, *ANET,* 151a)

21. *Contra* C. F. Burney, *Notes on the Hebrew Text of the Book of Kings* (Oxford, 1903), p. 253.

22. Cf. *ibid.*, p. xxiv.

23. *Contra* Seebass, *VT* 21 (1971), 382n, MT should be retained. As our literary-critical and form-critical discussion will indicate, לכן has an important function in its original narrative form (see below, pp. 28, 50 n. 22).

24. Inasmuch as οὐχ οὕτως for לכן occurs as an occasional non-*Kaige* reading (Gen. 4:15; 30:15; Judg. 8:7[A]; 11:8[A]; Job 20:2; Isa. 10:16; Jer. 2:33) and is supported by II Chron. 18:18, the usual LXX[B] equivalent is διὰ τοῦτο (cf. I Reigns 2:30; 27:6; Judg. 8:7[B]; 10:13; 11:8[B]), which *Kaige* characteristically uses for על כן and על זאת (Barthélemy, *Devanciers,* pp. 84f.). That οὐχ οὕτως should represent OG in our passage seems highly unlikely. Theodoret omits its first occurrence in vs. 19. In IV Reigns 1:3(4), 6, 16, [L] has OG διὰ τοῦτο for *Kaige* οὐχ οὕτως, omitted by [L] in 19:32 (cf. also 21:12; 22:20). Support for our position is expressed by Allen, *The Greek Chronicles,* II, 86.

25. *Contra* Burney, p. 255.

26. Cf. Allen, II, 83.

27. *Contra* Allen, I, 131.

28. Seebass, p. 380, argues that the second LXX variant, along with MT, represents a confused reading of the original preserved in the first variant (Heb. מבקר עד ערב). The elimination of this first reference to the king's death makes the second reference (37) meaningful while removing the awkwardness of a reference to post-mortem bleeding in vs. 35. Two criticisms of Seebass's suggestion are (1) that MT, vs. 37 is specifically intended as a resumptive summarization and (2) that the first LXX variant in vs. 35 must be a corruption from the second, rather than *vice versa,* because the narrative implies that the battle was too far along for the phrase "from the morning" to have any meaning in this context.

29. Cf. Burney, *Notes,* p. 258.

30. "Thou," "thy," "thee" render the Heb. second-personal singular pronouns. "You" and imperatives without these forms render the Heb. plurals.

CHAPTER THREE

Literary Analysis

1. EVIDENCES OF COMPOSITENESS

WE ARE PREPARED NOW TO INQUIRE INTO THE HOMOGENEITY OF THE material that has survived our text-critical scrutiny. Using MT Kings, minus the heretofore identified textual alterations and expansions, as our basic text, we immediately set aside vss. 1-2a as an undoubted redactional transition from chap. 20, which the Hebrew text transposes with chap. 21, belonging originally before chap. 20 (so LXX). We are similarly prepared to remove vss. 35bβ and 38 since there is nothing within the body of the intervening narrative that leads one to expect a denouement in the king's bloody disgrace rather than in the simple event of his death.[1]

What remains exhibits a meaninglessly complex and disjointed structure: Jehoshaphat visits the king of Israel, who, after consulting with his attendants, invites him to join him in attacking Syria at Ramoth-Gilead; Jehoshaphat first agrees, then demands an oracle; four hundred prophets advise advance, leading Jehoshaphat to request, and finally insist upon, the appearance of the evil-saying prophet, Micaiah; as Micaiah is being summoned, the two kings are described as sitting on their thrones while the prophets are described as in the process of prophesying; in their midst a certain Zedekiah delivers a symbolic-act oracle promising victory, and in this all the prophets acquiesce; meanwhile, the man summoning Micaiah advises him to speak as the others have spoken, to which Micaiah replies with an oath that what Yahweh says he will speak; yet when facing the kings he answers as the others have done, and only when chided by the disbelieving king of Israel recites the vision of scattered sheep having no shepherd; the king of Israel rightly interprets this as conveying evil, but Micaiah breaks in with a second vision concerning Yahweh's commission to a lying spirit in the mouth of the prophets of Ahab (here so named for the first and only time);[2] this now leads Zedekiah to strike Micaiah and reproach him, ending in the latter's cryptic, seemingly feeble repartee, "Behold, you shall observe it on that day, when you shall go into an inner chamber to hide." But the story goes on: after the king's harsh command for imprisonment and deprivation elicits from Micaiah another cryptic utterance, this time containing an ominous warning, "If you return in safety, Yahweh has not spoken by me," the two kings proceed to Ramoth-Gilead; because the king of Israel disguises himself, the Syrians are at first misled into attacking Jehoshaphat; by chance a bowman strikes the king of Israel with his arrow, forcing him to leave the fray and remain propped up until he dies; occurring just at sunset, his death is taken by his troops as the signal for their dispersal; the king "comes" to Samaria and is buried.

It is little wonder that the interpreters remain divided as to whether this should be called an historical report, a prophetic narrative, a fable, or whatever. Würthwein seeks to resolve the dilemma by severing the battle narrative from the prophet story. There are three places in the narrative where the development seems particularly retarded and confused: at vs. 10, where the setting for the narration that has already been proceeding is first set forth; at vs. 19, where Micaiah, not expressly named in the text at this point, interrupts the king's remonstrance with his second vision; and at vs. 25, where Micaiah delivers his seemingly lame reply to Zedekiah.

Evidences of internal disunity that have impressed Würthwein as possessing significance for documentary reconstruction are the following: (1) that vss. 4b-5 twice introduce Jehoshaphat as speaking, but with inconsistent content; (2) the apparent shift of scene and inexplicably introductory description in vss. 10f.; (3) the unaccountable change of subject in vs. 19, leading to Micaiah's second vision-oracle in vss. 20ff.; (4) the fact that Micaiah is rebuked in vs. 24, then punished in vss. 26f. — suggesting parallel, mutually contradictory themes of opposition; and (5) the two separate but seemingly climactic repartees in vs. 25 and vs. 28, respectively.

The fact that in vs. 5 Jehoshaphat is depicted as reversing what he said in vs. 4 and the fact that Micaiah, the central figure in vss. 5-28, disappears entirely from the story in its denouement of vss. 29-37, are taken by Würthwein as primary evidence that vss. 1-4, 29-37 were originally independent of the prophet narrative in the intervening verses. He argues further that vss. 19-22, with vs. 23 as a redactional transition, must be separate in origin from its immediate framework because it contains a second vision following immediately upon a first, and because it features a strange new matter, completely ungermane to its context.[3] This framework must in turn be separated into two strata, featuring respectively the confrontation between Micaiah and the king (vss. 5-9, 13-17, 18?, 26-28) and the confrontation between Micaiah and Zedekiah (vss. 10-12, 24-25). The king-versus-Micaiah account comes to a climax in Micaiah's prediction of the king's death (17) and ends in the report of the prophet's imprisonment; to this basic prophet stratum the Zedekiah-versus-Micaiah material, focusing the predicted calamity in terms of certain unnamed terrors coming upon Samaria, serves as a redactional corrective. The lying-spirit section, in turn, corrects Zedekiah's claim to possess the spirit of Yahweh. This complex prophet narrative, joined to the *Sage* of vss. 1-4, 29-37, at last turns the latter into a report of the fulfillment of prophecy, something its original composer never intended it to be.

There are a number of weaknesses in Würthwein's hypothesis. Divorced from the prophet material, the so-called *Sage* remains an enigma. It is a "fable" with a pointless polemic. Such feeble moralizing as Würthwein sees it making is quite unparalleled in this whole range of literature. Würthwein scarcely does justice to the subtle irony conveyed in the motif of the king's disguising himself. He fails to see that the pretext is continued in the king's propping himself up while his life ebbs away. But the highly complex redactional process to which the prophet narrative was subjected, according to Würthwein's hypothesis, is even more objectionable. The most damaging criticism is that, without vss. 1-4, it has no proper beginning; even if LXX^{L} should be followed in eliminating כיום in vs. 5, we find Jehoshaphat all too abruptly demanding an oracle. As a matter of fact, Jehoshaphat remains essentially without function in Würthwein's primitive prophet story, being introduced only as a device for bringing Micaiah into the narrative; we naturally ask, Why should it have to be Jehoshaphat? Why not someone else — such as one of the king of Israel's servants? And finally we ask, Where does the narrative go? In the end, Micaiah is consigned to prison, and we assume that the king of Israel goes off to war, presumably with Jehoshaphat, but nothing is resolved.

The solution that we would propose avoids the aimless complexities of Würthwein's hypothesis; but, rather than dismissing as irrelevant any of the inconcinnities that Würthwein has noted, we consider it essential to point out various new ones that he has not seen, or has ignored. These are the following:

(1) As some exegetes have insisted, the command to Jehoshaphat in vs. 30, *l^{e}bāš b^{e}gādéykā,* "put on thy robes," actually is inconsistent with vs. 10 and cannot be harmonized away by explaining that different garments were worn in battle than were worn on the throne. Those interpreters are wrong, however, who take this command to mean that Jehoshaphat was a flunky. The king of Israel simply advises him to do what is normal in battle, according him a priority that he in fact possessed, according to the conception of the narrative in its original form. This allows the king of Israel to resort to a trick aimed at avoiding the evil word that had been placed upon him.

(2) Not only is the singular address of vss. 10-12 inconsistent with

the co-ordination of the two kings at the beginning of vs. 10; so likewise vs. 15 in its original form.

(3) While it is certainly true that the phrase, "and all the prophets (were) prophesying," in vs. 10 is redundant after vs. 6,[4] it should also be noted that the prophets' advice in vs. 12b, particularly in its Septuagintal wording, differs in form from that of vs. 6.

(4) Whereas in vs. 9 the king of Israel summons a *śārîś* ("officer") to fetch Micaiah, it is a *mal'āk* ("messenger") who actually comes to call him in vs. 13.

(5) Micaiah is astonishingly, inexplicably inconsistent: in vs. 14 he swears an awful oath by Yahweh's very life, that what Yahweh will say[5] to him is what he will speak, yet immediately in vs. 15 he tells so palpable a lie that in vs. 16 the king has to chide him.[6] In vs. 22 Micaiah suggests that Yahweh has put a lying spirit in the mouth of the king's prophets, but fails to apply this same, very pertinent criticism to himself.

(6) The *lākēn* ("therefore," "as a consequence of the foregoing") with which Micaiah introduces his second vision-oracle presupposes something that he himself has just said, not the king of Israel's comment to Jehoshaphat (18).

2. THE IDENTIFICATION OF INDEPENDENT NARRATIVES

When we add these inconsistencies to the ones noted above, we find the thesis of homogeneity extremely difficult to defend. True, more or less plausible explanations may be devised for some of them, but several difficulties remain. The cautious scholar strives not to succumb to hypercriticism. By way of proposing a solution I here make use of a form-critical discovery that came out of my own earlier mentioned study of biblical time-designatives.[7] In the process of analyzing the function of past and future occurrences of the expression *bayyôm hahû'*, "in that day," it was observed that there are only two other passages in the Old Testament where past *bayyôm hahû'* and futuristic *bayyôm hahû'* occur together. These are Deut. 31:16-22 and I Sam. 3:1-21. In each of these the separate past and future references may be clearly drawn to distinct literary sources.[8] This observation, coupled with the recognition that *bayyôm hahû'* is a heavily weighted expression, occurring casually only in dissociated glosses (which are hardly in question here), means that the futuristic and the past *bayyôm hahû'*, appearing in climactic positions in vs. 25 and vs. 35, respectively, are certainly to be traced to separate, independent literary documents.

As compared with Würthwein's elaborate thesis, our solution is relatively simple. First of all, the words ויאמר יהושפט in vs. 4 are to be taken as a gloss influenced, like the several textual corruptions of this verse noted above, by II Kings 3:7. Since it can be argued that II Kings 3 is a late Jehuite polemic,[9] this insertion in I Kings 22:4 must be late. There is no reason whatever to regard the following words as an address of Jehoshaphat and to split vs. 5 from vs. 4.[10] It is the king of Israel, inviting Jehoshaphat to accompany him to Ramoth-Gilead, who goes on to say (with LXX^{L}; cf. Chron.), "As you are, so am I; as is your people, so is my people."[11]

It is uncertain whether the glossator of vs. 4 is the same as the redactor who has welded together two independent stories in the section, vss. 10-28. Our redactor incorporated a new account beginning in vs. 10. As the singularistic address reveals, this account is concerned only with Ahab, introduced here as "the king of Israel," but "Jehoshaphat the king of Judah" is at his side.[12] The redactor is responsible for the transitional ויאמר at the beginning of vs. 19 and for a harmonizing insertion in vs. 20, ויעל ויפל ברמת גלעד. Since this redactor was combining two somewhat disparate sources, he needed to resort to minor composition of his own in order to explain the jarring clash between Micaiah's oath in vs. 14 and that prophet's apparent willingness to mislead in vs. 15, as also to account for the double vision-oracle that resulted from the combination. Vs. 12a was originally composed to stand by itself, stating simply that "all the prophets" echoed Zedekiah (וכל . . . נבאים כן). The redactor put a saying into their mouths (12b) that is, according to the LXX, neither identical with what Zedekiah has just been saying here nor identical with what the four hundred say in vs. 6, though of course their saying does accord with the general tenor of each. In vs. 13 the redactor used his own substitute term, *hammal'āk,* as an interpretive equivalent to the *śārîś* of vs. 9, adding the resumptive link, אשר הלך לקרא מיכיהו; in his advice to Micaiah this "messenger" significantly refers to Micaiah's coming *words* (pl.; cf. "the *word* of one of them," i.e., single oracle) because in his new combination Micaiah was actually to deliver one oracle more than appears in each of the original parallel accounts.

The material that remains after the removal of these redactional transformations and supplementations falls meaningfully into two simple and internally cohesive accounts. What we may for the time being call Narrative A comprises the original Hebrew material in vss. 2b-4a, 4bβ-9, 15-18, 26-37; what we may for the time being call Narrative B is found in vss. 10-12a, 14, 19 (except ויאמר)-20aα, 20b-25. In both stories Micaiah is the chief protagonist, and the major theme of each is that of resistance to his word and its effect. Furthermore, both stories involve a king of Israel in the situation of pondering congenial prophetic advice respecting war against Syria. In other words, the historical background has to be the half-century of intermittent conflict between Israel and Syria from the end of the Omride dynasty (after 841 B.C.) until the final success of

Jeroboam II in the years after 790. Who our Micaiah was, we have no idea; though he has attracted no extensive cycle of narrative tradition to himself, he was evidently cast in the mold of an Elijah or an Elisha. Because our chapter has two separate stories about him, we may infer that Micaiah was indeed an historical figure; but just where he fits within the period mentioned, we can at this point only guess.[13] We need to examine each of the narratives and evaluate their separate structures in detail before we can assess the processes involved in the growth of tradition about him and trace them to a point of ultimate derivation.[14]

It is the intent of the following chapter to examine individually each of these Micaiah narratives in order to get their resemblances and differences into focus as a basis for further discussion. Once it is clearly seen that each exhibits a cohesive, meaningful structure it will be difficult to entertain the hypothesis that the redactor whose work we have here identified could have been inventing the one narrative to supplement and enlarge the other. Neither Micaiah narrative can be understood as a commentary on the other, for neither shows awareness of the other. They stand each alone as independent literary products (however much previously shaped in oral tradition), and though the redactor did create something new in his imaginative combination, the resulting story has been improved neither in aesthetic form nor in ideational clarity. We can only suppose that the redactor was dissatisfied with one or both of them — perhaps it was with Narrative B's lack of an historical resolution — or sought to improve each by using the one to fill out the other.

Admittedly, this sort of literary combination is rarely seen in the prophet narratives (see our analysis in Chapter Five), yet we must acknowledge the strong evidence for it here. The closest parallel to the literary methodology of our redactor may be the work of the editor who intertwined the Yahwistic and Elohistic narrations of the Pentateuchal history, who like our redactor probably lived and worked in Judah shortly after the fall of the northern kingdom, endeavoring to preserve by combination all that he knew of Yahweh's mysterious work in the life of his people.[15]

NOTES TO CHAPTER THREE

1. *Contra* Seebass, *VT* 21 (1971), 381f., vs. 17 most assuredly does imply the king's death; cf. vs. 28. Not only is the reference to the king's bleeding in vs. 35bβ functionless following the notice of his death; it disrupts the coalescence of temporal references intended by the original, according to which the king's dying became the signal for the dispersal. As has been noted, vs. 37 is a resumptive summary.

2. "All his prophets" (22) implies that Micaiah does not consider himself to have been affected by the coming of this lying spirit, in spite of the lie he told in vs. 15.

3. Citing Volz, Würthwein argues that the figure of *hārûaḥ* (= *rûaḥ šeqer*) in vss. 19-23 is "ein Gemisch von Volkstümlich Glauben und schriftstellerischer Reflexion" (Maass, ed., Festschrift Rost [1967], p. 250).

4. It is the new characterization and the aimless repetitiousness of vss. 10-12, not the participial construction of vs. 10 in itself, that lead us to identify vs. 10 as a new beginning. Although the participial construction, with subject foremost, is often a resumptive or transitional element, it occurs sometimes at the beginning of original narration, as in Judg. 4:4f.; I Kings 20:30b; II Kings 4:38, 42; 8:7 (see below), generally with noun clauses, providing an introductory exposition.

Being unfamiliar with the most recent criticism of our pericope, Hubert Cancik chooses I Kings 22 as a prime sample for analysis from the viewpoint of modern linguistics, assuming that it is an "offenbar recht alten und einheitlichen Partie" and that the participial construction characterizing the kings and prophets in vs. 10 is resumptive. This is on pp. 195-99 of Cancik's monograph, *Grundzüge des hethitischen und alttestamentlichen Geschichtsschreibung* (Wiesbaden, 1976). He attributes the repetitiousness to be observed in vss. 10-12 to the narrator's desire for embellishment: "Bemerkenswert an dieser Darstellung ist zunächst, dass von der Sache her die Wahl einer so komplizierter Erzählform nicht notwendig war. Die Prophezeiung der vierhundert Propheten wird schon in Vers 6 berichtet; der Erzähler hätte leicht die Prophezeiung Zedeqias an dieser Stelle einfügen können. Dass er eine gleichzeitige Handlung konstruierde, ist ein deutlicher Beweis für die Erzählfreudigkeit und Erzählkunst der früheren israelitischen Historiographen" (p. 199). But as we intend to show in Chapter Five, the earlier species of prophet legend regularly display a tightly drawn, highly functional structure, with no room for artistic display.

5. Cf. A. Šanda, EHAT, *in loco*. J. Fichtner, BotAT, *in loco,* offers an ingenious explanation of the imperfect and of Micaiah's initial "lie." It is too sophisticated to be considered as a probable solution.

The 3ms impf. of אמר, with the deity as subject, occurs in present reference in a variety of formulas, all distinct from the familiar herald formula used to introduce prophetic oracles, which employs the perfect. Introductory citation formulas appear in Isa. 1:11 (prophetic torah), 1:18 (controversy oracle), 33:10 (divine self-identification in a controversy oracle), 40:1 (proem to a hymnic collection), 40:25 (diatribe), 41:21 *bis* (controversy oracle). An oracle formula at the end of a salvation oracle has it in Isa. 66:9, and in Ps. 12:6 it occurs in an introductory citation formula within a salvation oracle in a psalm of individual lament. I Kings 22:14 (= II Chron. 18:13) has the futuristic reference common to the other passages containing the locution *'ašer yō'mar YHWH* (Exod. 8:23; Deut. 5:27; Jer. 42:20).

6. In I Kings 13:17 the words כחש לו are generally recognized as redactional; the old prophet of Bethel had a revelation in conflict with that of the Judahite man of God, but this does not mean that he consciously and deliberately lied. In II Kings 8:10 no lie is implied: that Ben-Hadad should recover was a true word, reported to the king in vs. 14. It would have been fulfilled, we may think, were it not for Hazael's treacherous act of vs. 15, which Elisha foresees in 10b. See the analysis of these two passages below, pp. 59ff., 64f. Cf. C. J. Labuschagne, "Did Elisha Deliberately Lie? — A Note on II Kings 8:10," *ZAW* 77 (1965), 327f.

7. *YTT,* pp. 112f., 292-95; cf. 63f., 69, 104f., 173, 286-89.

8. Deut. 31:16, 19-22 is a late composition intended as an introduction to chap. 32. In vss. 17f. a threefold futuristic *bayyôm hahû'* (cf. past, vs. 22) appears in a secondary expansion in which Yahweh personally threatens the evil that is objectively envisaged in vs. 21. Past *bayyôm hahû'* introduces original narrative material in I Sam. 3:2; the futuristic reference in vs. 12 is part of a late Zadokite polemic.

9. See our discussion of this passage in Chapters Five and Six. II Kings 3, accepting Jehoshaphat from this tradition, aims not at idealizing him (he is already present as a symbolic figure of ideal orthodoxy) but at depicting the apostasy of the northern king, himself symbolic of the Omride dynasty.

10. However Jehoshaphat may have entered into the tradition underlying our present narrative, neither this verse nor vs. 30 justifies the widely accepted view that this southern king was subject-vassal to Ahab. On this question, see Chapter Six.

11. Or, "As you shall act, so shall I; as your army shall act, so shall mine"; see above, p. 22. This form of the text certainly suggests Jehoshaphat's priority and explains why he was in a position to insist upon a reliable oracle. The king of Israel could act only if Jehoshaphat was willing to act.

12. We note that LXX[L] reverses the order of the two kings. Is it justifiable to suppose that "Jehoshaphat king of Judah" was added marginally in an early Hebrew *Vorlage* and was then copied in the wrong place by one of the variant recensions? We resist this on general grounds. Though it is conceivable that a scribe or redactor might have added these words to our second narrative to bring it into conformity with the first, the recognition of a common tradition for the two stories favors the likelihood that Jehoshaphat is original in the second story as well as in the first, even though this king has no further function in the structure of this second narrative as it develops.

13. In contrast to the interpretive addition in Chron. and LXX, Heb. את אחאב in vs. 20 is so secure textually that we are obliged to take it as the narrator's original identification of the "king of Israel" described in vs. 10. This in itself may be evidence that Narrative B reflects a somewhat advanced stage of tradition growth, in which the once anonymous "king of Israel" (so named throughout Narrative A) has now come to be equated with a legendary Ahab, notorious for his apostasy and resistance to the divine word.

14. See Chapter Six.

15. For further discussion of redactional processes, see Chapter Seven.

CHAPTER FOUR

The Independent Micaiah Narratives

1. NARRATIVE A

I. The problem: The need for supporting revelation

1. The proposal of "holy" war	
a. The physical situation	*Now Jehoshaphat king of Judah went down to the king of Israel.* (2b)
b. The political/military problem	*And the king of Israel said to his servants, "Do you know that Ramoth-Gilead belongs to us, yet we refrain from seizing it from the hand of the king of Aram?"* (3)
c. The invitation to Jehoshaphat	
(1) The question	*And he said to Jehoshaphat, "Wilt thou go with me to Ramoth-Gilead?"* (4a)
(2) The motivation	*And he added, "As thou shalt act, so shall I; as thy army shall act, so shall my army."* (4bβ)
2. The search for divine approval	
a. The demand for an oracle	*And Jehoshaphat said to the king of Israel, "Inquire thou first of Yahweh."* (5)
b. The favoring oracle: summons, question, reply	*So the king of Israel assembled the prophets — about four hundred persons — and said to them, "Shall I go up to Ramoth-Gilead to fight or shall I desist?" And*

they said, "Go thou up, and Yahweh will deliver it to the king's hand." (6)

3. The arrangement for confirmation

   a. The demand

   But Jehoshaphat said, "Is there not one other prophet here, so that we may inquire from him?" (7)

   b. Characterizing identification of Micaiah

   And the king of Israel said to Jehoshaphat, "There is yet a certain man from whom one may inquire of Yahweh, but I reject him because he does not announce good concerning me but evil: Micaiah son of Imlah." (8a)

   c. The summoning

      (1) Jehoshaphat's rebuke

      And Jehoshaphat said, "Let not the king say that!" (8b)

      (2) The king of Israel's command

      And the king of Israel summoned a certain officer and said, "Quickly, Micaiah son of Imlah!" (9)

II. The confrontation: conflict between a favoring and an evil oracle

1. The initial favoring oracle

   a. The inquiry

   And he came to the king; and the king said to him, "Micaiah, shall I go up to Ramoth-Gilead to fight or shall I desist?" (15a)

   b. The reply

   And he said, "Go thou up and succeed, and Yahweh shall deliver it into the king's hand." (15b)

   c. The rebuke

   And the king said to him, "How often must I adjure thee that thou art not to speak to me in Yahweh's name except in truth?" (16)

2. The superseding evil oracle

   a. The vision

   Then he said, "I saw all Israel scattered on the mountains, like sheep for

	whom there is no shepherd. (17a)
b. Oracular interpretation (thematic phrase: *yāšûbû 'îš l^{e}bêtô b^{e}šālôm)*	*And Yahweh said, 'They have no masters, they shall each return home in safety.' "* (17b)
c. The king's confirmatory characterization	*And the king of Israel said to Jehoshaphat, "Did I not say to thee that he does not prophesy good concerning me but only evil?"* (18)
3. The interpretive diatribe	
a. Instructions for Micaiah's confinement	*And the king of Israel said, "Take thou Micaiah and bring him to Amon, the city governor, and to Joash the king's son.* (26)
b. Accompanying message (thematic phrase: *'ad bō'î b^{e}šālôm)*	*And thou shalt say, 'Keep this person in jail and feed him with scant bread and scant water until I come in safety.' "* (27)
c. Micaiah's repartee	
(1) Protasis: *'im šôb tāšûb b^{e}šālôm*	*And Micaiah said, "If thou indeed return in safety. . .* (28aα)
(2) Apodosis: *lō' dibber YHWH bî*	*Yahweh has not spoken through me."* (28aβ)
III. The resolution: fulfillment of the evil oracle	
Transitional: the scene shifted to Ramoth-Gilead	*Then the king of Israel and Jehoshaphat king of Judah went up to Ramoth-Gilead.* (29)
1. A subterfuge frustrated	
a. Dialogical instructions:	
(1) For disguise	*And the king of Israel said to Jehoshaphat, "With respect to girding for combat and entering into battle: dress thou thyself in thy robes." But the king of Israel girded*

	himself for combat and so went into battle. (30)
(2) For attack	*And the king of Aram ordered his chariot commanders, "Fight not with the small or the great, but expressly with the king of Israel."* (31)
b. Narrative sequel	
(1) The attack on Jehoshaphat ends with his recognition	*And it happened that, when the chariot commanders saw Jehoshaphat, they said, "Surely, he is the king of Israel!" So they turned to fight against him, and Jehoshaphat cried out. And it happened that, when the chariot commanders saw that he was not the king of Israel, they turned away from him.* (32-33)
(2) An accidental arrow strikes the king of Israel	*But someone drew the bow at a chance and struck the king of Israel between the scale armor and the breastplate.* (34a)
c. Confirmatory dialogue	*And he said to the charioteer, "Turn thou thy hand and bring me away from the battle line, for I have been wounded!"* (34b)

2. Denouement: the battle ends in the death of the king of Israel

a. The battle intensifies (transitional link with *bayyôm hahû'*)	*So the battle intensified THAT DAY;* (35aα)
b. The final subterfuge of seeming life	*and the king remained propped up in the chariot facing toward Aram, but at evening he died.* (35aβbα)
c. The army scatters	*And the alarm spread just as the sun went down, "Each man to his city, and each man to his land!"* (36)

3. Resumptive conclusion — *So the king died. And he came to Samaria, and they buried the king in Samaria.* (37)

The physical situation is one involving a visit of Jehoshaphat, the well-known king of Judah, to an unnamed king of Israel. A traditional geographical orientation between the place from which Jehoshaphat has departed and the place to which he has come is reflected in the verb ירד (so in northern documents; cf. II Kings 8:29; 9:16). Though presumably the place of visit is Samaria, this is not expressly stated. The lack of specificity regarding the name of the Israelite king and the place of his residence, viewed in light of marked specificity with regard to both these items in the Ahaziah-Joram narrative of II Kings 9, points to the probability that our story may be a secondary reflex from that narrative, hence without independent historical foundation — a hypothesis that is to be tested in the sequel. It seems certain that friendly relations did exist between the Judahite and Israelite kings throughout most of the period of the Omride and Jehuite dynasties. Jehoshaphat may have been chosen for his role simply because he was the best-known Judahite king of the period in question. Historically he above all others would have been in a position to have rendered military assistance to his northern colleagues; but, as we have seen, the text does not support the common assumption that he was a servile vassal. That he should be the one paying the visit, not the other way round, may simply be due to the northern orientation of our account.

The external threat is Syrian aggression, a condition pertaining for many decades. Though the border town of Ramoth-Gilead is said in II Kings 8:20f.; 9:14 to have been in Israelite hands, it is here identified as under occupation by the king of Syria. The historical sequence of these opposite situations is uncertain, but we may be confident that the memory of defeat and deprivation, as expressed here, can rest solely on historical reality.[1] It is the intolerable fact that Israelite territory has been violated that now inspires the Israelite king to aggressive counteraction, and he knows that he has every right to appeal to his Judahite colleague to take a share in upholding the ideals of the ancient holy war. In any event, the decision to go to war is not left to the outcome of his consultation with his subordinate commanders, but depends on Jehoshaphat's willingness (see above), which in turn depends not on the calculation of numbers but on the assurance that this is indeed a cause in which Yahweh will come to the assistance of his aggrieved people.[2] As the story unfolds, we see that the king of Israel is determined to enlist supernatural power in service of his aggressive aim, while Jehoshaphat is present to remind him that the will of God can never be made subservient to the will of man.

Whether or not the king of Israel would have consulted the four hundred prophets without Jehoshaphat's suggestion,[3] they are there to support him. The unanimous four hundred appear as an idealization of patriotic Yahwism, dedicated to the wholeness of Israel's sacral union. They cannot imagine that the king's proposal should be contrary to the will of Yahweh since it is the well-being of Yahweh's people that is in question.[4] We do wrong in suspecting them of cynical politicizing, an interpretation that arises only from the present arrangement of the text, in which Zedekiah and the king seem to work in collusion in reprimanding and then punishing Micaiah. Yet our narrator, in his time already aware of incipient ideological conflicts within the prophetic circles, introduces the figure of Jehoshaphat to voice the problem whether the well-being of Israel as a nation is necessarily identical with the ambitions of her kings. And when Jehoshaphat's scepticism about the reliability of the unanimity among the four hundred discloses the existence of yet one prophet unsummoned, the narrator makes clear in the way he phrases the reply of the king of Israel that he "hates" (שנא, "repudiates," "avoids," "rejects") him only because he has the alarming habit of making distinctions between Israel's interest and the personal interests of her political leaders ("he never prophesies good *concerning me* . . ."; so vs. 18). Here clearly identified is the major theme of our narrative: in promising the well-being of his people, Yahweh does not necessarily commit himself to the success of an individual leader seeking to impose his political will upon the people. The leader is expendable, though the people never are.

Such is the setting for the confrontation of vss. 15-18. To judge from *hᵃšîbēhû* ("bring him back") in vs. 26, Micaiah has been confined and is now brought from the jailhouse. As he appears in the presence of the two kings, his initial response to the request for an oracle is phrased as even more enthusiastically approving than that of the four hundred.[5] That Micaiah is speaking tongue-in-cheek, as some interpreters claim, is a conjecture contradicted by the king's reply in vs. 16; though vs. 15 does not mention the king's adjuration, it does clearly imply that the oracle had been formally requested according to a regular pattern involving an oath, putting the prophet under solemn obligation to utter divine words, not his private opinion. Nevertheless, the king's insistence upon *raq ʾᵉmet,* "pure truth," implies that, in his understanding, Micaiah has not spoken all that he should have spoken. That is to say, Micaiah is presented as responding with a message of victory for Israel arising from the same stance of solidarity with the nation that characterizes the four hundred, while leaving unsaid a pronouncement concerning the king's personal destiny. Of the promised victory, our narrative has henceforward nothing to report. It is superseded. The prophetic word that is to be put to the test is not this prediction (which turns out to be, in fact, wrong) but the personal oracle directed against the king. And the king knows that Micaiah has not given him *raq 'emet* so long as this promise of victory lacks any mention of his own individual fate.

From Micaiah's final repartee in vs. 28, "If you return in safety, Yahweh has not spoken by me," we are invited to understand his vision in vs. 17 as a revelation apprehended in his inner being but, because of its conflict with vs. 15, uttered with some misgiving that it might not actually have originated from Yahweh. Micaiah is anxious about the interpretation of the vision he has received. This is why he does not deliver it as his initial answer, and in the end he is prepared to allow historical occurrence to be the test. But, being pressed by the king, he now reports the vision, concluding not with his personal interpretation but with a report of what he has heard Yahweh (was it actually Yahweh?) say.[6] Micaiah's description of the visionary scene is probably intended as poetry in spite of an irregular meter; the oracular interpretation is almost certainly poetic. Both vision and interpretation agree in the affirmation that Israel is to behave like shepherdless sheep. Though the interpretation promises that the scattered people will return *b^ešālôm,* it is ominous in its negative insinuation — and thus the king receives it in his confirming word to Jehoshaphat (vs. 18). Micaiah has proven the correctness of the king's initial characterization: he is indeed dangerous to the king because he insists on separating the destiny of the king from the fate of the nation.

It is this that explains the king's harsh measures against Micaiah in vss. 26-28, which we are to understand as no personal recrimination but as a measure emerging out of a dynamistic, semi-magical conception of the prophetic word, one that sees it as an effective, operative extension of the numinous person uttering it.[7] Since Micaiah has now once again shown himself capable of delivering an omen against the king's own person, the king responds with an act of personal power directed against the person of the prophet. By locking him in jail and weakening his hold on life through symbolic starvation, the king intends to subvert the power of the prophet's new word. The king thus imagines himself able to hem in the operation of imminent disaster while he marches out to battle. Only when he returns *b^ešālôm,* which on the word of the four hundred he confidently expects to do, will it be safe to set Micaiah free.

The narrative moves to its resolution as events determine whether indeed the king can assure his personal *šālôm*[8] by these drastic measures. Micaiah on his part is quite content to allow fulfillment to be the test, hence from vs. 28 onward we hear no more of him. The story is not about him, as a matter of fact, but about the king — or, more precisely, about the divine word concerning the king. Our king proves to be no man of half measures. Once on the scene of battle, he resorts to a subterfuge designed to ensure his immunity from the evil oracle: while Jehoshaphat is urged to play out the usual role of recognized leader at the head of the combined armies,[9] the king of Israel obscures his identity by wearing his ordinary battle clothes.[10] The entire episode from vs. 30 to vs. 34, dealing with the frustration of this subterfuge, is a delaying element. It is set in chiastic arrangement, with dialogue in the preparatory instructions of vss. 30f. and confirmatory dialogue at the end surrounding the narration of vss. 32-34a. The first half of this narration dispenses with the peripheral matter of the attack upon Jehoshaphat, directing the reader's attention to the climactic occurrence, the seemingly accidental arrow striking the king of Israel. The reader knows full well that no such arrow is accidental: it is surely Yahweh's deed, powerfully fulfilling his word. The wounded king commands that he be brought away from the place of fighting,[11] a narrative signal that his personal fate has already been separated from the fate of his army. The story is already told: we have only to hear that while the battle intensifies,[12] the king remains propped up, still alive but at the gate of death. Once the day is over, this final subterfuge is played out. The king surrenders his life in fulfillment of Micaiah's ineluctable prophecy. Yahweh has indeed spoken through him. As the army scatters, the king "comes" home only to be buried.

2. NARRATIVE B

I. The revelatory confrontation at Samaria
   1. The situation
      a. The two kings sitting for consultation — *Now the king of Israel and Jehoshaphat king of Judah were sitting each upon his throne, clad in robes, in the open space at the doorway of the gate of Samaria;* (10a)
      b. "All the prophets" prophesying — *and all the prophets were prophesying before them.* (10b)
   2. Zedekiah's favorable oracle
      a. Symbolic action — *And Zedekiah son of Kenaanah made himself iron horns,* (11a)
      b. Interpretive announcement — *and he said, "Thus says Yahweh, 'By these shalt*

	thou push Aram to their destruction.' "(11b)
c. Confirmation by the assemblage	*And all the prophets prophesied the same;* (12a)
II. The revelatory confrontation in heaven	
1. Announcement of independent revelation	*but Micaiah said, "By Yahweh's life, I swear that whatever Yahweh shall say to me, that is what I will speak!"* (14)
2. Micaiah's unfavorable oracle Formal introduction (*lākēn* with summons to hear)	*And he said, "Therefore hear thou the word of Yahweh!* (19a)
a. The vision	
(1) The situation	
(a) Yahweh sitting for consultation	*I saw Yahweh sitting on his throne,* (19bα)
(b) "All the heavenly host" attending	*with all the host of heaven standing beside him, to his right and to his left.* (19bβ)
(2) The consultation	
(a) Yahweh's challenge	*And Yahweh said, 'Who shall deceive Ahab?' And one said this and another said that.* (20aαb)
(b) "The Spirit" volunteers	*Then the Spirit came forth and stood before Yahweh; and he said, 'I will deceive him.'* (21a)
(c) Establishment of the means	*And Yahweh said to him, 'How?' And he said, 'I will go forth and become a lying spirit in the mouth of all his prophets.'* (21b-22a)
(d) Yahweh's commission	*And he said, 'Thou shalt deceive him; indeed, thou*

	shalt succeed! Go and do it!' (22b)
b. Interpretive announcement (*w^{e}ʿattâ. . .*)	
(1) Explanation of the favoring oracle	*So now, look! Yahweh has appointed a lying spirit in the mouth of all these thy prophets;* (23a)
(2) Declaration of its implication (*w^{e}YHWH dibber ʿālékā rāʿā*)	*thus Yahweh has spoken evil against thee."* (23b)
III. The resolution: diatribe between Zedekiah and Micaiah	
1. Zedekiah's rebuke	
a. The blow	*And Zedekiah son of Kenaanah approached and struck Micaiah on his cheek;* (24a)
b. The challenge	*and he said, "In what manner did Yahweh's spirit pass from me to speak with thee?"* (24b)
2. Micaiah's rejoinder	
a. Zedekiah as witness to the day of fulfillment (*bayyôm hahûʾ*)	*And Micaiah said, "Behold, thou shalt be an observer of it ON THAT DAY,* (25a)
b. Zedekiah as object of wrath	*when thou shalt enter an inner chamber to hide!"* (25b)

This outline dramatizes the fact that word is being set against word, and that the conflict between each is to be resolved by a higher authority coming irresistibly to effect in a still-awaited historical event. The relationship between word and word is not that of supersession but of contradiction. Court stands opposed to court, king stands opposed to king, and it is plainly the heavenly court and the heavenly king who possess the higher authority and the greater power.

Verse 10 is structured like vs. 19, with participial noun clauses describing first the kings on their throne, then the activity (or attitude) of those waiting upon them. The king of Israel and Jehoshaphat have taken their seats, not in the throne-room of a palace, but in the traditional place for hearing cases and resolving public issues, an open area at the entranceway to the city of Samaria.[13] To symbolize their authority to decide and to act, they are clad in their official robes. Evidently the kings are present for counsel, though advisory officials are not mentioned.[14] The place of political administrators is taken in this story by "all the prophets." The problem at hand apparently lies beyond the scope of administering public justice or deciding matters of internal politics. There can be only one reason why "all" the prophets have been summoned; this is evidently a matter requiring revelation — some transcendent indication of Yahweh's will.[15] It can only be a matter of the "holy" war, a military threat from a foreign source directed against the nation and people of Yahweh.

While "all" the prophets are described as engaging in offering oracular advice,[16] one of them in particular, a man named formally for purposes of explicit identification (Zedekiah ben Kenaanah),[17] pushes himself to the front to dramatize his oracle in symbolic act.[18] Making horns of iron, he declares, *"bᵉ'ēlleh tᵉnaggaḥ 'et-'ᵃrām 'ad-kallōtām"* — which normally ought to mean, and undoubtedly is intended here to mean, "With these you shall gore (push) Syria until they are destroyed!" By this declaration the enemy is for the first time identified; yet the prediction made by Zedekiah is in no wise synonymous with the advice of the four hundred in Narrative A. A point overlooked by the exegetes is that a subtle ambiguity remains in Zedekiah's prophecy, for the pronominal suffix attached to an infinitive may be subjective as well as objective; i.e., *'ad-kallōtām* could possibly mean the opposite: "until they destroy (you)!"[19]

Vs. 12a, "and all the prophets prophesied similarly," indicates that Zedekiah's presentation is only the most dramatic and expressive of various others, all of which agree in promising success against the Syrians. But one single prophet emerges from this group — or alongside it — to bring a contradictory revelation. From the fact that he is introduced in vs. 14 simply as "Micaiah," with no patronym as in vss. 8f., we may infer that to our narrator he had become a legendary figure like Elijah and Elisha, needing no formal identification.[20] In the oath that he speaks Micaiah makes immediately clear that his oracle can be influenced neither by loyalty to nation nor by fear of king, but solely by the transcendent authority of Yahweh, to whom above all he is obedient. "By the life of Yahweh, what Yahweh is saying/will say to me,[21] that will I speak!" He is at this very moment in an intense state of ecstatic receptivity, burning with desire like Jeremiah (20:9) to declare what he is receiving, unwelcome as it may be to those who must hear it.

With this announcement of his intent,[22] Micaiah describes in vss. 19-22 his vision[23] of a revelatory confrontation going on in heaven[24] simultaneously with the one going on here in Samaria. The situation there corresponds to the situation here: Yahweh is sitting on his throne, while standing[25] in attendance upon him is *kol ṣᵉbā' haššāmayim,* "all the host of heaven." This is the earliest occurrence of this expression; whatever specific connotation it may come to receive in the deuteronomistic tradition (Deut. 4:19; 17:3; II Kings 17:16; 21:3, 5; Jer. 8:2; 19:13; Zeph. 1:5) and in late Old Testament literature influenced by it (Gen. 2:1; Isa. 40:26; 45:12; Ps. 103:21; 148:2; Dan. 8:10; Neh. 9:6), it is clear that this term is here intended to identify the heavenly counterpart(s) to the group of prophets in Samaria. These can be none other than Yahweh's attendants and advisers.[26] One might be tempted to critique this comparison with the observation that while the prophets could do no more than offer advice on which the king himself would be obliged to act, the *ṣᵉbā' haššāmayim* are expected to act more as ministers and agents of the divine will than as advisers. But to assume such is to miss completely the point that the "Spirit" who functions as Yahweh's agent also functions as the principle of inspiration producing in the mouth of the prophets the misleading advice that these in turn give to the king.

Unmistakable parallels to Micaiah's vision are Isaiah 6 and Job 1–2. The latter is a baroque elaboration of the deceptive-spirit theme. Isaiah's call-vision in Isa. 6 (sharing features of Ezekiel's more complex call-vision in Ezek. 1:1ff.) stands much closer to Micaiah's vision in terms of tradition development, featuring the same array of holy attendants, the emergence of a revelatory volunteer, and the effect of hardening (if not misleading or deceiving) the recipients of the revelatory message (Isa. 6:9f.; cf. Ezek. 2:3–3:11).[27] In challenging his advisers to volunteer to "seduce" or "deceive" (פתה pi.) Ahab,[28] Yahweh maintains his traditional image as a deity who not only superintends historical event but actually instigates the revelatory incitement to such event. There is no place in biblical theology at this stage of development for a semi-independent principle of evil, a devil or satan who falls from heaven. Yahweh is the sole originator of all spiritual phenomena, even of such as must be classified as evil in their experiential impact (I Sam. 16:14; II Sam. 24:1; cf. Amos 3:6). In Micaiah's vision Yahweh is preparing to do precisely what Ezekiel claims for him with respect to such a prophet as mistakenly, albeit in all genuine sincerity, speaks a word in the name of Yahweh: deceive him (14:9, פתה pu., pi.). Yahweh is preparing to do what Jeremiah so angrily accuses Yahweh of doing to himself when the Deity allows the prophet's stern messages of judgment to go unfulfilled (20:7, פתה pi., niph.: "Yahweh, thou hast deceived me and I have been deceived!" Cf. vs. 10, pu.).

Neither textual nor literary criticism offers a firm basis for emending the proper name אחאב in vs. 20. Though our narrative has mentioned Jehoshaphat, it is not interested in him; he is quickly forgotten as the narrative sharpens its focus on the king of Israel, now named specifically. Along with a variety of similar indications emerging from our discussion of this narrative, this identification of Ahab as a well-known, almost legendary figure points unmistakably to a date appreciably later than that of Narrative A, where the king in question remains completely anonymous. Although hardly the active protagonist of baalistic apostasy depicted in Jehuite (I Kings 18:19; II Kings 10:18) and deuteronomistic (I Kings 16:31-33) redaction, Ahab has here developed into something more than the well-meaning but misguided monarch of the Elijah stories. Like Micaiah, he has become a typical figure, embodying a single-minded principle of political domination over prophecy, in the same way that Micaiah embodies the principle of prophetic supremacy over politics. It is, in the last analysis, the conflict between these two principles that is the central theme of our narrative.

There has been much discussion, and some aimless speculation, regarding *hārûaḥ* of vs. 21.[29] As the text offers no ground for identifying this figure as some kind of demon, it offers no basis for ignoring the determinative and translating "a spirit." Again, a comparison with vss. 10ff. may be helpful. There many prophets are prophesying but only one has revelation derived directly from heaven; here many attendants offer counsel *(wayyō'mer zeh bekōh wezeh bekōh)* but only one offers *effective* counsel, i.e., such as leads to the accomplishment of the desired result. Among "all the host of heaven" there is, in fact, only one who is able to volunteer for this action. It is "the Spirit" — the spirit of revelation. One and undivided is this revelatory spirit, a fact that Zedekiah too recognizes in his forthcoming reprimand to Micaiah.

As the consultation continues, "the Spirit" explains that he will deceive Ahab by becoming *rûaḥ šeqer* ("a lying spirit") in the mouth of all his prophets; i.e., he will inspire them with the word of prophecy, but it will be a false and misleading prophecy.[30] To this Yahweh gives his emphatic consent: "You shall deceive and you (i.e., your deceit) shall be successful *(tepatteh wegam tûkāl);* go and do it!"

Used in characteristic fashion to mark the transition from situation to consequence, *we'attâ* ("so now")[31] introduces Micaiah's own interpretation of the vision's meaning. The favoring oracle given by the prophets can only be a deception, produced by this *rûaḥ šeqer* speaking through their mouths (vs. 23a). This in turn leads to one unavoidable conclusion (vs. 23b): "so Yahweh has spoken against you (for) evil!" The reference to Yahweh's speaking is to be sought not in his initial challenge (vs. 20) or in his commission (vs. 22) but in the oracles of Ahab's own prophets, and most specifically in the word of Zedekiah. They had indeed spoken, and in good conscience, for Yahweh — but Yahweh had deceived them, and through them Ahab. Perhaps their unknowing deceiving and being deceived lay in the *double entendre* of Zedekiah's infinitive with its pronoun suffix; perhaps it lay only in their inability to discern between Yahweh's axiomatic concern for his people's well-being and the individual success of one of her political leaders. From our sophisticated point of view, it might more likely lie in the latter; but the original intent of our narrative may have been more subtle, while more primitive, than we would imagine.

If this were some kind of word-fulfillment story, like Narrative A, we would expect to hear next of Ahab's going to war with Syria and being defeated. But in fact the interest remains entirely in this elemental conflict between word and word, prophet and prophet. From the narrator's point of view, Micaiah's oracle needs no further authentication in terms of a narrative sequel. It has already received its full validation in the court of highest authority, heaven. The essential contrast is therefore between the two scenes of revelational occurrence. Zedekiah ben Kenaanah (so named for a second time) re-enters the narrative in vs. 24 to bring the conflict to a resolution. As we have argued, the originality of the more difficult Hebrew text maintains itself over against the variant readings of the ancient translations and ingenious emendations proposed by modern critics. Zedekiah's act of violence is, clearly, the strongest kind of rebuke (cf. I Kings 20:35, 37), expressing the extremity of his frustration and rage. Like the horns of iron, this blow on the cheek has symbolic force and is immediately interpreted in Zedekiah's challenge, "How did Yahweh's spirit pass away from me to speak with you?" Zedekiah means indeed to deny that Micaiah has received genuine revelation, but the basis of his denial lies in ideology rather than in verifiable fact. Since Zedekiah believes that he has himself been in genuine possession of Yahweh's spirit while prophesying to Ahab, he must question Micaiah's interpretation of that prophesying by demanding to know how the spirit that is said now to have been uttering falsehood through him could all the while have been a spirit of truth speaking authentically through Micaiah. It is not a question whether "the Spirit" is able to transform himself into a lying spirit; it is a question, rather, whether the same spirit may speak at the same time in two different prophets to absolutely opposite effects.

Micaiah's rejoinder (vs. 25) makes no attempt to deal with so theoretical a problem. Micaiah is, on his part, equally sure of his inspiration. The fact is that his vision has offered him a rationale for understanding why his antagonist could be inspired and deceived at the same time, supporting his own oracular announcement to Ahab, "So Yahweh has spoken against you (for) evil." Yahweh has spoken in Zedekiah — but he has spoken to produce evil.

Since Micaiah's vision, originating in heaven, is clearly Yahweh's most authentic and ultimate revelation, it must inevitably come to fulfillment (cf. Deut. 18:22), though paradoxically its operativeness is dependent upon the oracle of Zedekiah. Yahweh surely has a "day" for this to happen. When it will come no one knows, but *that* it will come is certain; it will come as a result of Zedekiah's deceptive oracle. To

Zedekiah Micaiah says, "Behold, you will be seeing (witnessing, observing) it (the evil consequences) on *that day* (the day when the consequences take effect)." Whom they will touch when the "day" comes, nobody can say. They may touch Ahab (one would think they would!), they may touch Micaiah, they may touch the whole nation. What matters at the moment is that they will surely affect Zedekiah, the designated witness to this day's coming, who will at last bear testimony to its reality by hiding in his innermost chamber.[32]

Not Amos 5:18-20, but this verse, may be the first emphatic reference to the futuristic "day of Yahweh" — though it is not called such here. If our narrative is any clue to its meaning, the day of Yahweh is no cataclysmic event at the end of the world but each and every day when the divine word takes effect in fulfilling event.[33] Everything in our narratives moves forward to this ultimate resolution. Revelation has been opposed to revelation, but in Micaiah's understanding the revelation in heaven determines the revelation of the *gōren* at Samaria. As Yahweh is sovereign and powerful to inspire prophetic advice leading to historical event, he is sovereign and powerful to direct the events of history to the climactic "day" that he has designed — and this will be the final demonstration of his profoundest, most ultimate purpose.

NOTES TO CHAPTER FOUR

1. *Contra* Miller, *JBL* 85 (1966), 441-454, it is precarious to identify the king of Israel in our story as Jehoahaz (II Kings 13:25) since our king's attack on Ramoth-Gilead led to defeat rather than victory.

2. On the persisting influence of holy war ideology long after the reality was dead, see G. von Rad, *Der heilige Krieg im alten Israel* (4th ed., Göttingen, 1965), pp. 33-50; cf. Fritz Stolz, *Jahwes und Israels Kriege; Kriegstheorien und Kriegserfahrungen im Glauben des altens Israels* (ATANT 60; Zurich, 1972), especially pp. 202f.

3. The original meaning of the locution *d^{e}raš YHWH,* "seek an oracle of Yahweh," has been elucidated in C. Westermann, "Die Begriffe für Fragen und Suchen im Alten Testament," *Kerygma und Dogma* 6 (1960), 2-30. Because it later was modified to mean "have a religious attitude toward Yahweh," a pious Hebrew scribe felt obliged to specify the original meaning by inserting in vs. 5 the word דבר, "oracle." The origin of the schematic figure 400 is obscure; cf. I Kings 18:19, which similarly features the theme of the many against the one.

4. On prophetic perpetuation of charismatic ideals from the period of the settlement and judgeship, cf. Robert Bach, *Die Aufforderung zur Flucht und zum Kampf im alttestamentlichen Prophetenspruch* (WMANT 9; Neukirchen-Vluyn, 1962), pp. 92-112; also Rolf Rendtorff, "Erwägungen zur Frühgeschichte des Prophetentums in Israel," *ZTK* 59 (1962), 145-167.

5. *'ᵃlēh wᵉhaṣlaḥ* versus the simple *'ᵃlēh* of vs. 6; cf. vs. 12. The first element of this battle oracle is often used in the meaning "attack," notably when the locale of battle requires ascending to a higher level (I Sam. 29:11; II Sam. 5:17, 19, 23; 23:9; II Kings 3:8); but contrast passages where it is necessary to *go down* to battle, e.g., I Sam. 23:4f. (cf. 2), 8. The second element, expressed as the hiphil of צלח, is often used in late passages within the general semantic range of "prosper." In the context of warfare it occurs elsewhere at Jer. 32:5 (neg., judgment oracle); II Chron. 13:12 (neg., Abijah's peroration against the *bᵉnê yiśrā'ēl*); 20:20 (stylized holy war peroration, par. אמן hiph.). The third element, "give into thy hand," is traditional; cf. I Sam. 24:10; 26:8, 23, etc.; cf. the favoring oracle in II Sam. 5:19. W. Eisenbeis is mistaken in supposing that the addition of *wᵉhaṣlaḥ* in our text reveals that Micaiah intended his urging as mere advice, not as revelation (*Die Wurzel* שלם *im Alten Testament* [BZAW 113; 1969], pp. 116-120). In vs. 12, directly identified as revelation, it is also used; though Micaiah does not expressly introduce his saying of vs. 15 as an oracle, it is the explicit evil oracle of vs. 17, not this favoring oracle, that he himself questions.

6. Though occasionally a prophet himself interprets his own vision (so here, vs. 23), vision reports very generally conclude with Yahweh's oracular interpretation, often in poetic form (cf. Jer. 1:12, 14; 24:4-10; Ezek. 3:4-11; 8:6, 12, 15, 17; 9:9f.; 11:2f.; Amos 7:8; 8:2f.; Zech. 1:14f.; 2:2, 4, 8f.; 5:4, 6, 11; 6:5f., 8). On the basis of E. Balla's study (*Die Droh- und Scheltworte des Amos* [Leipzig, 1926]), C. Westermann identifies vs. 17 as a *Seherspruch,* distinguished in kind from the usual *Botenspruch* of the prophetic literature (*Grundformen prophetischer Rede,* pp. 29f.; ET, *Basic Forms of Prophetic Speech,* pp. 42f.).

7. Cf. J. Pedersen, *Israel, Its Life and Culture,* I (London, 1926), 167f.; J. Lindblom, *Prophecy in Ancient Israel,* pp. 51f.; G. von Rad, *Old Testament Theology,* II (ET, New York, 1965), pp. 80-98.

8. Although Eisenbeis' treatment of this passage *(loc. cit.)* offers some helpful insights into the general bearing of this term, there are a number of stern criticisms that must be directed against it: (1) it fails to subject this passage to any kind of serious literary-critical scrutiny; (2) it fails to offer a form-critical analysis; (3) the linguistic discussion is weak and overdrawn: e.g., the supposed contrast between שוב בשלום and בוא בשלום in vss. 27f. is scarcely justified by study of the usage of these locutions elsewhere; so also with regard to *haṣlaḥ* as referring to human prosperity versus *šālôm* as divine blessing — subtleties are being read into the text that are scarcely justified by sober analysis; (4) the historical analysis is defective because of these other weaknesses; e.g., post-Jeremianic dating relies on a supposed familiarity with Jeremiah's use of *šālôm.*

9. Far from being forced into a role he would not normally have filled, Jehoshaphat is simply being given his proper right as a central figure, on whom the success of battle is dependent. Jehoshaphat's outcry (vs. 32) must be understood as a denial that he is the king of Israel in response to the shouts of the Syrians pursuing him — or simply as a cry of alarm by which the latter recognize that they have the wrong man. We can understand the statement that the Syrians returned *mē'aḥᵃrâw* only on the assumption that MT *wayyāsurû* is original (see Chapter Two).

10. If the suggestion of A. Malamat that חפש hithp. everywhere means "gird oneself for battle" ("Josiah's Bid for Armageddon," *Journal of the Ancient Near Eastern Society of Columbia University* 5 [Gaster Festschrift Volume;

1973], p. 278) is correct, an essential contrast is intended between the king of Israel's dressing as an ordinary soldier and Jehoshaphat's wearing the royal insignia.

11. Reading MT *maḥᵃneh* (see Chapter Two), i.e., not just the battle scene but the ranks engaged in combat. Although *maḥᵃneh* means "camp" in a great number of passages, it means "army" or "troop/troops" in Judg. 7:14; 8:10 *bis;* I Sam. 17:46; 28:19; II Sam. 1:3; Joel 2:11; II Chron. 14:12; we read of a *maḥᵃneh* in motion (hence no established camp) in Gen. 32:3, 9; 33:8; 50:9; Exod. 14:19, 20, 24; Num. 2:17; 4:5, 15; Josh. 10:5; 11:4; Judg. 4:16; 7:21f.; I Sam. 17:1; 28:1; 29:1; II Kings 5:15; 6:24; I Chron. 14:16. Judg. 4:15f. speaks of a *maḥᵃneh* (contrasted to *hārekeb,* "chariotry") actually engaged in battle action.

12. The locution *watta'ᵃleh hammilḥāmâ bayyôm hahû'* (vs. 35) is intended to epitomize the day as a whole; the entire day is seen as a day of intensifying fighting. At evening, at the setting of the sun, this day is finished. With it are finished both the fighting and the king's effort to subvert the word of doom directed against him. Cf. *YTT,* pp. 112f.

13. The combination פתח (ה)שער occurs also at Josh. 8:29; 20:4; Judg. 9:35, 40, 44; 18:16f.; II Sam. 10:8; 11:23; II Kings 7:3; 10:8; 23:8; Jer. 1:15; 19:2; Prov. 1:21. Since it seems unlikely that threshing would have actually occurred at the gate of Samaria (near the crest of the high hill on which Omri built his capital), the term *gōren* may have had a more primitive meaning, "open area," "bare space" (cf. Arabic cognate usage); this is the possible meaning also in Gen. 50:10f.; Judg. 6:37; II Sam. 6:6; I Chron. 13:9, as well as in 2 Aqht V, 7 (see above, Chapter Two, n. 20). In any event, II Sam. 15:2, speaking of Absalom, gives clear evidence that the king (David) was regularly expected to appear in the gate of the city, like the village elders, to hear disputes. This is the image presented by the mythological Daniel in the Ugaritic literature: he sits "before the gate, beneath a mighty tree on the 'threshing floor,' judging the cause of the widow, adjudicating the case of the fatherless." While the reference to a "mighty tree" (conjectured from Ugaritic *adrm*) in, on, or at a *grn* may make improbable a translation "threshing floor" (see above), it does evoke the biblical image of judges or kings sitting for consultation and decision beneath a numinous tree (so Deborah, Judg. 4:5; Saul, I Sam. 14:2; 22:6).

14. That court counsellors could function as quasi-revelatory agents is argued by G. von Rad in "Der Anfang der Geschichtsschreibung im alten Israel," *Gesammelte Studien zum Alten Testament* (1958; 3rd ed., Munich, 1965), pp. 167-69, 183-86; ET, "Historical Writing in Ancient Israel," *The Problem of the Hexateuch and Other Essays* (New York, 1966), pp. 184-86, 199-202.

15. The *gōren* of Araunah becoming the site of revelation is the major theme of II Sam. 24 (a theophany story legitimizing the Solomonic temple); so perhaps also the *gōren* of Gideon in Judg. 6:36-40. That a political personage might be expected to appeal to mysterious, revelatory event while confronting the people at the city gate is evident from II Kings 10:8-10, where Jehu offers the seventy heads, laid there during the night, as decisive evidence that Yahweh himself has judged the house of Ahab.

16. Fichtner, BotAT, *in loco,* errs in assuming that נבא hithp. suggests ecstatic dance or frenzy ("Raserei und Verzüchtsein"). Though this form is often used of ecstatic activity or of "false" prophecy, the more common niphal form is at times similarly used; contrariwise, the hithpael refers to (apparently) normative prophesying in Jer. 26:20; Ezek. 37:10, and is used of Micaiah himself in our passage at vss. 8, 18.

17. The narrative assumes that it is he who needs to be identified, not Micaiah (see below).

18. For a full discussion of this phenomenon, see G. Fohrer, *Die symbolische Handlungen der Propheten* (2nd ed., Zurich, 1968).

19. Unambiguously, II Kings 13:17, 19 reads the infinitive without object (*'ad-kallēh*). The observations in Gesenius-Kautzsch-Cowley, *Hebrew Grammar*, § 115[c], regarding subjective and objective uses of the pronoun suffix with the infinitive construct, are based on apparent, not demonstrated usage.

20. Wherever the given name of a prophet is expanded to include a patronym or a gentilic, the narrator appears to be introducing him as someone unknown and thus requiring identification; or he is placing special emphasis on his identity. Thus "Ahijah the Shilonite," I Kings 11:29; "Elijah the Tishbite," I Kings 17:1; 21:17 (28 LXX); II Kings 1:3, 8; "Elisha ben Shaphat," I Kings 19:19; II Kings 3:11 (LXX is corrupt); 6:31 (redactional); "Micaiah ben Imlah," I Kings 22:8f. (= II Chron. 18:7f.); "Isaiah ben Amoṣ," II Kings 19:20 (with "the prophet" in 19:2 = Isa. 37:2; 20:1 = Isa. 38:1). Occasionally the narrator wishes to specify the office of a named prophet in order to bring special emphasis on his prophetic power ("Nathan the prophet," II Sam. 7:2; "Ahijah the prophet," I Kings 14:2; "Elisha the man of God," II Kings 5:8; "Elisha the prophet," II Kings 9:1). Otherwise the prophet in question remains anonymous or is introduced with the single name, as well known and legendary. Anonymity occurs in I Kings 13:1ff.; 20:1ff.; 20:26ff.; 20:30ff. The single-name narratives are as follows: "Samuel," I Sam. 19:18ff.; "Nathan," II Sam. 12:1ff.; "Elijah," I Kings 17:17ff.; 18:21ff.; 19:1ff.; "Elisha," II Kings 2:1ff., 19ff.; 4:1ff., 8ff., 38ff., 42ff.; 6:1ff., 8ff., 24ff.; 8:7ff.; 13:14ff., 20f.; "Micaiah," I Kings 22:10ff. (= II Chron. 18:9ff.); "Isaiah," II Kings 20: 12ff. (= Isa. 39:1ff.).

21. See Chapter Three, n. 5.

22. Although the classical position of *lākēn* lies at the transition from accusation (invective) to announcement (threat), it may also bridge the gap from a definition of the situation to a formal statement of some kind (Gen. 4:15; 30:15; Exod. 6:6; Num. 16:11; I Sam. 28:2, etc.), as here (cf. Pedersen, *Israel*, I, 116-18).

23. The perfect *rā'îtî*, here as in vs. 17, is not to be given a past or pluperfect reference, as though Micaiah had received his vision at a prior occasion (cf. Fichtner, *in loco*). The perfect simply expresses an accomplished and assured fact whose effect continues into the present (the so-called stative perfect). That Micaiah intends his vision as oracular is clear not only from his interpretation (vs. 23) but also from the summons to hear in vs. 19a (*contra* Fichtner, pp. 331-33; cf. n. 47).

24. I am indebted to Conrad L'Heureux for calling my attention to a striking parallel in *Archives Royales de Mari* X, 9 (cf. H. W. Robinson, *JTS* 45 [1944], 151ff.; F. M. Cross, *Journal of Near Eastern Studies* 12 [1953], 247ff.), where a Mari *āpilum* overhears, and apparently sees, a council of the gods in action.

25. The singular is collective; cf. Chron.'s interpretive plural.

26. The argument of older commentaries (so now Hossfeld-Meyer, *Prophet gegen Prophet*, p. 33) to the effect that the notion of a heavenly court is necessarily late is countered by the recognition that it finds a close parallel in second-millenium B.C. Ugaritic mythology, like the *gōren* locale as the scene of earthly justice. Whether the motif of the heavenly court counterbalancing the earthly court is mythologically derived must remain obscure until specific parallels are discovered. Various indications have led recent criticism to identify

late pre-exilic Judah as the milieu in which mythological motifs were readily received — though in detoxified form — into biblical tradition.

On the angelic council, see now R. N. Whybray, *The Heavenly Counsellor in Isaiah xl 13-14* (Society for Old Testament Study Monograph 1; Cambridge, 1971) (on this passage, pp. 49f.). A detailed analysis of the locution *ṣᵉbā' haššāmayim* appears in C. Houtman, *De Hemel in het Oude Testament* (Franeker, 1974), pp. 135-143; in light of the fact that I Kings 22:19 shows no affinity whatever with the ideology of astral worship, Houtman's dictum that "the heavenly bodies *are* the heavenly inhabitants" (p. 137) begs the question that needs to be discussed.

27. The present study endeavors no independent treatment of Isaiah 6 and related passages in the prophetic books. The most important discussions of the relationship between I Kings 22 and Isaiah 6 are: M. Kaplan, "Isaiah 6:1-11," *JBL* 45 (1926), 251ff.; I Engnell, *The Call of Isaiah; An Exegetical and Comparative Study* (Uppsala and Leipzig, 1949), pp. 28ff.; H. Wildberger, *Jesaja* (BKAT X/1; Neukirchen-Vluyn, 1972), pp. 235-240; Annemarie Ohler, *Mythologische Elemente im Alten Testament; eine motivgeschichtliche Untersuchung* (KBANT; Düsseldorf, 1969), pp. 24-29. Cf. also G. von Rad, *Old Testament Theology,* II, pp. 63-65; Marie-Louise Henry, *Prophet und Tradition* (BZAW 116; Berlin, 1969), pp. 14ff., 22ff. On the form of the vision, see W. Zimmerli, *Ezechiel* (BKAT XIII/1; 1969), pp. 18-21. On the form of the prophet-call vision in general, the following are important: A. E. Rüthy, "Das prophetische Berufungserlebnis," *Internationale Kirchliche Zeitschrift* 31 (1941), 97-114; F. Horst, "Die Visionsschilderungen der alttestamentlichen Propheten," *EvT* 20 (1960), 193-205; N. Habel, "The Form and Significance of the Call Narratives," *ZAW* 77 (1965), 297-323; R. Kilian, "Die prophetischen Berufungsberichte," *Theologie in Wandel* (Festschrift Kath.-Theol. Fakultät Tübingen, 1967), pp. 356-376; R. Knierim, "The Vocation of Isaiah," *VT* 18 (1968), 47-68; B. O. Long, "Prophetic Call Traditions and Reports of Visions," *ZAW* 84 (1972), 494-500.

28. Though *mî yᵉpatteh 'et 'aḥ'āb* may mean "How shall one deceive Ahab?" (cf. Whybray, *The Heavenly Counsellor,* pp. 21-26), the usual meaning, "who," is more natural in the present context.

29. Cf. von Rad, *Old Testament Theology,* I (ET, New York, 1962), pp. 56f.; W. Eichrodt, *Theology of the Old Testament,* I (ET, Philadelphia, 1961), 319ff. Without mentioning I Kings 22, Lindblom, *Prophecy,* p. 57, discusses the heavenly council *(sôd)* and conflict within the prophetic circles (cf. pp. 113, 210-15).

30. Cf. M. A. Klopfenstein, *Die Lüge nach dem Alten Testament* (Zurich-Frankfurt a. M., 1964), p. 96.

31. See *YTT,* pp. 41f.

32. *Ḥeder bᵉḥeder* designates an interior chamber suitable for secrecy and hiding (I Kings 20:30; II Kings 9:2). For the image of hiding on Yahweh's eschatological day of retribution, cf. Isa. 26:20f. J. Fichtner, *in loco,* is far from the mark in suggesting that Micaiah's reply is "nur sein eigenes, menschliches Wort" (p. 335). This repartee, as the climactic epitome of the entire narrative, is supremely revelatory of God's ultimate intent, even though it is not cast in formal oracular style.

33. *YTT,* pp. 340-42.

CHAPTER FIVE

Analysis of Form and Ideology

1. THE GENRE "PROPHET LEGEND" AND ITS SUBGENRES

PREVIOUS DISCUSSION OF THE MICAIAH PERICOPE HAS NEGLECTED TO deal seriously with the question of genre (Ger. *Gattung*). Most present scholars appear ready to speak of "prophet narrative" or, forsaking Gressmann's all too vague and general term *Sage,* of "prophet legend." Klaus Koch in his influential book *Was ist Formgeschichte?* has offered an argument in defense of the latter designation,[1] but has encountered dissent from various quarters. The 1937 dissertation of Otto Plöger, *Die Prophetengeschichten der Samuel- und Königsbücher,* had earlier expressed criticism of the suitability of this designation.[2] Odil H. Steck's study of the stories featuring Elijah (1968) argued that at least these highly theological tales should be given some such name as "Jahwe-erzählungen."[3] Recently Alexander Rofé has suggested the need for a whole new series of names, based on the specific subject matter and literary development of the individual stories,[4] while Ronald Hals has disputed the applicability of the term "legend" to any kind of prophetic narrative.[5]

One can quibble over niceties, but the present writer's inclination is to retain the term "prophet legend" as a designation for the general genre involved in these and similar stories, because careful inspection confirms that each one of them proceeds from concern for fulfilling a purpose that is basically the same as that of the Christian legends from which the name has been borrowed. That purpose is to extol and inculcate admirable qualities and attitudes.[6] The prophets told legends about the great ones in their midst not to entertain, not to record history, but to explicate their ideals and exemplify their paradigmatic virtues.

The validity of this assessment can be seen when this general genre is further analyzed into subgenres.[7] By "genre" we mean here — to give a broad and generally applicable definition — a specific category of structural differentiation belonging to communicative material (whether spoken, dramatically enacted, or written), designed for a special purpose within a specific typical situation, and employing traditional formulas and/or a characteristic developmental structure that possess a communicative function along with the substantive content.[8] Since the genre designation "legend"[9] is too broad to be useful here, we define "prophet legend" as our basic genre, acknowledging that the qualifying term "prophet" does no more than define the circle of tradents and/or the subject matter involved. It will be impossible to describe the common structure or schema of the entire group of narratives belonging within this genre, except in the most sweeping of generalizations. This is not likely to prove very helpful in our specific task of examining the intertwined narratives of I Kings 22 against the background of similar prophet narratives; therefore it seems imperative to strive for the identification and definition of subgenres, by which we mean special subcategorizations belonging to this general classification.

Since, in our definition, genre is primarily functional, it seems essential that we search for functional differentiations within the general group and strive to devise appropriate names for the resulting subgenres in terms of the specific function of each. While identifying function, one should search for the intent or purpose of each specific type of narrative, and this can scarcely be done without defining the *Sitz im Leben* in very special terms. It will not be enough to observe that a specific narrative emerges from prophetic circles and inculcates prophetic ideals and virtues (the definition of "prophet legend"); the analysis of the Micaiah stories has made us aware that prophets could find themselves in a variety of situations — even the situation of internal conflict — while entertaining ideals that might be, or seem to be, mutually contradictory.

We offer the following outline as a provisional categorization for the various subgenres of prophet legend appearing within the Former Prophets collection. Obviously each individual pericope represented among them will eventually require the same detailed analysis that has been applied in the present study to the Micaiah story. Limits of scope naturally prevent this, but it is possible to offer tentative definitions, suggest appropriate names, and identify specific purposes.

I. From the schools of particular prophets:

1. *Power-demonstration narrative.*[10] A marvelous story exemplifying charismatic power. Purpose: provide edifying illustrations of what a model prophet can do.

   Type I, Marvelous act stories:

   I Sam. 19:18-24, "Overpowering Saul"
   II Kings 4:1-7, "Increasing the oil"[11]
   II Kings 4:8-37, "Reviving the dead boy"[12]
   II Kings 4:38-41, "Curing the pottage"[13]

II Kings 6:1-7, "Recovering the axe head"
II Kings 13:20-21, "Reviving the corpse"

Type II, Interpreted act stories:
II Kings 2:19-22, "Healing the water"
II Kings 4:42-44, "Increasing the loaves"

Type III, Prophetic word stories:
II Kings 2:23-24, "Cursing the irreverent boys"
II Kings 5:1-27, "Curing Naaman, cursing Gehazi"
II Kings 8:1-6, "Rendering justice to the woman and her son"

2. *Prophetic call narrative.* The story of a prophet's designation and empowerment. Purpose: identify the source of a particular prophet's charismatic gift.
   I Kings 19:19-21, "Elijah designates Elisha"
3. *Prophet-legitimation narrative.* A marvelous story demonstrating the scope and nature of a prophet's power. Purpose: identify a particular prophet as genuine.
   I Kings 17:17-19, 21-24, "Reviving the dead boy"
   II Kings 2:1-18, "Inheriting Elijah's power"

II. From prophetic circles in support of institutional authority:

4. *Charismatic designation narrative.* A story in which the gift of charismatic power confirms the anointing of a king. Purpose: demonstrate the authority of a "prophet" to impart his spirit to a secular leader.
   I Sam. 9:1 — 10:16a, "Samuel designates Saul"
5. *Historical demonstration narrative.* A modified holy war story in which a prophet identifies a coming event as an exercise of divine power. Purpose: enhance belief that Yahweh is in control of history.
   I Kings 20:1-21, "The siege of Samaria"
   I Kings 20:26-29, "The battle at Aphek"
   II Kings 19:9b-20, 32-36aα (= Isa. 37:9b-21, 33-37aα), "The siege of Jerusalem"

III. From prophetic circles in challenge to institutional authority:

6. *Succession oracle narrative.* A story in which a prophetic oracle specifies the terms of regal succession. Purpose: demonstrate the transcendent authority of Yahweh in the transfer of regal power.
   II Sam. 7:1-12, 16f., "Nathan's promise to David"
   I Kings 11:29aβb-31, 36abα, 37, "Ahijah's promise to Jeroboam"
   I Kings 14:1-6, 12-14, 17f., "Ahijah's threat against the house of Jeroboam"
7. *Prophet-authorization narrative.* A marvelous story demonstrating the power of a prophet to prevail over institutional

rivals. Purpose: enhance belief in prophetic authority to challenge usurpations of Yahweh's supremacy.

Type I, Word-fulfillment stories:

I Kings 13:1a, 2aα, 4, 6-18a, 19-32a, "The death of the Judahite man of God"

II Kings 6:24aβ-30, 32a, 33; 7:1-2, 6-7aαℵ, 14-17, "The death of the unbelieving captain"

Type II, Supplicatory power stories:

I Kings 17:1-16;[14] 18:1-3a, 5-9, 12, 15-18, 41-46, "Elijah challenges Baal as Israel's provider"

I Kings 18:21-30a, 31-39, "Elijah elicits the divine self-demonstration"

II Kings 1:2-17, "Elijah judges the idolatrous king"

II Kings 6:8-23, "Elisha dictates the terms of victory"

Type III, Theophanous commission story:

I Kings 19:1-18, "Yahweh re-establishes Elijah's authority"

8. *Regal self-judgment narrative*. A story in which a king's word or act determines his own judgment. Purpose: enhance the belief that Yahweh's supreme authority comes to paradoxical expression in the responsible deeds of the institutional holders of political power.

Type I, Oracle-manipulation stories:

II Sam. 12:1-7a, 9-10a, 13f., "David and the rich exploiter"[15]

I Kings 20:30b-43aα, "A king of Israel and the negligent soldier"

II Kings 13:14-19, "A king of Israel and the symbolic arrows"

Type II, Abusive action stories:

I Sam. 15:1-12a, 16-19, 27f., 35a, "Saul's neglect of *ḥerem*"[16]

I Sam. 28:4-16, 19aβb-25, "Saul's appeal to the occult"

I Kings 21:1-19, 27-29, "Ahab's usurpation of the vineyard"[17]

II Kings 20:12-19 (= Isa. 39:1-8), "Hezekiah's boasting to the Babylonians"

9. *Superseding oracle narrative*. A story in which a superseding oracle to a king is fulfilled in preference to one that it follows. Purpose: demonstrate how Yahweh's ultimate purpose in historical events takes priority over his mediate purpose.

Type I, Evil over good stories:

I Kings 22:2b-4a, 4bβ-9, 15-18, 26-28a, 29-35a, 36f. (= II Chron. 18:3-8, 14-17, 25-27a, 28-34), "The death of the king of Israel"

II Kings 8:7-15, "The death of the king of Syria"

Type II, Good over evil story:

II Kings 20:1-11 (= Isa. 38:1-8), "The recovery of Hezekiah"

10. *Instrumental fulfillment narrative*. A story in which the fulfillment of one element in a complex oracle is instrumental toward the oracle's ultimate fulfillment. Purpose: demonstrate that Yahweh ordains instrumental causes in the realization of his historical purposes, in rebuke to deviations from orthodox ideology.

    I Sam. 3:2-11, 13-18; 4:1-18a, 19-21a, 22, "The downfall of the house of Eli"[18]

    II Kings 3:5b-25a, "The defeat of Moab"

    II Kings 8:29b; 9:1-8a, 10-14a, 15b-16a, 17-25a, 27, 30-36aα, "The death of Jezebel"

11. *Word-controversy narrative*. The story of a contest between rival claimants to prophetic revelation. Purpose: demonstrate that Yahweh has power to counteract conflicting prophecy for the fulfillment of his historical purposes.

    I Kings 22:10-12, 19-20aα, 20b-25 (= II Chron. 18:9-11, 18-19aα, 19b-24), "Zedekiah versus Micaiah"

    II Kings 18:17-32a, 36f.; 19:1-8a, 9a, 36aβb-37 (= Isa. 36:2-17, 21f.; 37:1-8a, 9a, 37aβb-38), "The Rabshakeh versus Isaiah"[19]

2. THE ELUCIDATION OF RELATED SUBGENRES

As has been stated, the above categorization is tentative — designed to aid our ongoing analysis of the Micaiah narrative — and is not presented as proven or definitive. Although we have endeavored to derive subgenre designations, define their respective functions and purposes, and construct formal outlines from biblical examples as we understand them, there is as much art involved as science, as much spiritual empathy with the intent of the story-teller as cold reason. To elucidate what we have heard and seen, we offer the following explanations.

a. Power-demonstration narrative

Whereas the names given the various types belonging to the respective subgenres are determined solely in terms of dominant motifs, the subgenre names are, as far as possible, functional. It will be seen that all the power-demonstration narratives except I Sam. 19:18ff.[20] are told about Elisha and come presumably from his school. All tend to be highly supernaturalistic. They have each a simple theme and structure, moving directly from a statement of the problem to its resolution. II Kings 8:1ff. is somewhat more sophisticated than the rest, involving the element of marvelous coincidence and resolving the thematic element of crisis through analogy from the parallel element of crisis in an entirely independent narrative. II Kings 4:8ff. is simple in theme but expansive in its narrative elaboration.[21] II Kings 5:1ff. is not only expansive in treatment but involves an essential structure of opposition in which the prophet's power for performing evil is set over against his power for doing good. It is no doubt significant that precisely these three more-complex narratives involve the figure of Gehazi alongside Elisha. While the setting for most of these narratives is the private life of ordinary individuals — especially persons associated with the prophet movement — II Kings 5:1ff. and 8:1ff. draw the principal actors into intimate and essentially friendly relations with the court.

b-c. Prophetic call and prophet-legitimation narratives

I Kings 19:19ff. appears to be our only example of a prophetic call narrative. While the symbolic elements remind us of the story of Saul's empowerment in I Sam. 11, the present narrative shares with other prophetic call stories, such as Jer. 1:1ff., the motif of the prophet's initial reluctance (vs. 20). It is one of the most obvious products of the Elisha school, standing alongside what we have called a prophet-legitimation narrative, II Kings 2:1-18,[22] which has a more elaborate structure and a somewhat more sophisticated purpose. I Kings 17:17-19, 21-24, in its turn, is a prophet-legitimation narrative attached to the figure of Elijah. Both these subgenres differ from the strikingly more complex stories that we have named "prophet-authorization narratives"; they lack any specific element of confrontation with institutional authority.

d. Charismatic designation narrative

I Sam. 9:1–10:16a[23] is a genuine product of a prophetic school, one much earlier, to be sure, than the schools of Elijah and Elisha. In this early narrative Samuel is identified as a prophet, imparting some of his charismatic power to Saul through anointing. The fact that Saul ends up in prophetic rapture is evidence that the impartation was effective. The story is told not to legitimize him, however, but to demonstrate the working of prophetic power, for the inspiration and edification of adherents of the prophetic group associated with Samuel.[24]

e. Historical demonstration narrative

The three stories identified as historical demonstration narratives share with I Sam. 9:1ff. the characteristic of being designed in support of institutional authority. King and prophet are in full harmony, working together to relieve the distress of Yahweh's beleaguered people. The twin narratives of I Kings 20, originally separate, have been redactionally assimilated to each other. They share three striking similarities: (1) each features an anonymous prophet/man of God and an originally anonymous king of Israel;[25] (2) the situation of each is that of a military threat from Syria; (3) the structure of each is that of a modified holy war narrative in which Israel's peril is epitomized in mocking words placed in the mouth of the enemy (summarized by the man of God in vs. 28; vs. 23 is redactional), and in which the divine arousal to attack, a constitutional element in primitive holy war narration, is voiced by the prophet/man of God, each time (vss. 13, 28) concluding with a transparent statement of purpose, "so you shall know that I am Yahweh."[26] II Kings 19:9ff., a late modification of this subgenre, lacks the first two features but shares the third. The letter which Hezekiah receives from the Assyrians mocks Yahweh; the king's prayer expresses the theological purpose of deliverance and the function of this narrative: ". . . Save us . . . that all the kingdoms of the earth may know that thou, Yahweh, art God alone" (vs. 19).[27]

f. Succession oracle narrative

The three narratives assigned to this subgenre belong to prophetic circles in challenge to institutional authority. Though challenging public institutions may often involve coming into opposition to them, this is not necessarily the case. The purpose of each of the succession oracle narratives that we have identified, viz., II Sam. 7:1ff.,[28] I Kings 11:29ff., and I Kings 14:1ff.,[29] is to maintain Yahweh's prerogative for setting the terms of regal self-investment. In the first narrative, David's proposal to secure his tenure by building a temple is countered by the prophet's promise of dynastic succession; in the second, Jeroboam symbolically secures the ten tribes while the prophet retains two for the Davidides; in the third, Jeroboam's dynasty is symbolically terminated in the death of Abijam.[30] Notably, in each of these narratives the office of "prophet" is prominently mentioned.[31]

g. Prophet-authorization narrative

It will be necessary to devote careful attention to the next subgenre, "prophet-authorization narrative," because here the theme of conflict with institutional authority becomes a constant, apparently constitutive factor. There are three distinct types, each of which features its own special way for having the prophet in question authenticated and invested with Yahweh's power. The institutional authority under challenge is everywhere that of the king except in the Elijah-versus-Baal story of I Kings 18:21ff., where it is that of the rival cult.[32] However, it is only in I Kings 19:1ff. that the regal apparatus (through Jezebel) actually threatens the person of the prophet, requiring in this case an emphatic reinstatement of the prophet's power from Horeb itself.[33] In II Kings 1:2ff. a regal threat may be implied but is not expressly stated. In I Kings 17:1ff. it is a question of the king departing from orthodox ideals and in II Kings 6:8ff. of his usurping the prophet's prerogative of deciding the Syrians' fate. In II Kings 6:24ff. it seems to be a combination of these two, since the king refuses to wait for Yahweh and is determined to act without the prophet. In I Kings 13:1ff., finally, the king's threat is strictly symbolic and subsidiary, being no more than a narrative device for introducing the more central theme of prophetic opposition against the Bethel cult.

I Kings 13:1-32

Although considerations of space will forbid our entering into a separate analysis of each of the narratives in this group, our endeavor to find valid points of comparison with the Micaiah stories demands that we examine, at least briefly, the structure of one or two of the most representative among them. We take first I Kings 13:1ff., a prophet-authorization narrative structured upon the motif of the fulfillment of an oracular word (Type I).[34] As has been noted, this is the only narrative outside I Kings 22 (and Jer. 27–28) that explicitly sets one Yahweh prophet against another Yahweh prophet. But word against word is not its major theme, as will appear from the following outline, which we reconstruct from a careful study of the text:

I. The word against the Bethel altar
  1. The oracle uttered and substantiated
    a. The Judahite man of God denounces the altar, 1a, 2aα
    b. The king's reprisal frustrated
      (1) His hand stretched out, 4a
      (2) His hand withered, 4b
      (3) His hand restored, 6
  2. The communication of attendant revelation
    a. The king's invitation, 7
    b. The man of God's refusal and its explanation, 8-9
    c. Narrative sequel, 10

II. The testing of the attendant revelation
  1. The violation
    a. The Bethel prophet finds the man of God, 11-14
    b. His invitation refused
      (1) Invitation, 15
      (2) Refusal, 16

(3) Explanation, 17
c. His invitation accepted
(1) The countering revelation, 18a
(2) The man of God complies, 19
2. The punishment
a. Oracle of imminent death
(1) Narrative introduction, 20-21a
(2) Invective, 21b-22a
(3) Threat, 22b
b. Fulfillment
(1) The man of God's departure, 23
(2) His death by a lion, 24
(3) Report to the Bethelite prophet, 25
III. Confirmation of the prophetic power of the man of God
1. The Bethel prophet disposes of the body
a. Interpretive identification, 26
b. Burial in his own grave, 27-30
2. Preparation for his own burial
a. Instruction to his sons, 31
b. Explanation (confirmation of the word spoken against the altar of Bethel guarantees the numinosity of the Judahite man of God), 32a

An adequate understanding of this complex, much misinterpreted narrative depends on the recognition of three key elements: (1) the emphatic, thrice-repeated statement of attendant revelation, governing the procedure by which the Judahite man of God was to approach and depart from the target of his denunciation, the Bethel altar (vss. 9, 17, 22), recognized as genuine in the interpretive identification of vs. 26 because it had demonstrated that it possessed power for realization in the unfortunate man's death by means of the mysterious, very unlionlike lion; (2) the Bethelite prophet's deliberate self-fulfillment of the threat (no burial for the Judahite in his own grave) through his own action, designed to sanctify his own eventual burial; and (3) the latter's concluding explanation for wanting to be buried with the Judahite man of God: "For the word which he proclaimed by the word of Yahweh against the altar that is in Bethel will surely come to pass *(hāyōh yihyeh)*!" The Bethelite prophet is now certain that the seemingly outrageous oracle spoken against the ancient and prestigious Bethel shrine, provisionally guaranteed by the Judahite's miracle of restoration, will inevitably come to pass because the attendant revelation has been fulfilled in spite of the former's own efforts to test and subvert it. But this strange tale, told and preserved in a circle of Bethelite prophets,[35] is not at all concerned with the specific terms of the initial denunciation; in the unredacted form of the story these are not even mentioned, and there is no concern to describe an eventual fulfillment.[36] The story was originally told to establish the authority of the intruder to utter such an oracle, an indispensable prerequisite to its authenticity. The Bethelite prophet's command that he be buried with the Judahite bears eloquent witness to his conviction that the latter did indeed have such authority.

II Kings 6:24–7:17

That complexity and subtlety tend to be the dominant characteristics of this type of story is confirmed in an examination of the second narrative in our list, II Kings 6:24ff. Although previously I designated this as a "word-fulfillment narrative,"[37] I now recognize the appropriateness of calling it a prophet-authorization narrative. The reason is that the challenge of the captain (7:2a) questioning the man of God's ("Elisha's") power and authority to announce imminent relief (7:1) in rebuke to the king's impatience and unfaith, leading to his unilateral decision to surrender (6:33), becomes the occasion for a new prediction (7:2b) fulfilled at the ultimate climax of the story, 7:17. Through a depiction of the power of Yahweh's word to come to marvelous and timely fulfillment, this narrative is concerned in the last analysis with establishing prophetic authority to announce that word.

I Kings 17:1-16; 18:1-18, 41-46

If anything, the group of narratives designated as supplicatory power stories tend to be even more complex. I Kings 17–18, in which Elijah challenges Baal (introduced by Ahab) as provider for Yahweh's people, incorporates several subsidiary elements, including a power-demonstration story in 17:8ff. (the prophet-legitimation story in 17:17ff. has been added redactionally; see above). All is designed to demonstrate Elijah's power to bring to realization his dramatic, thematic announcement of 17:1.[38]

II Kings 1:2-17

We must pass this by and devote careful attention to a narrative featuring a more threatening situation for the prophet, II Kings 1:2ff. In opposition to Klaus Koch, who has analyzed this pericope as a combination of two originally separate narratives,[39] we defend the view that we have here a unitary composition, exhibiting like the Bethel narrative a meaningful and cohesive structural development:

I. The identification of Elijah as Ahaziah's[40] nemesis
  1. Elijah's encounter with the king's messengers
    a. The king's apostasy
      (1) His injury, 2a
      (2) His mission of inquiry, 2b
    b. The prophetic reproof
      (1) The angelic command, 3abαא

(2) The oracle of judgment
(a) Accusatory question (= invective), 3bαבβ
(b) Announcement of imminent death, 4a
(3) Report of compliance, 4b
2. The king's interview with the messengers
a. The report
(1) The king's query, 5
(2) Explanation of return
(a) The mysterious man of authority, 6aαא
(b) Repetition of his oracle, 6aαבβb
b. The search for the prophet's identity
(1) The king's query, 7
(2) The description, 8a
(3) The identification (*'ēliyyâ hattišbî hû'*), 8b
II. The authentication of Elijah as Ahaziah's nemesis
1/2. The first/second captain and his fifty
a. The imperious demand
(1) The king's dispatch, 9a/11a
(2) The captain's approach, 9b/11b
b. The devastating reply
(1) Supplication for fire, 10a/12a
(2) Fulfillment, 10b/12b
III. The vindication of Elijah as Ahaziah's nemesis
1. The third captain's humble plea
a. The king's dispatch, 13a
b. The captain's approach, 13b-14
2. Elijah's confrontation with the king
a. The angelic command, 15a
b. The oracle of judgment renewed, 15b-16
3. The king's death, 17aαא

Verses 9-12 are not thematically separated from the rest of the narrative, as Koch supposes,[41] but are functional toward producing the direct confrontation between Elijah and the king in which the oracle of death is for the third time, elaborately and with emphasis, repeated. We hear it first in Elijah's address to the messengers, then in the messengers' report. Meanwhile Elijah's identity, and hence his authority, is kept unrevealed: the messengers know him only as "a man" (vs. 6); through their description the king himself is able to say who he is (vs. 8). Now the question is whether the king's show of force can intimidate him, destroying the power of the evil oracle he has spoken, but Elijah demonstrates power more than abundant in his reply (vss. 9-12); he proves verily to be "a man of God." In the sequel he consents to accompany the third captain, not to be arrested and imprisoned, but to confront the king with a word that can no longer be withstood.

This narrative exhibits some striking parallels with Narrative A of

I Kings 22, such as the search for a favorable oracle and the delivery of one neither wanted nor looked for, a harbinger of the king's death; also the motif of jarring conflict between the prophet and the king. However, it is clear that in the present story all interest lies in the person and authority of the prophet. It is essentially in his role as prophet that he is vindicated, and only because of this vindication does the word that he finally speaks receive the full power of fulfillment. There is no concern to describe in detail how that word arrived at fulfillment, for this is taken for granted. So the story ends with the matter-of-fact statement, "And he died according to the word which Elijah had spoken." In the Micaiah narrative, on the contrary, all emphasis is placed on the question whether the word indeed has power to come to fulfillment in the face of the king's determined efforts to subvert it, while the question whether the prophet actually has the authority to speak such a word never comes to expression.

h. Regal self-judgment narrative

The narratives assigned to this category show a strikingly similar theme and development. Something that the king himself says or does determines his own judgment, as set forth in a climactic oracle by a prophet.[42] The element of sharp conflict does not seem to be essential here, though at best the relationship of prophet to king remains paradoxical, as in the symbolic arrows story of II Kings 13:14ff. In the first type belonging to this subgenre, the prophet actually functions as the agent by which the king's self-judgment is produced, but in the second the prophet functions only as spokesman for the interpretive oracle.

i. Superseding oracle narrative

Our arrangement is designed to show an increasing complexity and growing sophistication among the prophet legends. We come now to a subgenre in which, for the first time, word is set against word, although not yet in diametrical opposition, as in subgenre 11 to follow. Subgenre 9 is strikingly similar in structure to the instrumental fulfillment narrative (category 10) next to be discussed, like it involving a paradoxical situation in which multiple predictions interact for fulfillment. The important difference is that superseding oracle narratives feature separate and distinct oracles, one of which suppresses or neutralizes the other, whereas instrumental fulfillment narratives involve complex oracles in which the fulfillment of one or two subsidiary elements becomes the means by which the ultimate fulfillment occurs.

The element of opposition to the king does not seem essential to the superseding oracle narrative. Certainly II Kings 20:1ff. is friendly to the king, representing as it does a typical attitude toward the Davidic kingship on the part of the earlier Judahite prophets, particularly those associated with the figure of Isaiah. II Kings 8:7ff., which is not ostensibly hostile to the Syrian king, does nevertheless express a patently pro-Israel viewpoint. It is this narrative that shows the most striking formal similarities with Narrative A in I Kings 22.

II Kings 8:7-15[43]

I. The situation
   1. The king's illness, 7aβ
   2. His resort to revelation
      a. Report of Elisha's presence, 7b
      b. Ben-Hadad's instructions to Hazael, 8
   3. Hazael's approach to the man of God, 9a
II. The confrontation
   1. A query and its paradoxical answer
      a. The query, 9b
      b. The reply
         (1) An initial favoring oracle (*ḥāyōh tiḥyeh*), 10a
         (2) A superseding revelation of evil (*wᵉhir'anî YHWH kî môt yāmût*), 10b
      c. The resulting consternation, 11a
   2. A symbolic act and its interpretation
      a. The act
         (1) The man of God weeps, 11b
         (2) Request for interpretation, 12a
      b. The explanation (Hazael's forthcoming evil deeds toward Israel), 12b
      c. The interpretation
         (1) Hazael's objection, 13a
         (2) The ultimate meaning of the revelation (*hir'anî YHWH 'ōtᵉkā melek 'al 'ᵃrām*), 13b
III. The fulfillment
   1. The report to Ben-Hadad
      a. The king's query, 14a
      b. The initial favorable reply, 14b
   2. Action fulfilling the evil revelation
      a. The murder, 15a
      b. Hazael's succession, 15b

One is immediately struck by the similarity between this story and that of II Kings 1. Both stories involve a sick king anxious to know, "Shall I survive this illness?" (1:2; 8:8, 9: *'im/hā'eḥyeh mēḥᵒlî zeh*), and both feature a mission of inquiry to a foreign source of revelation. From that point, however, II Kings 8:7ff. goes its own way. Now we encounter a similarity to I Kings 22: the initial answer is affirmative. To the twice-repeated query, the man of God replies that Ben-Hadad shall surely live (vss. 10, 14), and this would presumably be fulfilled were it not for the intervention of an immediately countering revelation.[44] As in I Kings 22:17, the man of God reports something that he is at the moment seeing or has just seen. It has two distinct aspects: that Ben-Hadad should die (vs. 10) and that Hazael should become his successor (vs. 13). Far from delighting in the terms of this countering revelation, the Israelite man of God weeps (a symbolic act) to indicate the ultimate implications of this new revelation from Israel's point of view.

The fulfillment is intriguingly paradoxical. We may infer that were it not for Hazael's cynical intervention, the favoring oracle would have come to pass and Ben-Hadad's health would have been restored. But nothing of that is in the narrative! As in the Micaiah story, the favoring oracle would presumably have resulted in Israel's good because Ben-Hadad intended peace. But it was destined to give way to evil, both for him and for Israel. The striking difference between our two stories is that in I Kings 22 the king of Israel, the addressee both of the original and of the superseding revelation, works unsuccessfully to fulfill the first while preventing the second, whereas in II Kings 8 the king of Syria (Ben-Hadad) is the addressee of the original revelation while his murderer-to-be is the addressee of the revelation that supersedes it. In I Kings 22 the superseding oracle is brought to fulfillment by a stray arrow, but here in II Kings 8 Hazael, the counter-king, acts ruthlessly and designedly to prevent the fulfillment of the favoring oracle and ensure the fulfillment of the oracle of death.

From our modern point of view we would be inclined to say that the thought has become the father of the deed; the Israelite man of God put a deadly, Macbeth-like, self-fulfilling notion in Hazael's mind. But this sophisticated interpretation fails to explain what the Israelite man of God's motive could have been for instigating an act inimical to his own people's good. The profound point of the narrative is that Yahweh knows Hazael's plot, yet sovereignly ordains his wicked deed as an instrument for the realization of his own paradoxical purpose in the history of his people.

j. Instrumental fulfillment narrative

In order to assess the validity of our previous remarks about the complex structure of narratives belonging to this new group, it is necessary to exhibit the outlines of two that display close affinities with the interwoven narratives of I Kings 22. We pass by I Sam. 3–4 because of its extremely early date and because it lacks the theme of conflict with regal authority.[45] Our immediate interest lies in II Kings 3, which features our familiar Jehoshaphat alongside another aggressive Israelite king. Afterward we shall examine II Kings 9, with its central motif of another murderous arrow.

II Kings 3:5b-25a[46]

- I. The crisis
  - 1. Preparation for an attack on Moab
    - a. Measures against Moab's rebellion, 5b-6[47]
    - b. Alliance with Jehoshaphat, 7
    - c. The march, 8-9a
  - 2. Preparation for oracular assistance
    - a. The threat of thirst
      - (1) The lack of water, 9b
      - (2) The king of Israel's interpretive lament, 10
    - b. Request for a prophetic word
      - (1) Resort to Elisha ben Shaphat, 11-12
      - (2) Elisha's rebuff, 13a
      - (3) The king of Israel's interpretive rejoinder, 13b
- II. A complex oracle and its instrumental fulfillment
  - 1. The double word
    - a. Preparation
      - (1) Elisha's explanatory oath, 14
      - (2) Ecstatic inducement, 15
    - b. The divine answer to the request for water
      - (1) Characterization of Yahweh's power (*'ōśeh hannaḥal hazzeh gēbîm gēbîm)*, 16
      - (2) Announcement of abundant water, 17
    - c. The divine intent of victory
      - (1) Thematic characterization (*w^{e}nāqal zō't b^{e}'ênê YHWH*), 18a
      - (2) Promise of a punitive victory, 18b-19
  - 2. The superlative fulfillment of the promise of water, 20
- III. The ultimate fulfillment: victory over Moab
  - 1. Deception of the Moabites
    - a. Preparations for defense, 21
    - b. A misguided attack
      - (1) Water seen as blood, 22
      - (2) Misinterpretation inspires attack, 23
  - 2. Israelite victory
    - a. Successful counterattack, 24
    - b. Punitive devastation, 25a[48]

This story is not primarily about a marvelous gift of water in the desert, but about the way in which a gift of water led to the defeat of Moab. A scrutiny of the text shows that Jehoshaphat and Elisha, but not Joram,[49] are original in the story. Although the story reflects an historical situation in which the northern kingdom held the Moabites in subservience, while engaging Judah and Edom as allies,[50] its imaginative exaggeration[51] is as manifest as its antipathy toward Ahab (cf. especially vss. 13f.).[52] That its time and place are remote from the circumstances in which the historical Elisha lived is clear from his being sought in some unspecified site in "the wilderness of Edom."[53] The narrator seems designedly to make the king of Israel the exponent of unbelief; not only does he have him lament about the prospect of Yahweh deliberately giving "these three kings" into the hand of the king of Moab because there is no water (vss. 9f.), but he has him repeat his lament as a response to Elisha's suggestion that other gods (and prophets) might better have been consulted (vs. 13). This in turn provokes Yahweh's emphatic self-characterization in vs.16,[54] leading to the thematic declaration of vs. 18a[55] and the climactic prediction of ultimate fulfillment in 18b.

The structure of this narrative may be described as chiastic.[56] It begins and ends with the theme of military action against Moab; the threat of thirst, impeding this denouement, is dealt with first in terms of a marvelous gift of water; this in turn becomes the means by which the Moabites put themselves in a position of military vulnerability. The promise of the first is immediately interpreted as guaranteeing the second. Especially important as a clue to the structure of this narrative is the emphatic temporal equation between the instrumental fulfillment in vs. 20 (*babbōqer ka'ᵃlôt hamminḥâ*) and the ultimate fulfillment in vs. 22 (*wayyaškēm babbōqer*).

II Kings 8:29b–9:36a[57]

I. The oracular designation of Jehu
  1. A complex oracle of appointment
    a. Elisha's instruction to the young prophet
      (1) The situation in Jezreel, 8:29b[58]
      (2) The charge
        (a) Preparatory action, 9:1-2
        (b) Instruction for an oracle of anointing, 3a
        (c) Instruction for immediate departure, 3b
      (3) Report of compliance, 4
    b. The young prophet's expanded oracle
      (1) The isolation of Jehu, 5
      (2) The anointing
        (a) Narrative introduction, 6a
        (b) Oracle of anointing, 6b
        (c) Additional words of judgment
          1/ on the "house of Ahab," 7a
          2/ on Jezebel, 7b, 10a
  2. The acclamation (fulfillment of the oracle of anointing)
    a. Communication of the oracle
      (1) A diversion, 11

(2) The oracle paraphrased
(a) Rejection of the diversion, 12a
(b) Obfuscation of the word of judgment, 12bα
(c) Report of the word of anointing, 12bβ
b. Action of the company, 13

II. The attack upon the two kings (fulfillment of judgment on "the house of Ahab")
1. Jehu's rebellion against Joram
a. The conspiracy, 14a, 15b
b. Aggressive action against Jezreel, 16a
2. Reconnaissance frustrated
a. Discovery of the approaching force, 17a
b. The first reconnaissance
(1) The regal instruction, 17b
(2) The messenger's query, 18aα
(3) Jehu's symbolic invitation, 18aβ
(4) The watchman's report, 18b
c. The second reconnaissance
(1) The messenger's query, 19a
(2) Jehu's symbolic invitation, 19b
(3) The watchman's report, 20
3. The murder of the two kings
a. The uncovering of the conspiracy
(1) The kings meet Jehu, 21
(2) The confrontation
(a) Joram's query, 22a
(b) Jehu's symbolic reply, 22b
(c) Joram's panicky flight, 23
b. The death of Joram
(1) Jehu's arrow, 24
(2) Disposition of Joram's body, 25a[59]
c. The death of Ahaziah, 27

III. The attack upon Jezebel (fulfillment of ultimate judgment)
1. Report of Jehu's arrival in Jezreel, 30a
2. Jezebel's defiance
a. Her regal attitude, 30b
b. Her disdainful reproach, 31
3. The death of Jezebel
a. Jehu calls for help, 32
b. Jezebel thrown down and trampled, 33
4. Jezebel's nonburial
a. Instructions for burial, 34
b. The grisly remains, 35
c. Epitomizing interpretation, 36a

Our present comments on this narrative must be brief, though we shall return to it later. It has been outlined in detail because it incorporates the motif of a king of Israel (the last from the Omride dynasty) being killed by an arrow. Otherwise it shows but meagre affinity with I Kings 22. What is important to see is that the young prophet of vss. 4ff. drastically expands Elisha's oracle of vs. 3, whose fulfillment becomes merely instrumental toward the full and ultimate realization of this young prophet's words. Leaving aside deuteronomistic expansions, vss. 6-10 include three distinct elements: (1) the oracle of anointing; (2) prediction of the "striking down"[60] of the house of Ahab, i.e., of both reigning kings descended from Ahab, Joram and Ahaziah; and (3) prediction of gruesome vengeance on the queen-mother, Jezebel. Assuredly this narrative originated with prophets who honored Elisha, though perhaps not of his school (contrast I Kings 19:16, which ascribes the anointing of Jehu to Elijah), who saw Jehu's accession primarily as the prerequisite to achieving long-cherished vengeance for Jezebel's bitter persecutions against them.[61]

k. Word-controversy narrative

Here belongs Narrative B of I Kings 22. In this final category of prophet legend, the element of conflict is essential and constitutive. It is not merely a matter of supersession, with a new word from the same prophet coming irresistibly to fulfillment in preference to an initial word (category 9), but a matter of prophet pitted against prophet. Each claimant to revelation is backed by authority, but the higher authority prevails. It prevails by subversion and redirection. In light of the striking affinities between the "superseding oracle" subgenre and this new subgenre, it is no surprise at all to find that the Micaiah tradition should have been preserved in variants exhibiting both types. The phenomenon was rare and memorable enough to have produced these variants; yet, as our indication of the specific purpose of each subgenre has indicated, each proceeds from a subtly different concern and point of view. The superseding oracle narrative is concerned directly with fulfillment while the word-controversy narrative is concerned essentially with authority. The latter can be said to be more profound and sophisticated, reflecting the possibility of elemental differences within the ranks of those who equally appealed to Yahweh as the one God of Israel and laid equal claim to his spirit.

II Kings 18:17–19:37 (= Isa. 36:2–37:38)[62]

Although there is no close parallel to the Zedekiah versus Micaiah story, II Kings 18:17ff. does exhibit sufficient affinities with it to justify our placing it within the same subgenre. Observing that the passage of time has produced important but understandable modification, we offer the following outline for comparison with that of Narrative B in I Kings 22:

I. The confrontation
  1. The Rabshakeh versus the three officials
    a. Narrative introduction: the situation
      (1) Three Assyrian chieftains threaten Jerusalem, 18:17
      (2) Three Jerusalemite officials respond, 18
    b. The Assyrian king's message to Hezekiah
      Formal introduction, 19abα
      (1) Challenge, 19bβ-20
      (2) Hypothetical replies refuted
        (a) Egypt is a broken reed, 21
        (b) Yahweh is angry with Hezekiah, 22
      (3) A wager proffered, 23-24[63]
      (4) A revelation claimed, 25[64]
  2. The Rabshakeh versus the Jerusalemites
    a. Narrative introduction: the situation
      (1) The plea of the three officials, 26
      (2) The Rabshakeh's rebuff, 27
    b. The Assyrian king's message to the people
      Formal introduction, 28
      (1) Identification of false hopes, 29-30
      (2) Call to surrender, 31-32a[65]
      (3) The people's silence, 36

II. The resolution
  1. The eliciting of Yahweh's declaration
    a. Narrative introduction: the situation
      (1) The three officials report, 37
      (2) Hezekiah's reaction, 19:1
    b. Hezekiah's appeal to Isaiah
      Formal introduction, 2
      (1) Epitomizing characterization of the predicament, 3
      (2) The possibility of Yahweh's rebuke, 4a
      (3) Request for intercession, 4b
    c. Isaiah's oracle
      Formal introduction, 5-6a
      (1) Reassurance formula, 6b
      (2) Announcement of Yahweh's imminent action, 7
  2. The fulfillment, 8a, 9a, 36aβb-37

This late Jerusalemite narrative shows much more the style of the classical prophets. Its intricate structure involves a complicated administrative apparatus, in which the prophet appears only as a last resort, and then not to direct his word against the word of other Israelite prophets, or even against a king of his own people, but against the agent of a foreign king claiming for himself inspiration from Israel's god, Yahweh. This is its only important point of comparison with the Zedekiah versus Micaiah narrative, but it is an essential one. Whoever precisely the Rabshakeh may be,[66] his claim of revelation in 18:25 is taken seriously enough by the three officials that they do not want the people to hear it, by the people seriously enough that they do not know how to reply, and by Hezekiah so seriously that he can only appeal to Yahweh. This king makes the plea that Yahweh will pay attention to what the Rabshakeh has been saying and act to rebuke him (19:4). The oracular answer (19:7) corresponds directly to the Rabshakeh's challenge: as the latter has claimed that Yahweh directed the Assyrian attack against his own land (*'alēh 'al hā'āreṣ hazzō't wᵉhašḥîtāh,* 18:25), Yahweh now replies that he will put a spirit (*rûᵃḥ*) in the king of Assyria, causing a rumor (*šᵉmû'â*) which will provoke his return to his own land (*lᵉ'arṣô*) so that he may die by the sword there, in his own land (*bᵉ'arṣô*).

Nowhere in this narrative is the theoretical question dealt with, whether Yahweh had actually spoken to the king of Assyria.[67] Our storyteller is content to allow Yahweh to bring the crisis to a resolution by producing a counter-revelation, inducing the Assyrian king to do the opposite of what he had claimed he had been told to do. In short: if Yahweh can bring a foreign king against Yahweh's own land, he can surely send him away, causing him to die in the land of his origin, also under Yahweh's control.

Excursus: Jeremiah 27–28

Although it is natural to appeal to Jeremiah 27–28 as a parallel to the Zedekiah versus Micaiah narrative, a literary and formal analysis reveals here a complex structure combining a number of originally distinct literary elements. The motif of word against word is featured only in a secondary redactional combination. We offer the following outline:[68]

I. A prophetic collection of oracles concerning the yoke of the king of Babylon, styled in the first person:

Oracle A: To the envoys of Judah's allies, 27:2-10
1. Instruction for a symbolic act, 27:2
2. Instruction for an oracular message
   Introduction, 3
   a. Yahweh's decree, 5-6 (LXX)
   b. Yahweh's warning, 8-10abα

Oracle B: To Zedekiah, 27:12-15
Redactional introduction, 12aα
1. Command of submission, 12aβ
2. Explanation
   a. Why Judah should serve the king of Babylon, 14aβb-15aα
   b. Why the prophets prophesy falsely, 15aβb

Oracle C: To the people and priests, 27:16-22
Redactional introduction, 16aαא
1. Admonition, 16aαבβb˙
2. Challenge

a. Call to intercession, 18aαℵ
b. Yahweh's oracle, 19-20, 22 (LXX)

Expansion to C: Narrative report of Hananiah's countering oracle, 28:1-4

1. Narrative introduction, 28:1 (LXX)
2. The oracle
   a. Announcement, 2 (LXX)
   b. Prediction of weal, 3-4a (LXX)
   c. The divine purpose, 4b

II. Two narrative elaborations styled in the third person:

Report A: Hananiah's rebuff to Jeremiah, 28:5-11

1. Jeremiah's rejoinder to Hananiah
   a. Narrative introduction, 5
   b. Jeremiah's interpretation of Hananiah's oracle
      (1) A desire for its fulfillment, 6
      (2) The test of prophecy, 7-9
2. Hananiah's symbolic-act oracle
   a. The act, 10
   b. The interpretation, 11a
   c. Narrative conclusion, 11b

Report B: Jeremiah's rebuff to Hananiah, 28:12-17

1. Yahweh's instruction
   a. Narrative introduction, 12
   b. A double oracle
      Introductory command, 13a
      (1) The divinely provided symbol, 13b
      (2) The divine action, 14a
2. Jeremiah's address to Hananiah
   a. Accusation, 15
   b. Announcement of imminent death, 16
3. Report of fulfillment, 17 (LXX)

Here there is no longer any attempt to explain contradictory prophecy on the theory that Yahweh himself may actually be the source of deceptive revelation. What is implied in II Kings 18:17ff., viz., that the rival claimant to revelation is probably lying, is proposed in Jeremiah's words of 28:6-9 as a rational hypothesis requiring the test of history; but in the climactic oracle of 28:13ff. it is presented as an indisputable fact. Yahweh sets himself diametrically against Hananiah with the declaration, "You have broken wooden bars, but I[69] will make in their place iron bars." Yahweh's firm purpose can no longer be set aside by misleading interpretations of his intention, and the one who offers such must die.

3. EVALUATION OF AFFINITIES

If one were to insist that a common schema be established for every narrative belonging to the genre "prophet legend" before the existence of such a genre could be assured, the effort would by now have to be given up; the narratives we have listed exhibit such an amazing variety of structures that only the most forced and artificial sort of schematizing could possibly produce anything like uniformity. Nevertheless, all the narratives listed do reveal some basic structural similarities, such as the development from tension to resolution, the tendency to feature a single, typical prophet standing in conflict — or at least challenge — to opposing authority, and a delight in the element of paradox. Such common elemental characteristics might be sufficient to satisfy a general demand for uniformity in structure. In any event, our argument that function and purpose are more basic in defining genre than rigidity of form fully establishes the existence of "prophet legend" as a distinct genre. A more specific conformity to structural patterns may be expected of the distinct subgenres, each of which has a more specific *Sitz im Leben* and a more clearly defined function and purpose.

One is astonished at the ingenuity and inventiveness of Israel's early prophets in devising a great variety of forms for expressing their ideals. To demand of them a higher degree of structural uniformity would be to ignore the very genius of the prophetic spirit, charismatic freedom. With growing admiration the careful reader discovers that their skill in narration was quite proportionate to the unbridled power of their imagination. They cannot be inhibited from expressing their deepest convictions in powerful, moving figures. To them God is no sterile idea but One who lives and acts, while man himself works in opposition to him or in cooperation, but always somehow subject to his sovereign rule.

Reviewing the foregoing discussion, one finds that the subgenres here established for the two originally independent narratives of I Kings 22 each display a striking uniformity in structure. We must say this with some reserve with respect to the sole pericope assigned to Type II of subgenre 9; II Kings 20:1-11, a good over evil story, shares little in common with the two stories assigned to Type I apart from the "superseding oracle" pattern. Whether or not this is sufficient to establish an essential connection, we have found a high level of similarity in comparing the two Type I narratives with each other. We recall that Narrative A in I Kings 22 has the tripartite structure: I, Situation; II, Confrontation; III, Fulfillment. So also II Kings 8:7-15. In section II of the outline for Narrative A in I Kings 22 the further subdivision is: 1, Initial favoring oracle; 2, Superseding evil oracle; 3, Interpretive diatribe. In II Kings 8:7ff. it is: 1,

Paradoxical double oracle (including the favoring and the evil prophecy); 2, Interpretive symbolic act. At the crucial point in each narrative, where the superseding oracle impinges on the original favoring oracle, the prophet/man of God employs a special vision formula, *rā'îtî* or *hir'anî YHWH*. There are, as we have observed, significant differences, but the above structural and formulaic coincidences are sufficient to establish the identity of the subgenre "superseding oracle narrative" for at least Type I. The fact that I Kings 22 has an originally anonymous king alongside an emphatically named prophet, while II Kings 8 names the king with the counter-king, but in its probably original form leaves the man of God unnamed, may be stylistic or simply due to the vicissitudes of tradition. In the former passage Micaiah is emphatically identified because of the special element of interaction between him and the four hundred, from whom he has to be sharply differentiated.

Structural similarities are somewhat looser when we compare the two narratives assigned to subgenre 11, "word-controversy narrative," yet here too important coincidences establish the identification. Each moves from a first to a second identical element: confrontation and resolution. In each the confrontation scene is expanded in a distinctive way, but apparently in each instance with the purpose of delaying the resolution and thus augmenting the suspense. Although we have separated the first two scenes of confrontation in our analysis of I Kings 22, essentially they belong together as the first element in a two-part structure shared with II Kings 18–19. Thus I Kings 22, Narrative B, offers the outline: I, Revelatory confrontation in Samaria; II, Revelatory confrontation in heaven; III, Resolution. II Kings 18–19 has: I, Confrontation (1, Rabshakeh versus the three officials; 2, *idem* versus the people); II, Resolution. We note also that in each respective double scene of confrontation a description of the situation is followed by a message of some kind, by way of oracle or through an emissary. Furthermore, the resolution scene in each narrative has first a delaying element (I Kings 22, Zedekiah's reproof; II Kings 18–19, Hezekiah's appeal to Isaiah), then the definitive reply. In spite of the distinctively separate setting and provenance of each of these two narratives, their mutual similarity underscores their temporal and ideological affinity to each other.

We must list now the most important points of contact between Narrative A and Narrative B of I Kings 22, coming to light in our foregoing discussion of the most closely similar narratives belonging to each of the individual subgenres. First, Narrative A. We immediately see that it exhibits more similarities to other stories in our repertoire than does Narrative B. With the historical demonstration narratives as a group the connection is weak: it shares only a common holy war situation; and with the stories of I Kings 20 in particular it shares the scene of Syrian aggression. With the succession oracle narratives as a group it likewise has little affinity, except for the superficial element of prophetic opposition to the king as it appears in I Kings 14. With two pericopes belonging to Type I among the prophet-authorization narratives, viz., I Kings 13 and II Kings 6–7, Narrative A shares three important but nonessential elements: (1) a superficial element of regal opposition to the prophet; (2) a word-fulfillment motif; and (3) oracular complexity. The last-named passage adds the further elements of (4) a holy war situation and (5) the scene of Syrian aggression. One story of Type II within this subgenre, viz., II Kings 1, has four important but again nonessential points of affinity: (1) the motif of a king asking for a favoring oracle; (2) a prophetic oracle of imminent death; (3) the question of the prophet's identity; and (4) punitive measures taken against the person of the prophet to prevent the oracle's fulfillment. But this latter narrative is structured quite differently, employing these narrative elements for the distinct purpose of establishing the authority of the prophet in question. Even so, we should avoid conceiving of our genres and subgenres as so rigidly designed as altogether to exclude mutual influence upon one another.

To continue: Both types of the regal self-judgment narrative share with our Narrative A a basic motif and little more; viz., that a king's responsible action is involved directly in the determination of his own judgment. Again, mutual interaction of the respective subgenres is apparent. Yet there are subtle differences: in the narratives of subgenre 8 the king is the addressee and his own action is instrumental; in II Kings 8 the counter-king is an intermediary addressee whose action is instrumental; in I Kings 22 the king is the addressee, and although his action cannot be called instrumental, it is definitely contributory in spite of his own determined counter-action.

Finally we observe that it is the two examples of instrumental fulfillment narrative that reveal the most extensive and most essential similarities to Narrative A. II Kings 3 has (1) a more idealized and more central Jehoshaphat figure, (2) the request by Jehoshaphat for an oracle (in this case not for success in battle and not intended to counter a previous oracle, but simply for relief from thirst), (3) the motif of prophetic opposition to the king (ideologically aimed at the house of Ahab), and (4) the feature of oracular complexity. II Kings 9 shares (1) the background of Syrian aggression (this does not, however, provide the immediate problem),[70] (2) the same motif of prophetic conflict with the house of Ahab, (3) oracular complexity, and (4) the arrow.

Going through this same review with respect to Narrative B, we find that it shares with the historical demonstration narratives of I Kings 20 nothing but the holy war situation and the setting of Syrian aggression. With the succession oracle narrative of I Kings 14 it shares only the motif of prophetic perspicuity (prominent and thematic in the latter, incidental in I Kings 22). With the first type of prophet-authorization narrative, as represented in I Kings 13, Narrative B has the following striking, but again nonessential, affinities: (1) the element of a paradoxical testing of the validity of an oracular word; (2) the motif of prophet against prophet. Similarities with Type II, as represented by II Kings 6:8ff., are even more superficial: (1) the motif of prophetic perspicuity, which here becomes thematic; (2) the holy war situation; (3) Syrian aggression; (4) the stance of prophetic prerogative over against the king. With the regal self-judgment oracle, especially Type I, our narrative shares only one broad characteristic motif, that of prophetic power to guide or misguide the king in determining his own judgment. And with the instrumental fulfillment subgenre it appears to have virtually no affinity whatever, although it does share with II Kings 9 the general background of Syrian aggression.

Summarizing, we may say that Narrative A is related most closely to the word-fulfillment type of prophet-authorization narrative, as represented particularly in II Kings 6:24–7:17; to the supplicatory power type of this same subgenre, as represented especially in II Kings 1:2ff.; to the oracle-manipulation type of regal self-judgment narrative, especially to I Kings 20:30ff. and II Kings 13:14ff.; and, very strikingly, to the instrumental fulfillment narrative subgenre, especially as represented in II Kings 3:5ff. Evidently the respective purposes of these three distinct subgenres, viz., (1) enhancing prophetic authority for challenging usurpations of Yahweh's supremacy, (2) enhancing belief in Yahweh's transcendent authority at work in the responsible deeds of political leaders, and (3) demonstrating that Yahweh ordains instrumental causes in the realization of his historic purpose, closely interact with the specific purpose of the superseding oracle subgenre, viz., to demonstrate that Yahweh's ultimate purpose takes priority over his mediate purpose. As a matter of fact, each of the above may be identified as important presuppositions on the part of Narrative A in I Kings 22, as well as in II Kings 8:7-15. Yet none of these distinct subgenres shares sufficient structural similarity to the last two narratives to justify setting aside the definitions that have been established. It is surely significant that the majority of individual narratives showing the greatest measure of affinity with Narrative A emerge from approximately the same historical background, and evidently also from the same general circle of tradents. The time and place are those that witnessed Aramean aggression against the northern kingdom, with Samaria as geographical center. The tradents are the Elisha and related schools of prophets (whose prestige is reflected even in the relatively late narrative, II Kings 3, strikingly reshaping the figure of Elisha). Meanwhile, it is significant that the two historical demonstration narratives of I Kings 20, while sharing similarity in time and place, exhibit more the ideology of the four hundred than that of Micaiah ben Imlah.

Narrative B, on its part, shows its greatest number of affinities with the word-fulfillment type of prophet-authorization narrative, represented chiefly by I Kings 13, which in fact comes from an isolated group of prophets, those associated with the Bethel shrine. It is also closely related to II Kings 6:8ff., a representative of the supplicatory power type of prophet-authorization narrative; also in some measure to the oracle-manipulation type of regal self-judgment narrative — though in neither of the latter are the similarities thematic. It is clear that the closest affinities on the part of Narrative B lie not with traditions of the late ninth-century north, but with later traditions of southern origin, especially those that have produced II Kings 18:17–19:9, 36f., together with the call-vision of Isaiah. It may not be too daring to deduce from these coincidences that our Narrative B has been shaped by a group of predeuteronomistic prophets friendly to the north but living in Judah in the years following the downfall of Samaria. Our narrative shares, then, with the core of Deuteronomy and the prophecies of Hosea a similar origin, stance, and destiny. Of this, more will be said in Chapter Six.

Finally, the closest observable similarities on the part of the two distinct Micaiah narratives lie with each other. While their mutual structural resemblances are no more than general, i.e., both move from tension to resolution, introducing a vision as the decisive element, they also share the same holy war situation, the same scene of counter-action to Syrian aggression, the same motif of a resort to prophetic advice, the same central theme of a conflict between a favoring versus an evil oracle. Above all they share the same heroic protagonist, Micaiah, who is in all likelihood historical.[71] These coincidences are surely sufficient to guarantee that our two stories derive each from the same source. When all has been said, we have to do with the same prophet, the same Israelite king, the same favoring and unfavoring oracle, the same interprophetic controversy, the same tragic outcome.

Yet the two narratives differ significantly from each other. Incidental disagreements are that in Narrative A the king opposes the prophet while in Narrative B it is a prophet who is pitted against his fellow prophet; that in the first narrative the prophets are summoned after the preliminary discussion while in the second the prophets are initially present; that the one story depicts Micaiah as absent in the beginning while the other depicts him as most probably already present. Seen from the perspective of possible historicity, these material differences are not necessarily irreconcilable or mutually exclusive. More essential, however, are the structural differences. Not only is the content of the definitive vision different in each case; the vision of Narrative B is far more complex and sophisticated. Narrative A emphasizes the specific identity of the dissenting prophet in order to call attention to the specialness of his superseding oracle, whereas in Narrative B he is typical, emerging as someone unannounced, familiar, and taken for granted. In Narrative A the thematic tension is between Micaiah's two self-contradictory oracles, magnified in the king's resolute but futile action, while in Narrative B the thematic tension is between two types of prophets and two courts of authority. In Narrative A the conflict is resolved through fulfillment, but in Narrative B it is resolved in terms of (1) identification with the higher authority and (2) a rational principle of inspirational deception.

In the final analysis we see that a measurable ideological gap lies between Narrative A and Narrative B. The first has discovered that in certain instances prophecy may find itself contradicting itself because competing ideals of Hebraic religion are no longer fully reconcilable with one another. This dilemma has been produced by the emergence of incongruous elements in Israel's public life: no longer is Israel to be rallied simple-mindedly to the old cry of self-defense against external attack, without consideration to conflicting motivations occasioned by the power-presence of the political establishment. To be sure, the prophets as inheritors and preservers of the charismatic tradition fulfill the ancient role of rousing the people to Yahweh's cause. Yet in their new role as advisers and superintendents over military politics they are caught in ambiguities; they are being forced to distinguish between the people's ultimate good and the opportunistic aims of monarchical ambition. This serious conflict is most understandable within the disruptive military crisis produced by the first serious foreign threat against the northern kingdom following the period of Baasha, viz., the series of Syrian incursions beginning in the reign of Joram. The northern kingdom was now being forced to decide whether the aim of resisting a formidable foreign power was fully commensurate with the aim of supporting the policies of its own specific rulers — a problem that continued to trouble the Israelite kingdoms to their end, and to arouse ongoing debate among the various groups of prophets endeavoring to ascertain Yahweh's plan and purpose in an increasingly chaotic age.

Narrative B reflects a more highly developed situation in which definite parties and groupings have emerged within the prophetic movement as a whole. Individual cadres of prophets have identified themselves with specific ideologies. Some support the political institution, others challenge it. Narrative B dramatically marks the beginning of elemental conflict identified with these specific groups. From now on there will be constant tension between *Heilspropheten* and *Unheilspropheten*. The first are destined to perish with the nationalistic structure; the second are destined to recite the nation's elegy. Yet from the latter's ranks will emerge men like Ezekiel who will call their forlorn people to witness Yahweh's new creation. The eschatological image of a repossession of the promised land is, for them, posited on the cessation of political independence. They know that Israel will live again solely by the transcendent vision of Yahweh's eternal favor.[72]

NOTES TO CHAPTER FIVE

1. Neukirchen-Vluyn, 1964, pp. 209f. (ET, *The Growth of the Biblical Tradition* [New York, 1969], p. 186). See also Gene Tucker, *Form Criticism of the Old Testament* (Philadelphia, 1971), pp. 26-41. While calling attention to certain difficulties in the application of this term to the narratives under consideration, W. Eugene March's essay on "Prophecy" in John H. Hayes, ed., *Old Testament Form Criticism* (Trinity University Monograph Series, 2; San Antonio, 1975), accepts this as the most meaningful classification (pp. 172-74).

2. Plöger prefers the more general term "Prophetengeschichten." Though he discusses formal criteria, his sub-classifications are determined essentially by considerations of content (1. "Prophetenwort-Geschichten"; 2. "Prophetentat-Geschichten"; 3. "Prophetengeschichten als Teilausschnitte aus der israelitische Geschichte").

3. *Überlieferung und Zeitgeschichte in den Elia-Erzählungen* (WMANT 26; Neukirchen-Vluyn, 1968), p. 143; so likewise G. Fohrer in *Elia* (ATANT 31; Zürich, 1957; 2nd ed. ATANT 53; 1968).

4. "The Classification of Prophetical Stories," *JBL* 89 (1970), 427-440. In making content a basic criterion, Rofé does not advance significantly beyond the procedure of Plöger. The genres or subgenres that he identifies ("simple legenda," "literary elaboration of the legenda," "vitae") seem designed more from nonbiblical parallels than from the biblical material itself.

5. "Legend: A Case Study of Old Testament Form Critical Terminology," *Catholic Biblical Quarterly* 34 (1972), 166-176. Hals follows Gunkel in insisting on the element of the *imitabile* as essential to the definition of legend (so the martyr legends of Christianity, Daniel), criticizing Koch for applying this name to the prophet narratives because the acts related in them are not intended to be imitated. But it is the *ideology* of these narratives that is exemplary, not the specific acts ascribed to individual prophets.

6. See A. Jolles, *Einfache Formen* (Halle, 1930; 2nd ed., Tübingen, 1958).

7. What follows is intended as a serious response to the challenge for redefinition voiced by Rofé in *JBL* 89 (1970), and by B. O. Long in his article, "2 Kings iii and Genres of Prophetic Narrative," *VT* 23 (1973), 337-348. An extended argument in support of our categorization will be offered in a projected book studying the prophet legends as a special group.

8. Definitions of the parallel terms *Gattung,* "genre," "literary form," are generally concerned with structure and style as identifying criteria; cf. *Lexikon für Theologie und Kirche,* IV (1960), col. 686, *s.v.;* see also W. G. Doty, "The Concept of Genre in Literary Analysis," *Proceedings of the Society of Biblical Literature,* 1972, II, pp. 413-448, summarizing the debate as to whether form or content should be definitive for genre identification, but scarcely perceiving the crucial role of function.

While certainly form and content, prominent especially in the more artificial literary types, help differentiate the various genres and subgenres, in the literature of the common people it is function that determines the form to be employed, not form the function. So W. Eugene March, in his treatment of prophecy in Hayes, *Form Criticism,* p. 176; cf. Jolles, *Einfache Formen,* pp. 1-22. On the special problems involved in defining biblical genres cf. W. Richter, *Exegese als Literaturwissenschaft* (Göttingen, 1971), pp. 140f.

9. Because the fathers of modern form criticism, Hermann Gunkel and Hugo

Gressmann, could go no further in analyzing the prophetic stories than to define them as imaginative narratives containing certain characteristic elements, their far too broad term *Sage* confuses contemporary discussion. Cf. Jay A. Wilcoxen on Gunkel's concept of "legend" (pp. 78f.) in the context of his treatment of *Sage*, pp. 57-98 ("Narrative") in Hayes, *Form Criticism*.

10. The term "legend" may be substituted for "narrative" in each category.

11. Cf. R. Kilian, "Die Totenerweckungen Elias und Elisas — eine Motivwanderung?" *Biblische Zeitschrift* N.F. 10 (1966), 44-56; E. Haller, "Märchen und Zeugnis. Auslegung der Erzählung 2 Könige 4, 1-7," *Probleme biblischer Theologie* (Festschrift G. von Rad; 1971), pp. 108-115.

12. *Contra YTT*, p. 235.

13. Cf. J. Heller, "Tod im Kopfe (2 Kön 4, 38-41)," *Communio Viatorum* 10 (1967), 71-76.

14. *Contra YTT*, p. 228.

15. Cf. H. Seebass, "Nathan und David in II Sam 12," *ZAW* 86 (1974), 203-211; W. Richter, *Exegese*, pp. 127-132. We identify here the following structure:

I. The regal pronouncement of judgment
   Narrative introduction, 1bα
   1. Report of a fictitious crime
      a. The general situation, 1bβ-3a
      b. Tender love for the ewe lamb, 3b
      c. Its rapacious slaughter, 4
   2. David's double decree
      Introduction, 5a
      a. The oath of death for the culprit, 5b
      b. The demand for restitution, 6

II. The prophetic oracle of judgment
   1. Identification of the culprit, 7a
   2. The oracle
      a. Invective, 9
      b. Threat, 10a

III. Prophetic interpretation of the regal decree
   1. Death for the culprit
      a. David's contrition, 13a
      b. Announcement of absolution, 13b
   2. Death for a substitute (= retribution for injury to Uriah), 14

The original judgment oracle has been expanded redactionally in vss. 7b-8, 10b-12, developing the theme of David's superabundant lust. With the use of transitional links at vss. 1a, 15a, this prophet legend has been incorporated into the ongoing throne-succession narrative, with its sequel in vss. 15ff.

16. Although many interpreters have agreed that I Sam. 15 seems overfull, no consensus has been reached on how to identify independent sources. Our treatment of *hayyôm* in vs. 28 appearing in *YTT*, pp. 198f., accentuates its epitomizing function. In the light of the fact that epitomizing *hayyôm* comes regularly at the climactic conclusion of various types of primitive narrative, we are now prepared to identify vss. 12b-15, 20-26, 29-34, 35b, along with 13:8-15, as a theologizing expansion polemicizing against Saul and the Saulides in the partisan interests of the Davidic dynasty, parallel to similar expansions in II Sam. 28 (see *YTT*, pp. 208f.). The remaining verses in I Sam. 15 assign to Samuel the

prerogative of determining dynastic succession, similarly to the role of Nathan and Ahijah in the succession oracle narratives heretofore identified. But this is a regal self-judgment narrative — albeit of markedly primitive conception — because in it Samuel delivers the invective (= the accusatory question of vs. 19) while Saul's own act of tearing Samuel's robe determines the terms of the threat (vs. 28). That this original narrative originated within the prophetic circle with which Samuel was identified — not with the Davidic court — is evident not only from close affinities with I Sam. 9–10 but also from the fact that Samuel establishes his credentials in vs. 1 by identifying himself as a spokesman of Yahweh-Sebaoth, a designation deriving from the Shiloh tradition.

The structure of the original narrative is as follows:

- I. Saul violates the Amalekite *ḥerem*
    - 1. Samuel's instructions to Saul
        - a. The identification of his authority, 1
        - b. The oracle
            - (1) Yahweh's purpose to punish, 2
            - (2) The command
                - (a) Smiting Amalek, 3aαא
                - (b) Utter destruction, 3aαבβb
    - 2. The fight against Amalek
        - a. The preparation
            - (1) The mustering, 4
            - (2) The separation of the Kenites, 5f.
        - b. The battle, 7-8a
        - c. The aftermath (= incomplete *ḥerem*), 8b-9
- II. The word of judgment
    - 1. The oracle of divine disapproval
        - a. Yahweh's announcement to Samuel
          Formal introduction, 10
            - (1) Yahweh's repentance, 11aα
            - (2) Its ground: Saul's disobedience, 11aβ
        - b. Samuel's anger, 11b
    - 2. The confrontation with Saul
        - a. Samuel's approach, 12a, 16
        - b. Samuel's reproach
            - (1) Saul's appointive responsibility, 17-18a
            - (2) Rehearsal of the command
                - (a) Utter destruction, 18bαא
                - (b) Smiting to extinction, 18bαבβ
            - (3) The accusation, 19
        - c. The determination of judgment
            - (1) Symbolic act: the tearing of the robe, 27
            - (2) Interpretation: the transfer of the kingship (epitome with *hayyôm*), 28
    - 3. Sequel: Perpetual estrangement between Samuel and Saul, 35a

17. See the discussion below, pp. 115f., 131f. n. 18. Recent literature on this passage includes the following titles: Fohrer, *Elia*, pp. 24-29; Steck, *Überlieferung*, pp. 32-77; K. Baltzer, "Nabaoths Weinberg [etc.]," *Wort und Dienst* 8 (1965), 73-88; M. Weitemeyer, "Naboths Vingård," *Dansk Teologisk Tidsskrift* 29 (1966), 129-144; F. I. Andersen, "The Socio-Juridical Background of the Naboth Incident," *JBL* 85 (1966), 46-57; A. Jepsen, "Ahabs Busse [etc.]," *Archäologie und Alte*

Testament (Festschrift K. Galling; 1970), pp. 145-155.

18. Cf. *YTT*, pp. 287-89. I Sam. 2:27-36 is no independent prophet legend but a contrived piece of Zadokite polemic. An abbreviated outline of the original narrative is the following.

I. The revelation
1. Preparation of the boy recipient
a. The first summons, 3:2aβ-5
b. The second summons, 6f.
c. The third summons, 8f.
2. Reception of a portentous oracle
a. Narrative introduction, 10-11aα
b. A word of double judgment
(1) For Israel, 11aβb
(2) For the Elides, 13bαבβ-14
3. The delivery of the divine message
a. Narrative introduction, 15f.
b. The communication to Eli, 17f.
c. Conclusion, 14:1a (MT)

II. Instrumental fulfillment: Israel's disaster
1. The ark is brought to battle, 1b-5
2. The Philistines recoup, 6-9
3. Result: victory and defeat, 10f.

III. Ultimate fulfillment: the power of the evil report
1. Its impact on Eli, 12-18a
2. Its ominous interpretation
a. Phinehas' wife's portentous death, 19f.
b. The child receives a symbolic name, 21a, 22

19. Cf. II Chron. 32:9ff.

20. Cf. N. Poulssen, "Een lach en een traan om Saul. Het volksverhaal van 1 Sam 19, 11-17 als Woord van God," *Tijdschrift voor Theologie* 12 (1972), 3-27.

21. Rofé, *JBL* 89 (1970), 433-35, overly concerned with psychological subtleties in this story, hesitates to call it a legend. But this is not saga, in which character tends to remain undelineated; it is designed as an unsolicitated demonstration of the prophet's wonder-working power.

22. Rofé, pp. 436-39, is probably right in insisting that the latter narrative is relatively late. It is surely one of the most programmatic and sophisticated among the Elisha collection. However, Rofé errs in designating it a "vita," for it deals with a single episode in the prophet's life. Cf. also R. A. Carlson, "Elisée — le successeur d'Elie," *VT* 20 (1970), 385-405; K. Galling, "Die Ehrenname Elisa in die Entrückung Elias," *ZTK* 53 (1956), 129-148; E. Haag, "Die Himmelfahrt des Elias nach 2 Kg 2, 1-15," *Trierer Theologische Zeitschrift* 78 (1969), 18-32; C. A. Canosa, "Eliseo sucede a Elías (2 Re 2, 1-18)," *Estudios Bíblicos* 31 (1972), 321-336; M. A. Beek, "The Meaning of the Expression, 'The Chariots and the Horsemen of Israel' (2 Kings 2, 17)," *OTS* 17 (1972), 1-10. See also *YTT*, pp. 233f. An outline developed from the narrative's own structure reveals clearly the aim of legitimization:

I. A demonstration of Elisha's fitness
1/2. The test at Bethel/Jericho
a. A challenge to Elisha's fidelity, 1f./4
b. A challenge to Elisha's prescience, 3/5

II. A demonstration of Elisha's inspiration
  1. The crossing of the Jordan
    a. A challenge to Elisha's fidelity, 6
    b. Transitional: the prophetic guild as witnesses, 7
    c. The parting of the waters, 8
  2. The designation of a test
    a. The offer of a parting gift, 9a
    b. The request for a prophetic birthright, 9b
    c. The condition: inspired sight, 10
  3. The test fulfilled
    a. Elijah's rapture, 11
    b. Elisha sees, 12a
    c. Confirmation: Elisha exchanges his garments for Elijah's mantle, 12b-13a

III. A demonstration of Elisha's empowerment
  1. A testing of his miraculous power
    a. Striking the water with Elijah's mantle, 13b-14a
    b. The parting of the waters, 14b
    c. Recognition by the prophetic guild, 15
  2. A vindication of his authority
    a. The prophetic guild request permission to seek Elijah, 16
    b. The search permitted, 17
    c. Elisha's remonstrance, 18

23. On this passage cf. the following recent literature: M. Bič, "Saul sucht die Eselinnen," *VT* 7 (1957), 92-97; V. Eppstein, "Was Saul also among the Prophets?" *ZAW* 81 (1969), 287-304; J. Sturdy, "The Original Meaning of 'Is Saul also among the Prophets?'," *VT* 20 (1970), 206-213; B. C. Birch, "The Development of the Tradition of the Anointing of Saul in I Sam. 9:1–10:16," *JBL* 90 (1971), 55-68.

24. By comparison, the story of Samuel's anointing of David, I Sam. 16:1-13, cannot be regarded as a genuine product of a prophetic school. Though it features Samuel as the legitimator of the king taking Saul's place, Samuel functions mechanically, being in fact constantly corrected by Yahweh. While the spirit comes mightily upon David as a result of his anointing, the narrative displays no concern to tell of any characteristically prophetic manifestations of that spirit, as in the Saul story. I Sam. 16:1ff. is ideological and propagandistic, being part of an elaborate redactional rewriting measurably later in date than the actual period of David's life (see S. J. De Vries, "David's Victory over the Philistine as Saga and as Legend," *JBL* 92 (1973), 23-36.

25. On the redactional intrusion of "Ahab," see below, p. 123.

26. On these narratives see *YTT,* pp. 231-33; also W. Zimmerli, *Gottes Offenbarung* (Munich, 1963), pp. 54-56, 122-25, 128-131. The following abbreviated outlines reveal a development in sophistication from the second to the first, the second being essentially a holy-war story adapted to the theme of prophetic intervention:

I Kings 20:1-21

I. The crisis
  1. Initial negotiation
    a. The military situation, 1

b. The sharpened demand, 2-6
c. Rejection and defiance, 7-9
2. Subsequent confrontation
a. The threat, 10
b. The counter-threat, 11
c. Order for attack, 12
II. The encouraging oracle
1. Oracle
Narrative introduction and herald formula, 13aα
a. Situational query (= invective), 13aβ
b. Announcement, 13bα
c. Historical demonstration formula, 13bβ
2. Interpretive instruction, 14b
III. The fulfillment
1. The preparation
a. Mustering, 15
b. The approach, 16-17a
c. The Syrian strategy, 17b-18
2. The battle
a. The approach (resumptive), 19
b. Slaughter and pursuit, 20a
3. Epitomizing conclusion, 21

I Kings 20:26aβ-29

I. The crisis
1. Syrian advance, 26aβb
2. Israelite preparation, 27a
3. Unequal strength, 27b
II. The encouraging oracle
Narrative introduction and herald formula, 28aαא
1. Invective, 28aαבβ
2. Threat (announcement), 28bα
3. Historical demonstration formula, 28bβ
III. The fulfillment
1. A seven-day encampment, 29a
2. A single-day victory, 29b

27. For a differing analysis see B. S. Childs, *Isaiah and the Assyrian Crisis* (Studies in Biblical Theology 2nd ser. 3; Naperville, 1967), pp. 73ff.

28. Recent titles reflecting the intensive discussion of this crucial passage include the following: M. Simon, "La prophétie de Nathan et le Temple [etc.]," *Revue d'Histoire et de Philosophie Religieuses* 32 (1952), 41-58; H. van den Bussche, "Der dynastische Prophetie van Nathan," *Collationes Gandavenses* 1 (1951), 285-303; E. Kutsch, "Die Dynastie von Gottes Gnaden [etc.]," *ZTK* 58 (1961), 137-153; L. Randellini, O.F.M., "Il significato del vaticinio di Nathan," *BeO* 3 (1961), 130-35; L. B. Gorhulho, O.P., "A Profecia de Natan em 2 Sam 7, 1-17," *Revista de Cultura Biblica* 6 (1962), 59-70; A. Caquot, "La prophétie de Nathan et ses échos lyriques," *SVT* 9 (1963), 213-224; M. Tsevat, "Studies in the Book of Samuel [etc.]," *Hebrew Union College Annual* 34 (1963), 71-82; D. J. McCarthy, "II Samuel 7 and the Structure of the Deuteronomic History," *JBL* 84 (1965), 131-38; M. Tsevat, "The House of David in Nathan's Prophecy," *Bib* 46 (1965),

353-56; J. Coppens, "L'union du thrône et du temple d'après l'oracle de Nathan," *Ephemerides Theologicae Lovanienses* 44 (1968), 489-491; J. G. Trapiello, "La profecia de Natán," *Cultura Biblica* 224 (1969), 3-42.

29. Cf. the following recent titles concerning I Kings 11 and 14 (16): A. Caquot, "Ahiyya de Silo et Jéroboam 1er," *Semitica* 11 (1961), 17-27; Ina Willi-Plein, "Erwägungen zur Ueberlieferung von I Reg. 10,26–11,20," *ZAW* 78 (1966), 8-24; J. Debus, *Die Sünde Jerobeams; Studien zur Darstellung Jerobeams und der Geschichte des Nordreichs in der deuteronomistischen Geschichtsschreibung* (FRLANT 93; Göttingen, 1967), pp. 3-18, 49-54; H. Seebass, "Tradition und Interpretation bei Jehu ben Chanani und Ahia ben Silo," *VT* 25 (1975), 175-190 (superseding *idem,* "Die Verwerfung Jerobeams I. und Salomos durch die Prophetie des Ahia von Silo," *Die Welt des Orients* 4 [1968], 163-182). Identifying the expression in 14:10, *'āṣûr w^{e}'āzûb,* as predeuteronomistic, Seebass proceeds to relegate vss. 7-8a, 9bβ, 10aβ, 11a, 12f., 15aα to early tradition. But W. Dietrich's analysis of redactional terminology (*Prophetie und Geschichte; eine redaktionsgeschichtliche Untersuchung zum deuteronomistischen Geschichtswerk* [FRLANT 108; Göttingen, 1972], pp. 51-54) has demonstrated that much of vss. 7-11 reflects the strongly formulaic pattern of deuteronomistic expansions in I Kings 16, 21, II Kings 9, and elsewhere.

30. I Kings 14 stands clearly within the tradition of I Kings 11. As we have shown in *YTT,* p. 152, the final words in MT vs. 14 (unattested in LXX), זה היום ומה גם עתה, constitute a late gloss. They were added to smooth a jarring transition from original material preceding them in vs. 14 to the deuteronomistic addition in 15f. The original introduction to this narrative has been lost (cf. LXX 12:24). The theme of unmasking the sick child's identity through his mother is essential to the purpose of making that child's death symbolic of the end of the dynasty. We must not be misled by the superimposed deuteronomistic invective into exaggerating the intensity of Ahijah's opposition. The point is that the prophet cannot be surreptitiously diverted from his prerogative of determining the terms and conditions of dynastic succession.

31. The oracle of Jehu ben Hanani recorded in I Kings 16:1-4 (cf. vs. 7), identified in Seebass, "Jehu ben Chanani," pp. 170-79, as original, although cast entirely in deuteronomistic language, reflects the tradition of what may have been a similar succession-oracle narrative.

32. Important treatments of this pericope are Fohrer, *Elia,* pp. 13-20; Steck, *Überlieferung,* pp. 9-19, 28-31; A. Alt, "Das Gottesurteil auf dem Karmel," *Kleine Schriften,* II (1953), pp. 135ff.; O. Eissfeldt, *Der Gott Karmel* (Berlin, 1953); C. A. Keller, "Wer war Elia?" *Theologische Zeitschrift* 16 (1960), 298-313; C. Kopp, "Il sacrificio di Elia sul Carmelo," *BeO* 2 (1960), 11-13; H. H. Rowley, "Elijah on Mount Carmel," *BJRL* 43 (1960), 190-219; D. R. Ap-Thomas, "Elijah on Mount Carmel," *PEQ* 92 (1960), 146-155; E. Würthwein, "Die Erzählung vom Gottesurteil auf dem Karmel," *ZTK* 59 (1962), 131-144; A. Jepsen, "Elia und das Gottesurteil," *Near Eastern Studies in Honor of W. F. Albright* (1971), 291-306.

References to Ahab in this narrative are redactional or belong to the surrounding narrative. On the structure of the narrative, see S. J. De Vries, *Journal of The Methodist Theological School in Ohio* 9/2 (1971), 9ff. It is concerned to show Yahweh's power to answer (the thematic word *'ānan* is constantly repeated) and is ultimately designed to demonstrate that Elijah is Yahweh's true prophet, authorized and empowered to challenge the vacillating Israelites (cf. vss. 36b, 21).

33. Recent literature on I Kings 19:1-18 includes S. Weissmann, "The Narrative of the Theophany on Horeb" (Heb.), *Bet Miqra* 11 (1965), 140-43; R. A. Carlson,

"Elie à l'Horeb," *VT* 19 (1969), 416-439; O. Eissfeldt, " 'Bist du Elia, so bin ich Isebel' (I Reg 19, 2)," *Hebräische Wortforschung* (Festschrift W. Baumgartner; SVT 16; 1967), 65-70; G. Fohrer, *Elia*, pp. 20-24; Steck, *Überlieferung*, pp. 20-28, 90-125.

34. Recent studies on this passage include M. A. Klopfenstein, "I Könige 13," *Parrhesia* (Festschrift K. Barth; 1966), pp. 639-672; A. Jepsen, "Gottesmann und Prophet," in Festschrift G. von Rad (1971), pp. 171-182. Cf. also Hossfeld-Meyer, *Prophet gegen Prophet*, which offers a cursory examination on pp. 21-27, affirming the essential unity of I Kings 13 with identification of deuteronomistic elements at the beginning and conclusion. On p. 35 this narrative is defined as "eine Lehrerzählung über Ungehorsam und Strafe eines Propheten." The "lying" is accepted as unproblematical.

35. Though this narrative was readily interpreted as anti-Bethelite (to this it owes its preservation as a vehicle for deuteronomistic ideology), it cannot have originated in Judah since the events recorded transpired in and near Bethel, and the sole Judahite witness to them died. See below, p. 101.

36. Regarding deuteronomistic adaptation to the specifications of Josiah's reform, see *YTT*, pp. 290f. Cf. M. Noth, *Könige I* (BKAT IX; 1968) *in loco*. W. Dietrich, *Prophetie und Geschichte*, pp. 114-120, 138, offers a persuasive argument that I Kings 13 contains a fairly old legend adapted to the concerns of Josiah's reform. His argument that the narrative was not present in the original deuteronomistic document is not proven by the identification of supplemental redactional notations, which may be isolated additions rather than the vehicle of a programmatic redactional supplementation (see further Chapter Seven, n. 1).

37. *YTT*, pp. 235-38; cf. S. J. De Vries, "Temporal Terms as Structural Elements in the Holy War Tradition," *VT* 25 (1975), pp. 80-105. An abbreviated outline is as follows:

- I. The crisis
  - 1. Prolonged siege and famine
    - a. Introductory characterization, 6:24aβb-25
    - b. Anecdotal example: the cannibalistic mothers, 26-30
  - 2. The king's despair
    - a. Narrative introduction: the king appeals to Elisha, 32a, 33a
    - b. The king's plea, 33b
- II. The double oracle
  - 1. Announcement to the king (epitome of abundance *kā'ēt māḥār*), 7:1
  - 2. Demonstration with the captain
    - a. The captain's unbelief, 2a
    - b. A symbolic reproof, 2b
- III. The double fulfillment
  - 1. Yahweh's saving act, 6-7aαא
  - 2. Confirmatory reconnaissance, 14f.
  - 3. Fulfillment of the word
    - a. Abundant food, 16
    - b. The captain's death, 17

38. On this passage see Fohrer, *Elia*, pp. 7ff.; Steck, *Überlieferung; YTT*, pp. 227-231. An abbreviated outline is the following:

Thematic announcement, 17:1

- I. Demonstrations of providential care
  - 1. Nature's creatures summoned

a. The divine instruction, 2-4
b. Narrative of compliance, 5f.
2. Nature's elements renewed
a. The divine instruction, 7-9
b. Interview: the widow's need, 10-12
c. Oracle of abundance, 13f.
d. Narrative of compliance, 15
e. Interpretation, 16

II. The confrontation with Ahab
1. The preparation
a. Elijah comes to Ahab, 18:1-2a
b. Obadiah searches for water, 2b-3, 5
c. Elijah instructs Obadiah, 7-9, 12, 15
2. The encounter
Narrative transition, 16
a. Ahab's accusation, 17
b. Elijah's counter-accusation, 18

III. Resolution: Elijah's word brings rain
1. The disposition of Ahab
a. Instruction to symbolic action, 41
b. Narrative of compliance, 42a
2. Elijah's supplication
a. The prayer, 42b
b. The search for the answer, 43-44a
3. The divine answer
a. The coming of abundant rain, 44b-45a
b. The triumphal return to Jezreel, 45b-46

39. *Was ist Formgeschichte?* pp. 212-14; ET, *Growth of the Biblical Tradition,* pp. 187f.; so also, among others, Eissfeldt, Fohrer, Pfeiffer, Dietrich.

40. On the problem of Ahaziah's originality in this narrative, see below, pp. 98f.; cf. Noth, BKAT IX, p. 87. Recent studies of this narrative are Fohrer, *Elia,* pp. 29-33; Steck, "Die Erzählung von Jahwes Einschreiten gegen die Orakelbefragung Ahasjas," *EvT* 27 (1967), 546-556.

41. Cf. also Steck, *EvT, loc. cit.*

42. See the analyses of I Sam. 15; II Sam. 12; I Kings 20; I Kings 21, in the present volume. II Sam. 14, employing the "wise woman" of Tekoa as revelatory intermediary (cf. vss. 13f.), may be a significant parallel. Cf. D. M. Gunn in *VT* 26 (1976), 218ff.

43. Cf. B. O. Long's simplified outline in *VT* 23 (1973), p. 343. On Balaam parallels in the recently deciphered Deir 'Alla texts, see J. Hoftijzer in *Biblical Archaeologist* 39 (1976), 11ff.

44. There is nothing in the narrative to indicate that the man of God was speaking tongue-in-cheek or offering offhand advice. The oracular reply is meant as genuine revelation, but is superseded by the more authoritative vision. Cf. Chapter Three, n. 6.

45. See above, n. 18; cf. *YTT*, pp. 287-89.

46. On this passage see J. Liver, "The Wars of Mesha, King of Moab," *PEQ* 99 (1967), 14-31; J. R. Bartlett in D. J. Wiseman, ed., *Peoples of Old Testament Times* (Oxford, 1973), pp. 235ff.; cf. A. H. van Zyl, *The Moabites* (Leiden, 1960), p. 18.

47. It is difficult to account for LXX^{L}'s omission of βασιλεύς and βασιλεῖ in vs. 5 except on the supposition that the MT, followed by LXX^{B}, added them under the influence of vs. 4. Since "Joram" is probably not original in this narrative (see below), it seems unlikely that Ahab would have been named in the original version of it; therefore vs. 5b is almost certainly the original beginning. Vs. 5b stated the simple fact that "Moab rebelled against Israel," and vs. 6 stated only that "the king" went out of Samaria (ביום ההוא is a late gloss; cf. *YTT,* pp. 59f.) to muster "all Israel" as a result of this rebellion. Vss. 4-5a (along with 25b-27) is part of a later historical framework, transforming our prophet legend (similarly with one of the same subgenre in II Kings 8:29b and following) into political propaganda (see Chapter Seven on the redactional procedures involved).

48. No other explanation of vss. 25b-27 makes sense than that it is a secondary expansion. Vs. 25a emphatically fulfills the prediction of vs. 19, in which the ruining of the land is thematic rather than any specific action against the Moabite king. It makes little sense, following a report of total ruin upon Kir-hareseth (Q^{e}riho?), to narrate the battle against it as though it were still standing (cf. the wall of vs. 27), hence the explicative insertion in LXX^{L} before the final phrase of vs. 25a. The reference to the stones in Kir-hareseth is itself meant as climactic and illustrative; it becomes the focus for what is unmistakably a secondary expansion in vss. 25b-27, part of a redactional framework that includes vss. 4-5a, tying the entire episode to a specific Moabite and Israelite king. In II Kings 1:1 the deuteronomistic redactor has rephrased this framework's reference to Ahab (*wayyipša‘ mô'āb b^{e}yiśrā'ēl 'aḥ^{a}rê môt 'aḥ'āb* is substituted for [*wayhî k^{e}môt 'aḥ'āb*] *wayyipša‘ melek mô'āb b^{e}melek yiśrā'ēl*), inserting it as a transition to narrative material concerning Ahaziah (vss. 2ff.).

49. *Contra* Noth, *Überlieferungsgeschichtliche Studien,* p. 83, n. 7; and Shenkel, *Chronology and Recensiónal Development,* pp. 93-101, *inter alii* (cf. *YTT,* p. 60), the name "Jehoshaphat" has to be original in the three contexts where it appears without the title "king of Judah," unless we are to suppose that it has been substituted for another proper name — an arbitrary assumption. The proper name is needed at the beginning of vs. 11 because three potential speakers (including the king of Edom) are there present; so again in 12a. In vs. 12b it appears in coordinate position alongside the formal designations "king of Israel" and "king of Edom." Much of Shenkel's argumentation in favor of the chronology followed in LXX^{L} (see Chapter Six) depends on the observation that this recension substitutes either "the king of Judah" (vss. 11f.) or the proper name "Ahaziah" (vs. 7a) for the MT's "Jehoshaphat," adding "Ahaziah" in two places where no proper name appears in the MT (vss. 7b, 9) and simply removing the proper name in vs. 14. Though Shenkel argues that the insertion of "Jehoshaphat" in the MT is arbitrary and tendentious, it is in fact LXX^{L}'s substitutions that deserve this description. It is perhaps reasonable to raise the possibility that one proper name might have been systematically substituted for another, resulting in a tendentious MT reading, but it is hardly likely that if "the king of Judah" had been original in vss. 11f. the MT would have suppressed this title in order to substitute a proper name. Here and elsewhere LXX^{L} shows evidence that it has carried out a programmatic recasting of the text in order to improve upon what it considered to be a mistaken MT chronology; the insertion or substitution of alternate terms for MT's "Jehoshaphat" are part of this program; so also the insertion of "Joram" in vss. 8 and 9 and the elimination of J(eh)oram's synchronism in vs. 1. It is probable that the MT's reference to "the king of Judah" in vs. 9 (without the proper name) is a deliberate device for the formal co-ordination of the "three kings," whereas in vs. 12 the proper name is offered in place of the

title because Jehoshaphat has been the principal speaker in the intervening section (see further M. Weippert, *Edom; Studien und Materialien zur Geschichte auf Grund schriftlicher und archäologischer Quellen* [Tübingen, 1971], pp. 314-320).

Elisha is firmly anchored in the three places where he is mentioned (vss. 11, 13, 14), the first time with patronym and typifying description. It is J(eh)oram who is textually questionable; he is not named in vs. 5 and in vs. 6 the proper name follows the fully adequate המלך (LXX[L]'s reading "Joram the king of Israel" is explicative, guarding against the misunderstanding that the J(eh)oram in question might be the Judahite king of that name). This proper name was inserted into the Hebrew text as part of — or as a result of — the redactional reference to Ahab's death in vs. 5a.

50. On the historical problems see now *PEQ* 99, *loc. cit.;* van Zyl, *The Moabites;* Bartlett, in Wiseman, *Peoples, loc. cit.;* also K.-H. Bernhardt, "Der Feldzug der drei Könige," in Bernhardt, ed., *Schalom* (Festschrift A. Jepsen; Stuttgart, 1971), pp. 11-22. The Moabite stele (*ANET*², pp. 320f.) offers a contemporary witness to the Moabite point of view. No precise chronological information may be deduced from lines 7-9, referring to Omri's and Ahab's (?) occupation of Medeba. On the probable date of composition, see Chapter Six.

51. Schematic elements abound: the three kings, the seven-day march, the conquering of "every" city, the systematic destruction. The three main characters are each highly typical: Elisha is one "who poured water on the hands of Elijah," the model prophet who serves Yahweh of Hosts; Jehoshaphat is the king who insists on an oracle and identifies Elisha as one who has the word of Yahweh; the "king of Israel" is functionless except as the person who organizes the march and who twice interprets the drought as the instrument of Yahweh's malevolent design. Highly fantastic is the notion of water coming from Edom (the most unlikely source) to fill the land without wind or rain, and especially the interpretation ascribed to the Moabites, viz., that the morning sunlight shining on all this water should be blood flowing from the wounds of dead soldiers.

52. Elisha's praise for Jehoshaphat has generally been interpreted as evidence for a Judean provenance (so Jepsen, *Nabi,* p. 89). This narrative's resemblance to I Kings 22, and especially to II Kings 9, argues instead for a Jehuite connection. The derogation of the king of Israel (who has to be Joram even though the name is textually secondary) in vss. 13f. is intended not as a polemic against the northern kings in general but specifically against the Omrides, who are here typified as less than orthodox with respect to Yahweh's historical purpose. Elisha's suggestion that the king "go to the prophets of your father and the prophets of your mother" (compare the Deuteronomist's note about Joram's comparative piety in vs. 2) is meant as a denunciation of the baalistic eclecticism prevalent under Ahab and Jezebel (LXX[B]'s eccentric omission of the latter phrase is probably motivated by piety, removing from Elisha's mouth the offensive suggestion that a false prophet be consulted). The king of Israel's refusal to follow this advice (vs. 13), emphatically reaffirming that it is Yahweh who has led the three kings astray, and who must therefore be consulted for a solution, retains a subtle innuendo, to the effect that the false prophets might indeed be consulted if another god were actually responsible.

53. The phrase (vs. 9) *wayyāssōbû derek šib'at yāmîm* is deliberately enigmatic, and no attempt to give it historical meaningfulness (as in Bernhardt, *Schalom,* pp. 12-14) can succeed; so also the reference to the kings "going down" to Elisha (vs. 12). Somehow the army gets east of Moab, for in the morning the Moabites see the sunlight glaring on the water (vs. 20).

54. The syntax of vs. 16b makes sense only by vocalizing עשה as an active participle.

55. A probable pun is intended between *hannaḥal hazzeh* (16) and *wenāqal zō't* (18). Our passage reflects the influence of Num. 11:23.

56. Compare a more conventional outline in Long, *VT* 23, p. 342.

57. On the relationship of this passage to I Kings 21, cf. the extensive discussion in Steck, *Überlieferung*, pp. 38-71.

58. Vs. 29b shows no awareness of 28-29a. Ahaziah's "going down" to Jezreel reflects the same orientation as I Kings 22:2; Ahaziah is here introduced by name and patronym, though identified only pronominally in the verses following 8:25 ("king of Judah" and "son of Ahab" are post-Septuagintal glosses); his motivation was to visit Joram "because he was sick" (חלה); cf. נכה hiph., 8:29a; 9:15. 8:29b is the original introduction to the prophet legend, bringing the two Omride kings together in Jezreel as a precondition to the development of this story. The Jehuite redactor responsible for 8:29a and 9:15a uses the locution *yôrām hammelek* in place of the legend's and the Deuteronomist's (8:28) single name; also, he refers to the place of Joram's wounding as "Ramah" instead of the legend's and the Deuteronomist's "Ramoth-Gilead."

59. Vss. 25b-26 are part of the Jehuite redaction (including 8:29a; 9:8a, 15a, 16b, 36b-37; 10:1-28) that expanded this prophet legend into a political manifesto. The Deuteronomist is responsible for 8:23-28; 9:8b-9, 14b, 28; 10:29ff.; a late gloss is 9:29; cf. 8:25 (deuteronomistic) (see Chapter Seven). Though the Jehuite redactor knows the tradition of vengeance on the Omrides at some place associated with Jezreel, it is certain that he was not acquainted with I Kings 21, which incorporates an independent prophet legend from the early post-Omride period (cf. vs. 29). The latter is intended as a legitimization of Jehu's insurrection, but is unfamiliar with our present narrative (cf. the extensive argumentation in Steck, *Überlieferung*, pp. 40-53, 71-77). We cannot accept the argument offered by J. M. Miller in "The Fall of the House of Ahab," *VT* 17 (1967), 309-324, interpreting the violent deed committed against Naboth as of recent occurrence (a literal *'emeš*, "yesterday"!) and accordingly identifying I Kings 21 as a late, entirely fanciful reconstruction.

That vss. 25b-26 are secondary in II Kings 9 is especially apparent from the fact that the conclusion laconically repeats the command of 25a. The original prophet legend is too tightly drawn, and its narrative development too impetuous, to have allowed the introduction of an extraneous motif of this sort — one never hinted at in the introductory sections. Nevertheless, the Jehuite redaction, which in our view arose soon after the prophet legend in point of time, eagerly seized upon this mention of Naboth as an opportunity to incorporate the tradition of a divine oracle against Ahab (delivered by a prophet whose name was not remembered) threatening him because of his crime against Naboth (and his sons). I Kings 21, a prophet legend belonging to the regal self-judgment subgenre and deriving from among those who preserved the revered memory of Elijah, takes a stance in support of the Jehu revolt similar to that of I Kings 19:1-18. Though I Kings 21 shows a development that is imaginative and not altogether logical (see our treatment on pp. 115f., 131f.), we are not convinced by Steck (pp. 53-71) that Jezebel could not have played the historical role assigned her there of engineering Naboth's judicial murder. There can be no serious question, in any event, about Ahab's involvement, since it is remembered in II Kings 9:25f. and forms the core of tradition in I Kings 21 (cf. Steck, pp. 40ff.)

60. For Heb. נכה hiph., LXX reads כרת hiph.

61. So Miller, *loc. cit.;* cf. B. D. Napier, "The Omrides of Jezreel," *VT* 9 (1959), 366-378. The fact that both royal lines were now descendants of Ahab, and hence protectors and proteges of the hated Jezebel, fully explains why the prophet legends (cf. also I Kings 21:29) polemicize against "the house of Ahab" rather than against "the house of Omri." That Assyrian records of the period actually refer to Israel as "Bit-Ḫumri" emphasizes the historical stature of Ahab's father. If the polemic of the prophets had been dynastically oriented, it would therefore surely have mentioned Omri as the founder of the line of kings descending from him. Compare the Deuteronomist's assault upon "the house of Jeroboam" (I Kings 14:14) and "the house of Baasha" (I Kings 16:3, 7) although it was, in fact, the respective son of each who perished in fulfillment of the prophecies introduced into the deuteronomistic account.

It is important to realize that both Joram and Ahaziah had to meet their deaths in this story in fulfillment of judgment on "the house of Ahab," as now represented in both regal lines; further, that only such a wide-ranging purge could fulfill the ultimate purpose of vengeance on Jezebel. The clever hypothesis of John Strange in "Joram, King of Israel and Judah," *VT* 25 (1975), 191-201, to the effect that Joram of Israel was in reality Jehoram the son of Jehoshaphat, falls foul of this realization. That Strange must interpret 9:22's reference to Jezebel as Joram's "mother" in a nondynastic sense, and that he fails to deal with the evidence of II Kings 3, to the effect that Joram of Israel is there Jehoshaphat's opposite number, implicitly identified in vs. 13 as Ahab's and Jezebel's son, puts his argument under heavy suspicion.

62. On this passage, see the somewhat differing analysis of Childs in *Isaiah and the Assyrian Crisis,* pp. 73ff. Cf. C. van Leeuwen, "Sanchérib devant Jérusalem," *OTS* 14 (1965), 245-272.

63. Vss. 23f. are parenthetical, reporting a wager that the Rabshakeh offers to make for the king of Assyria, in the king's own words.

64. The same *w^{e}'attâ* that introduces vs. 23 introduces vs. 25 (confirmed by LXX and Isaiah), directing attention to the king's final and climactic argument.

65. 18:32b-35 is a secondary expansion from 19:10-13.

66. The Hebrew represents the Babylonian *rab-šakē*, "chief of officers," or *rab-šākē*, "chief of the cupbearers." On the Babylonian military administration cf. B. Meissner, *Babylonien und Assyrien,* I (Heidelberg, 1920), 103; also H. W. F. Saggs, *The Greatness that was Babylon* (New York, 1962), p. 260.

67. Upon the possibility that the Assyrians might have made a claim to Yahweh's help, new light has been shed by Morton Cogan's study, *Imperialism and Religion; Assyria, Judah and Israel in the Eighth and Seventh Centuries B.C.E.* (Society of Biblical Literature Monograph 19; Missoula, Mont., 1974). Cogan summarizes the situation in the following words: " 'Ashur and the great gods' were not the only divine authors of Assyria's victories; the Assyrian conqueror acknowledged that local foreign gods, in control of the destinies of their adherents, were also active in Assyria's behalf. The traditional Mesopotamian literary motif of divine abandonment was incorporated in annalistic boasts that disaffected gods of the enemy had stopped protecting their devotees, thus exposing them to the onslaught of Assyrian armies" (p. 111).

68. Elements are listed as in the LXX, with the omission of MT pluses.

69. MT "you" is a pious alteration.

70. "At Ramoth-Gilead" is a gloss in I Kings 22:20; see Chapter Two.

71. Micaiah's historicity is made more probable by the fact that his name was evidently not sufficiently popular to attract extraneous traditions to itself, like Elijah and Elisha. The figure of Elijah has usurped the traditions of increasing the food (I Kings 17:10ff.), raising the dead boy (I Kings 17:17ff.), and anointing Hazael and Jehu (I Kings 19:15f.) from the Elisha cycle. It is very probable that some of the legends speaking of Elisha as a "man of God" were originally anonymous. But there is nothing in the text of I Kings 22 to suggest that Micaiah may be a substitute for an anonymous prophet or for one with a different name. Unlike Chronicles, Kings does not invent unhistorical names for its prophetic heroes.

72. For a comprehensive analysis of the development of salvation preaching within classical prophetism, see S. Herrmann, *Die prophetischen Heilserwartungen im Alten Testament; Ursprung und Gestaltwandel* (BWANT 85; Stuttgart, 1965).

CHAPTER SIX

The History of the Micaiah Tradition

1. THE IDENTIFICATION OF THE TWO KINGS

a. Chronological problems

IN ORDER NOW TO ANCHOR FIRMLY THE MICAIAH TRADITION TO ITS historical point of origin, it is necessary to identify those elements in our variant narratives that are historical. We have already seen that the setting of the Syrian wars is historical, also the existence of a prophet named Micaiah ben Imlah. The central question is the problem of the two kings. Jehoshaphat is securely tied to the text of Narrative A, Ahab to the text of Narrative B; but recognition of the typical function of the latter, reducing the element of his historicity in this narrative, raises the question whether Jehoshaphat is not also typical in Narrative A, as he very possibly is in II Kings 3 as well.

Although a solution to the problem of the historicity of either of these two kings cannot be found in isolation from the problem of the other, we may begin with Jehoshaphat by observing that if Ahab is indeed the Israelite king in question, Jehoshaphat, beginning his twenty-five-year reign in Ahab's fourth year (I Kings 22:41f.), would have been contemporary with Ahab for seventeen of the twenty-two years with which Ahab is credited (I Kings 16:29). This in itself leaves unresolved the question of Jehoshaphat's historicity in our narrative because, once Ahab had been identified — implicitly or explicitly — as the Israelite king in question, a narrator with a knowledge of the just-mentioned contemporaneity would naturally have assumed that Jehoshaphat was the Judahite king in question.

We find no mention elsewhere of familiar relations between Jehoshaphat and Ahab. As a matter of fact, I Kings 22:48f. seems to suggest that this Judahite king was not altogether willing to work in harmony with the kings of the Omride line. The fact that this passage depicts him as refusing to join Ahaziah, Ahab's son, in a shipping venture is, at the least, evidence that those historians are wrong who assume that the

Judahites were at this time nothing but complaisant vassals of the Omrides. Jehoshaphat's reluctance may be explained, however, as deriving from the wrecks mentioned in this same passage, not necessarily as being motivated by animosity. Certainly this text does not preclude the possibility of Jehoshaphat's act of joining Ahaziah's father in a military expedition against Syria.[1] Hostilities between the Judahites and Israelites seem to have long subsided — ever since Asa, Jehoshaphat's father, summoned Ben-Hadad I to invade the northern borders as his ally (I Kings 15:16-22).

Thus far there is nothing impossible in our narrative's association of Ahab with Jehoshaphat, but rather much to favor it. It must be clearly seen, however, that, apart from the specific names (one in the one narrative, the other in the second), there is nothing in the text that demands a historical background within the period when these two kings were together on the throne. We are faced with the challenging information provided by II Kings 8:28f., associating a grandson of Jehoshaphat and a son of Ahab in battle against the Syrians. There are four points of close correlation between this passage and I Kings 22: (1) it states that Ahaziah of Judah accompanied Joram of Israel to make war against the Syrians; (2) it mentions Ramoth-Gilead as the scene of battle; (3) its identification of Hazael, much more aggressive than his predecessor (cf. II Kings 8:12; 13:3, 22), as the Syrian king suggests that the Syrians may have actually been occupying Ramoth-Gilead — a condition presupposed in I Kings 22:3; and (4) it makes a point of stating that the Israelite king was wounded (compare *kî ḥōleh hû'*, II Kings 8:29, with *kî hoḥ°lêtî*, I Kings 22:34).

Joram ben Ahab is clearly the only other candidate for identification as the original king of Israel in I Kings 22, for the coincidence of Joram's and Ahaziah's deaths, an emphatic element in the instrumental fulfillment narrative of II Kings 8:29b–9:36a,[2] marks the beginning of both Jehu's and Athaliah's reigns (cf. II Kings 10:17; 11:1). This synchronism is supported by II Kings 11:21; 12:1, which state that the seven-year-old Jehoash began to reign in Jehu's seventh year. Inasmuch as Jehoshaphat's son Jehoram is credited with an eight-year reign (II Kings 8:17), and Jehoram's son Ahaziah is credited with one year (II Kings 8:26), Jehoshaphat himself clearly could not have accompanied Joram ben Ahab to battle in the last year of that king's twelve-year reign (II Kings 3:1). If the latter was indeed the actual king of I Kings 22, the reference to Jehoshaphat cannot be anything but unhistorical.

TABLE ONE

CHRONOLOGY FROM ZIMRI TO AZARIAH

Scriptural references	Judahite rulers (Tishri yrs.)	Dates B.C.	Israelite rulers (Nisan yrs.)
		885/84	Zimri
I Kings 16: 10, 15			ac 27 (LXX^{L} 22, LXX^{B} om) Jehoshaphat a/d
"			r 7 days (LXX^{B} years)
		885/84	Omri-Tibni rivalry
I Kings 16:23			Omri r 12 yrs. a/d
		880	Omri alone
"			ac 31 Asa a/d
		874/73	Ahab
I Kings 16:29			ac 38 Asa a/d (LXX 2 Jehoshaphat)
"			r 22 yrs. a/d
	Jehoshaphat coregent	873/72	
cf. II Chron. 16:12	(= 39 Asa a/d)		
I Kings 22:42 (= II Chron. 20:31)	r 25 yrs. p/d		
	Jehoshaphat alone	870/69	
I Kings 22:41	ac 4 Ahab p/d		
I Kings 16:28+	(LXX 11 Omri)		
cf. II Kings 1:17	Jehoram coregent	854/53	
		853	Ahaziah
I Kings 22:51			ac 17 (LXX^{L} 24) Jehoshaphat a/d
"			r 2 yrs. a/d
		852	J(eh)oram
II Kings 1:17 (LXX 18)			ac 2 Jeroham (coregency a/d (MT, LXX^{L})
II Kings 3:1			ac 18 Jehoshaphat a/d (MT, LXX^{B}; LXX^{L} om)
"			r 12 yrs. a/d
	Jehoram alone	848	
II Kings 8:16	ac 5 Joram a/d		
II Kings 8:17 (= II Chron. 21:5, 20)	r 8 (LXX^{B} 40; LXX^{L} 10) yrs. a/d		
	Ahaziah	841	
II Kings 9:29	ac 11 Joram a/d		
II Kings 8:25	ac 12 (LXX^{L} 11) Joram a/d		

TABLE ONE—(CONT.)
CHRONOLOGY FROM ZIMRI TO AZARIAH

Scriptural references	Judahite rulers (Tishri yrs.)	Dates B.C.	Israelite rulers (Nisan yrs.)
II Kings 8:26 (= II Chron. 22:2)	r 1 yr. a/d		
	Athaliah	841	Jehu
II Kings 10:36			r 28 yrs. a/d
II Kings 11: 3-4 (= II Chron. 22: 12; 23:1	(r 7 yrs. a/d)		
	J(eh)oash	835	
II Kings 12:1 (= II Chron. 24:1)	ac 7 Jehu a/d		
"	r 40 yrs. a/d		
		814/13	J(eh)oahaz
II Kings 13:1			ac 23 Joash a/d
"			r 17 yrs. a/d
		798	J(eh)oash
II Kings 13:10			ac 37 Joash p/d
"			r 16 yrs. p/d
	Amaziah	797/96	
II Kings 14:1	ac 2 Jehoash p/d		
II Kings 14:2 (= II Chron. 25:1)	r 29 yrs. p/d		
		793/92	Jeroboam coregent
II Kings 14:23			r 41 yrs. p/d
	Azariah coregent	792/91	
II Kings 15:2 (= II Chron. 26:3)	r 52 yrs. p/d		
		782/81	Jeroboam alone
II Kings 14:23			ac 15 Amaziah p/d
	Azariah alone	768/67	
II Kings 15:1	ac 27 Jeroboam coregency		

Legend: a/d = antedating p/d = postdating ac = accession r = yrs. of reign

Table One offers a schematic view of the chronology of the period with which we are concerned.[3] There has been extensive discussion of the chronology of this period in recent literature, but nothing that would essentially augment or diminish the choice stated above.[4] It would not be important to enter into the chronological problem at all, were it not for the question of references to Ahab and Jehu in the records of Shalmaneser III of Assyria. The Monolith Inscription of this king (*ANET*, p. 278) claims a victory at Qarqar over Ahab as a member of a western confederacy in Shalmaneser's sixth year, 853 B.C., while the annals of the latter's eighteenth year, 841 (*ANET*, p. 280; cf. the Black Obelisk, *ANEP*, p. 122), claim that he received tribute from Jehu in this year. Since Ahaziah ben Ahab is credited with a two-year reign (I Kings 22:51), we are faced with the necessity of fitting two years for Ahaziah and twelve years for his brother Joram into the interval between 853 and 841. This problem can be readily solved on the basis of antedating, which counts parts of each accession year in the total length of reign, but we are in any event required to assume that Shalmaneser dealt with Ahab in this king's last year, then with Jehu in Jehu's first year. It seems reasonable — indeed, probable — that Jehu might have taken immediate measures, upon the success of his revolt, to have consolidated his external alliances by paying tribute to Shalmaneser,[5] but a problem remains with respect to Ahab. How are we to understand his being allied with the Syrians at Qarqar and then, very shortly thereafter, attacking them? Various explanations have been offered, but the only attractive solution is that it was not Ahab who attacked the Syrians, but his son.[6]

b. "Ahab slept with his fathers"

A crucial problem is the meaning and bearing of the deuteronomistic closing formula for Ahab found in I Kings 22:39f. The Deuteronomist winds up his account of Ahab's reign in the usual way, alluding to two ambitious building projects as that king's most remarkable achievements and referring the reader to his documentary source, *sēper dibrê hayyāmîm l^emalkê yiśrā'ēl*, for further information. He then adds the customary transitional formula, "So Ahab slept with his fathers (*wayyiškab 'aḥ'āb 'im 'ᵃbôtâw*) and Ahaziah his son reigned in his stead." The remarkable thing about the "sleeping with one's fathers" formula is that it is nowhere except in our passage applied to a king who is reported to have died a violent death.[7] A present consensus agrees that this statement, along with most other elements among the framework formulas, is no free invention of the Deuteronomist but a stereotyped datum extracted from the sources.[8] The only statements that do represent programmatic deuteronomistic composition within the framework, viz., the theologizing assessments of the respective kings, appears as a result of the recent work of Helga Weippert to have resulted from two successive phases of commentative activity within the editorial process.[9] From this we conclude that the "sleeping with one's fathers" formula is pre-deuteronomistic; and, since it is entirely possible that the Deuteronomist as redactor did not fully understand its meaning, we would scarcely venture to conclude, with J. Maxwell Miller,[10] R. H. Pfeiffer,[11] W. Dietrich,[12] and others that I Kings 22:1-38 could not have belonged within the original deuteronomistic corpus. If we are to assume that a postdeuteronomistic redactor would have been unfamiliar with this formula's meaning, what is to prevent us from assuming the same for the original Deuteronomist? *Hypothesi non multiplicanda sunt*. As we intend to show, every argument favors the early redactional insertion of I Kings 22:1ff. as part of a special prophetic collection.

The Judahite kings to whom this formula is applied[13] are Rehoboam, Abijah, Asa, Jehoshaphat, Jehoram, Jehoash, Azariah, Jotham, Ahaz, Hezekiah, Manasseh, and Jehoiakim, all of whom died of so-called "natural causes." In addition, II Kings 14:22, reporting a memorable deed of Azariah, times it "after the king (*hammelek*) slept with his fathers." The reference here is apparently to Azariah's father Amaziah, but this verse is clearly a gloss. The wording does not conform at all to the usual form, seen in the regular conclusion for Amaziah in vs. 18, where the "sleeping with one's fathers" formula is missing.

The Israelite kings to whom the "sleeping with one's fathers" formula is applied are Jeroboam I, Baasha, Omri, Ahab, Jehu, Jehoahaz, Jehoash, Jeroboam II and Menahem. Again, all are reported to have died of natural causes except — apparently — Ahab. With respect to five of these kings, viz., Baasha, Omri, Jehu, Jehoahaz and Jehoash, we find a following notice concerning the burial; that Ahab's obituary lacks it seems to have no special significance because three prominent colleagues, Jeroboam I, Jeroboam II and Menahem, along with the Judahite Hezekiah, are in this same situation. That the burial notice is independent from the "sleeping with one's fathers" formula may be deduced from the fact that five Judahite kings lacking the latter (Ahaziah, Jehoash, Amaziah, Amon and Josiah) have the former.

The Judahite rulers who lack the "sleeping with one's fathers" formula are the five just mentioned, plus Athaliah, Jehoahaz, Jehoiachin and Zedekiah. The last three were deported; the others died a violent death. The same is true of all but one of the Israelite kings for whom this formula is lacking: Nadab, Elah, Zimri, Jehoram, Zechariah, Shallum, Pekahiah, Pekah and Hoshea. The last mentioned was deported; the others died victims of assassination.

The only Israelite king who was neither deported nor killed, yet lacks the "sleeping with one's fathers" formula, is Ahaziah the son of Ahab. In the prophet legend about him, II Kings 1:2-17a,[14] his death is reported as occurring through two special circumstances: (1) it is the result of a serious accident; (2) it is interpreted as a divine judgment upon his apostasy. Nicholas J. Tromp, who has recently studied all the Hebrew expressions for death,[15] suggests that our formula is "an indirect *testimonium pietatis*" reserved for persons of distinction, the circumstances of whose death (in peace and honor) were a witness to the quality of their lives. We read in I Kings 11:21, for instance, that Hadad heard that David "slept with his fathers" while Joab, who had been executed, "was dead (*mēt*)." From this we can understand why Ahaziah did not rate our formula. Apparently the chronicles from which the Deuteronomist was working did not have it; the scribe who had made the original entries regarding Ahaziah had concluded from the untimely death that what the prophet legend affirms was true: the apostate king bore in his death a clear divine judgment upon his life.

Thus we have confirmation that even this exception proves the rule. Those kings who are recorded as having "slept with their fathers" were kings who died at home, in peace, and with honor. It seems blind and arbitrary to ignore the imposing evidence for the meaning of this phrase when it comes to Ahab, and the very fact that his seemingly irregular case is directly juxtaposed with the seemingly irregular case of Ahaziah lends the more emphasis to it. We cannot escape two important conclusions: (1) although I Kings 22:1-37 was in the definitive deuteronomistic corpus, and was understood to refer to Ahab, it was not interpreted as being in conflict with vs. 40 because the Deuteronomist did not appreciate the implications of the "sleeping with one's fathers" formula; (2) since this formula, as applied to Ahab, was in the deuteronomistic sources and implies a peaceable death for Ahab, the king of Israel who dies in vss. 1-37 could not actually have been Ahab.

Thus in the final analysis we see no escape from the claim that I Kings 22 has been developed from the historical background of the events recorded in II Kings 8:28ff. Joram ben Ahab is the only other candidate for the role of "king of Israel." His Judahite counterpart was Ahaziah. But the persons who preserved the Micaiah tradition in its early form (Narrative A), having no name for their Israelite king, no doubt soon came to believe that the king in question would have been none other than Ahab, who with Jezebel was held responsible by the Jehuites for all the gross apostasies that had necessitated and justified their insurrection. Though the name "Ahab" does not actually appear in this narrative (only in its later variant, Narrative B), it is this understanding that must have determined the naming of Jehoshaphat as his colleague. That the normative recollection of what had happened at Ramoth-Gilead, preserved in the chronicles used by the Deuteronomist in II Kings 8:28 and in the introduction to the Jehu accession narrative in II Kings 8:29a, spoke specifically of Joram and Ahaziah, ruled out the possibility that so divergent a version of this event as is recorded in our prophet legend could have been attributed to the same set of kings. It had to be Ahab and Jehoshaphat, then. And why not — for more and more Ahab had come to exemplify apostasy, as Jehoshaphat had come to represent orthodoxy.

2. THE PROBLEMS OF DATE AND HISTORICITY

It is now our task to raise the questions of the date and level of historicity for the two narratives comprising our passage, I Kings 22:1-37. How are we to go about determining the answers to these questions? One thing is settled: the *terminus a quo* is 841 B.C., the date of Jehu's coup, not 853, the end of Ahab's reign. From 841 we have at least another fifty years of Aramean hostilities. We need to develop sound principles for deciding where in this or succeeding periods our legends are to be placed, and from this to propose a reasonable theory of redaction.

a. Criteria

It would seem to be sound method to develop controlling data from a comparison with other prophet legends. Narrative A belongs to subgenre 9 and Narrative B to subgenre 11, but these numerical designations are arbitrary, suggesting no more than relative sophistication, and having nothing to do with date or historicity. Regarding the latter problem, we need to assert at the very beginning that the presence or lack of the wondrous and the supernaturalistic says nothing directly about historicity. It is true that a high level of the supernatural may make unlikely a significant element of historical factuality in a given narrative. But a narrative reflecting a high level of historicality may well contain striking elements of wonder, introduced as the basis of theological interpretation, depending on the narrator's ideological framework for the interpretation of historical event. Contrariwise, a narrative without the element of wonder may be purely schematic and without factual historical foundation. We do well to remind ourselves that there were no mechanists in ancient Israel. God was active in every event. In this sense nothing was uniquely miraculous because everything was miraculous. Certain groups did tend to be more imaginative than others in their way of interpreting divine action in human experience, but all groups believed without question that Yahweh was sovereignly at work in every event, whatever the mode of causality.

(1) There are several criteria that may be applied to individual narratives as tests for their relative level of historical actuality. The first criterion is whether a narrative can have any meaning without an essential orientation toward historical fact. An example for the affirmative application of this criterion would be seen in II Kings 8:1-6. Though, of course, there is nothing to prove the historicity of this narrative in itself — it is assuredly too trivial and private to have been recorded as historically meaningful — there are two elements that at least require that the tradition underlying this narrative antedate the narrative itself: (1) it is structured around a fulfillment that is defined outside the structure of this particular narrative; and (2) the narrative on which this one is based is

completely independent of and separate from it, finding its full structural development in itself. Our story introduces the problem of a dispossessed woman trying to get the king to render her justice. Presumably the king will not be inclined to grant favorable consideration to her as a helpless stranger. But her trouble has come as a result of her obedience to supernatural instruction formerly received, hence the tension-element in the story is whether the prophetic power that produced her dilemma can now resolve it. That Elisha is dead may be deduced from the fact that his servant Gehazi is alone with the king, telling deeds that his master has done. Yet the power of Elisha's previous work in raising this very woman's son from the dead (II Kings 4:8-37) has effect even now, as Gehazi identifies the woman and her son to the king, who is thereby moved to render the woman her due and thus resolve her problem.[16] But, as we say, II Kings 4:8ff. is structurally independent of this narrative; it is told of Elisha in his lifetime, with Gehazi at his side, and moves from problem to complete resolution on its own terms.

(2) A second criterion of historicity is the preservation of inimical elements. A narrative that retains traditions that are in opposition to the interests of its own tradents may be presumed to be historical, for how else would it have been developed and preserved? An excellent example is found in the story about the Judahite man of God in I Kings 13.[17] That this story had an independent existence until taken up by the Deuteronomist to bolster his propaganda in favor of Josiah's reform may be deduced from the fact that in his account of that reform (II Kings 23:15-20) this late seventh-century redactor incorporated narrative elements that were somewhat at variance with the details offered in I Kings 13.[18] The etiological element of the early story, viz., a tomb near Bethel containing the bones of a Judahite man of God (cf. II Kings 23:17f.), explains its preservation. But, as we have argued, this story was not initially preserved in Judah, for no surviving Judahite had been on the scene to witness, and we can scarcely think of Bethelite tradents passing it on to Judahites until after the fall of the northern kingdom. The original tradents were the Bethelite prophets, who preserved the story in connection with the tomb as a testimony to the validity of an element essentially invidious to the very shrine with which they were associated. Though these persons are not to be thought of in simplistic terms as cult prophets, they would have had no reason to have preferred the Jerusalem temple to the more ancient, hallowed shrine at Bethel. They remembered the word of the Judahite because he had proven in the manner of his death to be "a man of God" indeed, and because their prime loyalty was to Yahweh, sovereign even to judge a shrine at which he himself was worshiped.[19]

(3) A third criterion for relative historicity is the absence of tendentious elements, chiefly the following: the idealization of individual figures, moving toward typifying treatment; artificial embellishment; schematic

structuring. Wherever these particular elements are prominent, the likelihood of historical actuality is greatly reduced; wherever they are minimal or completely absent, the presumption is increased that a narrative may be reporting factual occurrence. In sum: the more unaffected and unschematic a story is, the closer in fact and perhaps in time it is likely to be to the events marking its historical emergence.

An example of how this third criterion may become a basis for relative dating and relative historicity can be seen in a comparison between I Kings 22 and II Kings 3. We recall the several elements of high schematization, typification, and outright fancifulness identified in the latter passage.[20] This argues that the common elements shared by the two stories, viz., a military alliance, the participation of Jehoshaphat, the threefold comparison, the demand for an oracle, and the reproach delivered by the prophet to the Israelite king, most likely derive from the former passage in the direction of the latter, not vice versa. Accordingly, we must again judge those critics wrong who attribute Judean influence to the I Kings 22 narrative. It is not even present, as we have argued, in II Kings 3. At the same time, II Kings 3 reveals its relative lateness and relative artificiality in its strong ideological bias against the Omrides, drawn from the same circle of tradition but upon a far weaker historical basis than the highly realistic account of II Kings 8:29ff.

A word now about the latter. We can surely be confident in agreeing with a consensus that attributes a high historicity to what we have called "the Jehu accession narrative" appearing in the just-mentioned passage. It draws upon the "instrumental fulfillment narrative" told by the prophets and upon several other narrative elements, welding them into a meaningful, factual redactional combination, producing an effective apologia for Jehu's bloody takeover. This composite narrative clearly meets the first of the criteria that we have identified, viz., meaninglessness except on the basis of a high level of historicity. In distinction from all other non-annalistic materials in the section, I Kings 17 through II Kings 10 (13), the Jehu accession narrative is clearly a political instrument, geared closely to recently experienced, clearly remembered political and military actualities. It would have had no effectiveness in justifying Jehu's revolt if its account of events were largely imaginary. This is not to deny the presence of propagandistic structuring. Quite on the contrary, its propagandistic bias is very strong and clear, and it is the fact that this bias was shared by a large segment of the populace supporting the coup, who saw this narrative as a factual, verifiable account of the events as they saw them and participated in them, that argues the most powerfully for its historicality. Its hero, Jehu, is thoroughly realistic and believable, but is drawn in such a way as to elicit sympathy and support. That his interests, and not those of the prophetic circle that supported him, dominate the redacted narrative may be seen in that the prophet who anoints Jehu[21] is only one element, alongside the army, the Rechabites and the general populaces of Samaria and Jezreel, aiding him to seize the kingdom.

Applying now the criteria that we have developed to the two independent narratives of I Kings 22, we find that the first two offer little definite help, while the third suggests only the relative lateness of Narrative B, as compared with Narrative A. We can say of neither narrative that historical factuality is an essential clue to meaning: either would be effective and theologically meaningful as an imaginary, though typical, example of how Yahweh determines prophecy in control of history. We are, furthermore, unable to point to any inimical element similar to that preserved in I Kings 13. We can detect in Narrative A something of the propagandistic bias that appears so pronouncedly in the Jehu narrative, though without question the former remains a prophet legend in its unredacted form, explicating prophetic rather than political ideals, and does not take on the shape of political propaganda until recast by the redaction. In Narrative B the element of antipathy toward the king has been entirely redirected toward the prophets who advise him and oppose their prophetic protagonist. Here we find a level of idealization and accentuated typification that is relevant to the developing situation of prophetic controversy as experienced after the downfall of the northern kingdom. Its situational background is far removed from the political-military setting of Narrative A.

b. The origin of the Micaiah narratives

We are prepared now to draw the confident conclusion that neither Narrative A nor Narrative B in I Kings 22 directly records historical events. Yet we must take the trouble to examine specific points shared by the two in order to determine just how wide apart they actually are.

It is clear that the two narratives do derive from a common tradition and ultimately from an historical occurrence. The respective levels of departure from that ultimate source may be judged from the following parallel elements: (1) points of close affinity between Narrative A and several varieties of prophet legend associated with the Elijah and Elisha schools are completely lacking of Narrative B, whose nearest associations are with the Hezekiah/Isaiah traditions, in particular the heavenly court, the word-controversy form, the deceiving/hardening motif, and the accentuated problem of internal prophetic controversy; (2) Narrative A reflects a clear and specific military aim, viz., to retake Ramoth-Gilead, whereas Narrative B defines this merely as "to push Syria," attributing the initiative for this vague action to a prophet in place of the king; (3) Narrative A preserves an anonymity for the Israelite king characteristic of virtually all the stories from the early prophetic circles featuring the motif of conflict with the royal office, but Narrative B (at first leaving the Israelite king unnamed) specifically names Ahab as the paradigmatic evil king who is misled by equally paradigmatic, untrustworthy prophets; (4) Narrative A features a more specific, essentially historical procedure from the primitive holy-war tradition, retaining in its original meaning the *d*[e]*raš YHWH* element common in this tradition from early monarchical days; (5) in Narrative A, Jehoshaphat has an active and realistic role (cf. the pious stereotype in II Kings 3), but in Narrative B he appears only in the initial scene and is then dropped; (6) Narrative A reveals a strong, and again very specific, interest in Aramean military arrangement, armament, and tactics, while Narrative B omits all reference to a military denouement except for its ultimate personal effect on the contending prophet; (7) Narrative A incorporates a subtly epitomizing past *bayyôm hahû'*, following the clear tradition — if not the usual structure — of sagas and holy war stories from the early period, whereas Narrative B's futuristic *bayyôm hahû'* is unparalleled in early literature but is widely copied in the eschatological announcements of classical and postclassical prophetism.[22]

Narrative A shows so great a departure from the events of 841, accurately and straightforwardly recorded in II Kings 8:28ff., that one would scarcely dare assume that it came into being in the early years following the death of Joram and Ahaziah. The Jehu accession narrative, designed as an apologia for Jehu's bloody deed and suffused with retributive hostility toward Jezebel and the whole "house of Ahab," quickly established itself as the normative account of these stirring events. But the intriguing motif of prophetic instrumentality in the ineluctable fate of an Israelite king found a fertile variant background in the memory of close association between the Israelite kings and the Judahite kings since the days of Ahab and Jehoshaphat, who as eponyms of the two ill-starred lines eventually came to be identified, implicitly and at last explicitly, as the two kings joined in combat at Ramoth-Gilead. Since Narrative A is a prophet legend, not a political propaganda piece, it presents a genuinely prophetic theme. It substitutes divine control and intervention for Jehu's own ruthless act. Thus the nameless Syrian bowman of I Kings 22 introduces an accentuated transcendental dimension in which Yahweh's deed takes the place of Jehu's. As we have seen, the schema of Narrative A is that of the superseding oracle narrative, paralleled only in II Kings 8:7ff., which likewise has to do with the theme of prophetic interaction in the ominous exchange of power from Ben-Hadad I to Hazael, the villain of the latter passage as well as the enemy king named in II Kings 8:28f. Since the Micaiah narrative required a counterpart Judahite king who would serve the function of demanding an oracle endangering the life of the king of Israel, our tradents were naturally inclined to choose the relatively orthodox, untainted Jehoshaphat in preference to his successors, who through intermarriage had become sullied with the sins of the house of Ahab.

We certainly need to assume that Narrative A was shaped in quite different prophetic circles than those that might have been involved in the origin of II Kings 8:29–10:28. There is no reason to associate the latter narrative directly with the Elisha school, though it was probably contemporary with it.[23] Narrative A, together with all the prophet legends contained in I Kings 10, 13, needs to be evaluated against the background of the ongoing Aram-Israel warfare, involving the various Israelite kings from Omri through Jeroboam II. Of course, much of what we profess to know of this involvement has been drawn from the prophet legends whose association with the notices concerning the respective kings came about only in the process of deuteronomistic redaction. Yet we recognize that the court records employed by this redaction themselves produced comparable information of generally high historical reliability. Particularly important are the notices in II Kings 8:28; 10:32f.; 12:18f.; 13:3-5, 22f., recording the aggressions of Hazael, and II Kings 13:25; 14:25-27, recording the successes of Jehoahaz and Jeroboam II against the Syrians. Without attempting here to enter into all the problems of Assyrian correlations, and the question whether there was in fact a third Ben-Hadad,[24] we may roughly divide the whole period of struggle into three subperiods: (1) the reign of Ben-Hadad I (from the time of Asa until shortly before Jehu), who apparently carried out raids against the Israelite borders and kept the Omrides in a state of dependence, though not of outright vassalage; (2) the reign of the usurper Hazael (mentioned in the annals of Shalmaneser III's eighteenth year as a "son of nobody"), who entered into a campaign of depredations in northern Israel and even in Judah, marching down the Philistine coastline to threaten Jerusalem; and (3) the reign of the latter's son, another Ben-Hadad (which is accordingly a probable throne-name, meaning "representative" or "worshiper" of the god Hadad), who lost in three battles with Jehoash the cities that his father had taken from Israel (II Kings 13:25; cf. vss. 14-19).[25] It is in the middle period that Narrative A belongs, reflecting the significance of a crucial event at the transition from the first period to the second. The date is toward the end of the ninth century B.C.

Narrative B is approximately one century younger. It reveals no concern whatever for contemporary political problems. Unlike the book of Hosea, which for the large part originated in northern Israel during the last tumultuous decades of that realm and was subsequently transported to Judah for preservation, our Narrative B reveals no special antipathy toward the Jehuite kings (cf. Hos. 1:4f.) and makes no mention of the chaos wrought by their nondescript successors. The institution of the Israelite kingship is no longer a problem for Narrative B; whether, on the other hand, the Judahite kingship, represented typically in Jehoshaphat, is now taken as normative, remains unclear. It is possible that we have here a valid *argumentum e silentio* for a pre-Hezekian origin, since

Jehoshaphat, not Hezekiah, appears as the ideal orthodox king. Anyway, Narrative B's concern is with the question of how kings can go astray even under prophetic leading. The sad history of the northern realm, now defunct, has been precisely a relevant example of this. No doubt there were prophets to guide each one of the northern kings, yet somehow they had all gone astray and ultimately ruined the kingdom. Hosea and Deuteronomy — which many scholars now believe originated in the northern kingdom at approximately this same period[26] — tried to solve the problem in terms of an antique model, the model of Moses, Israel's ideal prophet from the time of its wilderness wandering (cf. Deut. 18:15-22; Hos. 6:4-6; 9:7-9; 12:8-11, 13-15).[27] Our recast Micaiah narrative, for its part, looks upward rather than backward — that is, to heaven rather than to Sinai. The appeal to heaven may bring no more satisfying a solution to the problem of prophet against prophet and the problem of prophet against king, but it does interject greater subtlety and sophistication. Thus does Narrative B pioneer the way toward the profundities of Israel's great classical prophets.

c. *Historicity and theological relevance*

Now that our study has resulted in drastically reducing the element of historical actuality in the Micaiah story (stories), a word of caution needs to be said with respect to possible negative judgments about its theological relevance and validity. Alongside those who have long lamented to see brought into question the literal inerrancy of the very words of Scripture, there are others who accept biblical criticism but resist any reduction of historical facticity because, as they imagine, if Yahweh did not actually perform every event as the narrative describes, the element of revelational occurrence may be seriously threatened if not utterly lost. Not so: a narrator may in one place record accurate, "objective" facts, though this may be less for their theological significance than for their pragmatic value as political documentation, as in the case of the Jehu accession narrative. A narrator may somewhere else build up a highly imaginative tale, including perhaps striking elements of wonder, departing freely from the factual historical background of the event he is recounting, yet the particular narrative he tells may gain in theological meaningfulness through this artful process of imaginative expansion. As we have said, biblical narrative sometimes develops the element of wonder for dramatic effect, but the concept of Yahweh working everywhere in nature and in history remains the same. In the Bible nothing can be uniquely miraculous because everything is miraculous. Even where the explicit element of wonder is altogether lacking — as in our earliest Micaiah tale — the decisive role of Yahweh is unmistakable. That "accidental" arrow was Yahweh's arrow: make no mistake about it! Thus this story — and its later variant, Narrative B — remains theologically potent. It preaches the sovereignty and omnipresence of the biblical God. What happens to "Ahab" is a model for what can and does happen to every man who seeks to determine his course in defiance of the divine will. Whatever measures one may take — even if one should appeal, like Saul, to alternative sources of transcendental revelation — *he must meet his God* (cf. Amos. 4:12)![28]

Since the implications of the foregoing analysis of historical and traditional development can best be appreciated in the context of the redactional handling of the pertinent material, they will be summarized at the conclusion of the following chapter.

NOTES TO CHAPTER SIX

1. How far one may be led astray by erroneous presuppositions is illustrated in Julian Morgenstern's article, "Chronological Data of the Dynasty of Omri," *JBL* 59 (1940), 385-396. Taking his point of departure from I Kings 22:1f., Morgenstern remarks: "It is almost self-apparent that at the moment of his meeting with Ahab, Jehoshaphat knew absolutely nothing of Ahab's plan for the Ramoth-Gilead campaign. . . . Therefore it is almost certain that Jehoshaphat had not come down to meet Ahab attended by his army and all prepared for war. Yet the continuation of the narrative certainly implies that the campaign against Ramoth-Gilead followed immediately upon Ahab's proposal to Jehoshaphat and with the latter's either having the time or facing the necessity of mustering his army and bringing it down from Judah" (385f.). With this last supposition we may compare Josephus' statement in *Antiquities* viii.399, to the effect that Jehoshaphat *did* wait for his army. Morgenstern's conclusion is that II Chron. 18:1f. must be preferred to Kings: Jehoshaphat visited Ahab only to celebrate the wedding feast of Jehoram and Athaliah. How the Ramoth-Gilead narrative nevertheless got into the text, Morgenstern does not explain. His interest is aimed solely at applying the three-year figure of I Kings 22:1 (cf. II Chron. 18:1 *l^eqēṣ šānîm*) to the interval preceding the marriage feast, not the Ramoth-Gilead battle, thus justifying his date of 874/73 for the events of I Kings 20 and a date after Qarqar (853) for the Ramoth-Gilead battle.

2. See above, pp. 67-69.

3. Cf. S. J. De Vries, "Chronology of the Old Testament," *IDB,* I (also "Chronology, Old Testament," in the Supplementary Volume). The chronology offered here is essentially that developed by E. R. Thiele, *The Mysterious Numbers of the Hebrew Kings* (rev. ed., Grand Rapids, 1965).

4. Although, as we have seen in Chapter Two, LXX^B from I Kings 22 onward has been normalized toward the MT, reflecting the *Kaige* recension, it departs from the MT in some of the figures for the kings of this period. The MT is evidently counting by postdating when it dates Jehoram's and Ahaziah's accessions in Joram ben Ahab's fifth and eleventh years, respectively; also when it ascribes to the first of these kings an eight-year, and to the second a one-year reign. This fits precisely the 12+ years between 853 and 841, but LXX^B throws the whole pattern out of kilter by giving Jehoram of Judah forty years. LXX^L, giving Jehoram ten years, is still beyond the bounds of reason.

J. D. Shenkel, *Chronology and Recensional Development*, has been somewhat anticipated by J. Maxwell Miller in his article, "Another Look at the Chronology of the Early Divided Monarchy," *JBL* 86 (1967), 276-288, in claiming that the chronology of LXX^{L} is definitely superior to that of the MT. Shenkel, who has most extensively argued the case, makes much of the fact that LXX^{L} rejects the MT/LXX^{B} synchronism for Joram ben Ahab in Jehoshaphat's eighteenth year (MT, II Kings 3:1; LXX^{B}, II Kings 1:18+; 3:1), preserving only the MT synchronism in Jehoram of Judah's second year, found in II Kings 1:17 (LXX^{L} 1:18+). Although Shenkel recognizes that the name "Joram" has been added secondarily to the text of II Kings 3, he assumes that the identification of the Israelite king is historically accurate because no other candidate (Ahab, Ahaziah, or Jehu) is suitable. This means that the name "Jehoshaphat" has been tendentiously substituted in the MT and LXX^{B} for an original "Ahaziah," preserved in LXX^{L}. From this observation Shenkel argues that LXX^{L}, not the MT, is right in the figures it preserves for the entire succession of kings from Asa/Elah to Ahaziah/Joram. But it has been established above (Chapter Five, n. 49) that Jehoshaphat is not in fact secondary in the text of II Kings 3. It is rather LXX^{L}'s "Ahaziah" whose appearance is suspicious. Besides the fact that LXX^{B} and LXX^{L} have an addition at I Kings 16:28+ that reveals itself as a secondary adaptation from 22:41ff., showing that the Greek textual tradition follows a corrective program over against its Hebrew *Vorlage* (cf. D. W. Gooding's review of Shenkel in *JTS* N.S. 21 [1970], 118-131), clear evidence that LXX^{L} has altered the original text at II Kings 3:1 may be seen in that it retains the entire deuteronomistic redactional introduction to Joram's reign, including a statement of the length of his reign that otherwise regularly occurs in the Deuteronomist's framework formulas with respect to orderly successions, while simply omitting the synchronism. On the problem of the double synchronism for Joram ben Ahab and related chronological questions, see my argumentation in the dictionary articles mentioned in n. 3.

5. This would have been designed as a measure to get the Assyrians to force Hazael to cease his aggressions against the Israelite borders. The Shalmaneser annals for this period indicate that Hazael remained alone in opposing the Assyrians, who eventually besieged Damascus and wrought heavy devastation in the countryside.

6. Cf. A. Malamat, "The Aramaeans," in Wiseman, ed., *Peoples of Old Testament Times*, pp. 144f.: "A war between Ahab and Ben-Hadad at Ramoth-Gilead (as in I Kings 22) is unlikely so short a time after the battle of Qarqar, for this western alliance of kings seems to have remained intact, meeting Shalmaneser III again in 849, 848, and 845 B.C. Only Hazael, who overthrew the Ben-Hadad dynasty, reversed the Aramaean policy towards Israel, clashing with Ahab's son Joram in 842 B.C. at Ramoth-Gilead (2 Kings 8:28f.; the alleged encounter here in the days of Ahab probably reflects this later event)."

7. Since the work of Hölscher (in *Eucharisterion H. Gunkel*, I [1923], pp. 158-213) the significance of this fact has been generally recognized (Steuernagel already understood the historical implication of this expression; see his *Lehrbuch der Einleitung in das Alte Testament*, p. 362); but it was B. Alfrink who drew out its full implications in his article, "L'expression שָׁכַב עִם אֲבוֹתָיו," *OTS* 2 (1943), 106-118 (cf. N. J. Tromp, *Primitive Conceptions of Death and the Nether World* [Biblica et Orientalia 21; Rome, 1969], pp. 169-171).

8. See Shoshana R. Bin-Nun, "Formulas from Royal Records of Israel and Judah," *VT* 18 (1968), 414-432. In spite of weak English style, this is a cogent if

not altogether persuasive presentation, arguing that the framework formulas are directly derived from king-lists (not "annals"). The author's argument that the respective source documents would not have synchronized a given king's accession on the basis of another line of kings involves an unwarranted assumption.

9. "Die 'deuteronomistischen' Beurteilungen der Könige von Israel und Juda und das Problem der Redaktion der Königsbücher," *Bib* 53 (1972), 301-339. Weippert carefully argues that the theological evaluations for Jehoshaphat to Ahaz, paralleled by those from Joram to Hoshea, belong to a primary redactional phase dating in the reign of Hezekiah, *ca.* 700; the theological evaluations for the remaining kings of the respective realms belong to a second and third phase of redactional activity. She does not speculate with respect to the relationship between this commentative material and other elements among the framework data. We seem to have few options except to suppose that, if Weippert is correct respecting her date for the redactional labor of this "first Deuteronomist," it was he who made the extracts for his framework material, binding together the structure of the ongoing narrative from Solomon to Hoshea/Ahaz. That he began his theological evaluation first with Jehoshaphat and Joram ben Ahab appears to have been occasioned by a desire to compare these two kings with the apostate house of Ahab (we note that Joram is specially excused from the sin of "his father and mother," II Kings 3:1; cf. the "second Deuteronomist's" note on Ahaziah in I Kings 22:52). It is very likely that this same early redactor was responsible for the expansions upon prophetic oracles condemning a number of kings in the preceding narratives (Jeroboam, I Kings 14:7-11; Baasha, I Kings 16:1-4; Ahab, I Kings 21:21f., 24); see Chapter Seven.

10. *VT* 17 (1967), 307ff.

11. *Introduction to the Old Testament,* p. 409.

12. *Prophetie und Geschichte,* p. 135.

13. On the application of our formula to the Judean kings, cf. E. J. Smit's harmonistic treatment, "Death and Burial Formulas in Kings and Chronicles Relating to the Kings of Judah," *Ou-Testamentiese Werkgemeenschap van Suid-Afrika,* 1966, pp. 173-77.

14. See above, pp. 61-63.

15. *Primitive Conceptions, loc. cit.* In analyzing this expression, Tromp acknowledges dependence on Alfrink's article in *OTS* 2, and on G. R. Driver, "Plurima Mortis Imago," in *Essays and Studies in Honour of Abraham A. Neuman* (Leiden, 1962), pp. 137-143.

16. Although we have labeled this story as Type III, prophetic word narrative, in subgenre 1 (power demonstration), it shows some development toward what we have called the regal self-judgment narrative. The prophetic deed and word (living on in Gehazi's identification) are instrumental in getting the king to render judgment, not on himself in this instance but on behalf of a suppliant.

17. See above, pp. 59-61.

18. The only reasonable explanation for the fact that II Kings 23 differs significantly from I Kings 13 is that, as we have asserted, the latter originated independently and was transmitted to Judahite custodians prior to Josiah's reform. Elements of the tradition underlying I Kings 13 survived in oral form until this event and found their way into the Deuteronomist's account of it. It is this disparity that refutes the theory of A. Jepsen in *Nabi,* p. 178, to the effect that I Kings 13 is a programmatic composition by a late member of the deuteronomistic school,

designed as a polemic against the effort to restore the Bethel altar following Josiah's reform, perhaps even in the exile period.

19. Though the tradition underlying I Kings 13 cannot be directly connected with the ministry of Amos, it is possible that it passed into Judahite hands soon after the fall of the northern kingdom (not the final destruction of the Bethel shrine, which continued in operation until the time of Josiah) demonstrated the validity of that particular Judahite's prophecies against the north. The fact that the northern prophet Hosea also had harsh judgment for Bethel (5:8; 8:5; 10:5, 8; 13:2; cf. 12:4, 6) would have confirmed this interpretation. From the deuteronomistic notice at II Kings 17:28 we are to infer that Bethel continued as a relatively orthodox center of Yahweh worship after the northern deportation, having been designated by the Assyrians as a special shrine for preserving and propagating the original religion of the land.

A further argument for the essential historicity of I Kings 13 is the fact that it makes no reference to the golden calf, for which the Deuteronomists so vehemently condemn all the northern kings. If Jeroboam I did in fact introduce the golden calf in Bethel, as I Kings 12:26-32 asserts, one of two things must be true: (1) either he erected it after the event of I Kings 13 or (2) the Judahite man of God, together with the Bethelite prophets, did not consider it odious to primitive Yahwism. In any event, if our story had been invented by the Deuteronomists, it surely would have included an invective against the calf; the deuteronomistic additions at vss. 2b-3 speak only of the altar because the original was directed solely against it.

20. Chapter Five, n. 52.

21. Although Elisha is identified as the ultimate source of Jehu's prophetic designation, it is pointedly a young man belonging to his entourage who anoints him. Therefore this story did not originate as part of the Elisha cycle. It is surely significant that our two instrumental fulfillment stories, II Kings 3 and II Kings 8:29ff., reflect the ideology of the Jehu movement; yet, as we have argued, the former passage is clearly derived from the latter, having been influenced by I Kings 22 as well.

22. Cf. *YTT*, pp. 297ff.

23. See our following discussion regarding the redaction history of the prophet legend material (Chapter Seven).

24. See below, p. 124.

25. The relevant data on the Ben-Hadads and Hazael are summarized in R. A. Bowman's articles in *IDB, s.v.*

26. Cf. A. C. Welch, *The Code of Deuteronomy* (London, 1924); K. Galling, "Das Gemeindegesetz in Deuteronomium 23," *Festschrift A. Bertholet* (Tübingen, 1950), p. 191; *idem,* "Das Königsgesetz im Dt.," *TLZ* 76 (1951), 138; A. Alt, "Die Heimat des Deuteronomiums," *Kleine Schriften,* II, 250-275; G. von Rad, *Studies in Deuteronomy* (ET London [SBT 9] and Chicago, 1953), pp. 60ff., cf. 68 (German ed., pp. 46ff.); G. Seitz, *Redaktionsgeschichtliche Studien zum Deuteronomium* (BWANT 93; Stuttgart, 1971). Helga Weippert argues in *Bib* 53 (*loc. cit.)* the likelihood of an initial deuteronomistic redaction of the historiographic materials among refugees from the north during the reign of Hezekiah.

27. On Hosea's historical background and theological program, cf. H.-W. Wolff, "Hoseas geistige Heimat," *TLZ* 81 (1956), 83-94; *idem,* BKAT XIV/1[2],

p. xxvi; ET, *Hosea* (Hermeneia; Philadelphia, 1974), p. xxxi; also R. Rendtorff, *ZTK* 59 (1962), 145-167.

28. On the hermeneutical problem of interpreting legendary material, see the helpful and perceptive discussion by Thomas L. Thompson, "Historical and Christian Faith," pp. 326-330 in *The Historicity of the Patriarchal Narratives; the Quest for the Historical Abraham* (BZAW 133; Berlin-New York, 1974).

CHAPTER SEVEN

Redaction History

ONE MORE RESPONSIBILITY REMAINS: TO ACCOUNT FOR THE PROCESS BY which the Micaiah narratives got where they are and into their present form. Any effort to reconstruct this process will seem arbitrary and superficial without some effort to deal with redactional development in the entire prophet legend complex, I Kings 17 through II Kings 10 (13). Therefore, avoiding needless complexities, we shall attempt to offer a simple but thorough survey of the entire problem.[1]

Certain theories of the past have established genuine possibilities. For one thing, it seems entirely likely that Jepsen was correct in identifying a documentary collection of prophetic narratives as one of the written sources drawn upon by the deuteronomistic redactors for their history of the Israelite kingdoms.[2] Evidence for this is the presence of internal editorial handiwork within the several collections. The consensus seems to be correct, furthermore, in defining a significant delimitation between an Elijah collection, an Elisha collection, and a third collection — given various names[3] — interposed in the present order of the text between the first two.[4] A question that remains is that regarding the origin and date of these three separate collections; also whether each was in itself a unified composition prior to further redactional combination. We shall adduce evidence, item by item, with the aim of suggesting resolutions to these problems.

1. REDACTIONAL LINKAGES

First let us examine the connective links between these major collections. The Elijah cycle does not end with the account of Elijah's rapture in II Kings 2, but with II Kings 1. Chap. 2 belongs to the Elisha cycle,[5] having been designed as a legend for that prophet's legitimation.[6] This chapter in its turn does not mark the beginning of the Elisha collection. It introduces Elijah and Elisha as already well known, presupposing the prophetic call narrative of I Kings 19:19b-21. That this latter narrative is no direct continuation of the pericope to which it is presently connected can be demonstrated from the fact that in vss. 15f. Elijah is commanded to anoint (משח) Elisha, along with Jehu and Hazael, while in vs. 19 Elijah does no more than cast his mantle over him. Nevertheless this effort to associate the narrative of Elisha's call with that element in the Elijah cycle which mentions the latter's anointing clearly marks the point at which the two cycles have been redactionally welded together. Although, as we shall see, the Elisha cycle itself consists of various subcollections, the itinerary notice introducing vs. 19, "and he departed from there,"[7] makes it very probable that our redactor is the same person who made similar links at II Kings 2:23a, 25, joining several legends in an early legitimation collection. Since I Kings 19:19 is connected to a relatively complete form of the Elijah cycle — a form produced by redactors from Jehu's time — the initial Elisha collection cannot have been added before Jehu's reign, and, as we shall see, there is strong evidence that it may have been added in the time of Jehu's successors.

The just-mentioned concern to connect the Elisha call story with I Kings 19:16 would no doubt have been important enough in the redactor's mind to have led him to place this story in a position preceding the actual conclusion of the Elijah cycle as it presently exists. There is nothing to prove that II Kings 2 was ever directly linked to I Kings 19:19-21; the Ahaziah story of II Kings 1 may very well have separated the two in the redactor's initial combination. One might be inclined to conjecture that, inasmuch as the name "Ahaziah" appears only at vs. 2, the original narrative was anonymous, in which case it might be assumed that the story came only secondarily to be associated with Ahaziah, having been placed here by the Deuteronomist because this late redactor had at this point terminated his narration of Ahab's reign. But there is no textual evidence to support the conjecture that "Ahaziah" is secondary. One needs to recall our previous argument that the omission of any reference to Ahaziah's "sleeping with his fathers" in the annalistic extract at vs. 17b almost certainly reflects the factual recollection of an ignominious death for this king, and this would argue for the correctness of his identification as Ahaziah.[8] A third possibility is, therefore, that the Ahaziah story — while rightly identified with that king — was not part of the Elijah cycle as it was known to the early redactor who joined it to the initial Elijah collection. Since it has no internal redactional linkage to I Kings 19:1-18, it is this third possibility that deserves our preference. Although it is theoretically possible that the Deuteronomist added it, making a transition modeled after II Kings 3:5 for his insertion of 1:1, then adding extracts from his sources at 1:17b-18 as a transition back to the Elisha cycle, it is not at all likely that the Ahaziah story would have remained unattached until so late a period. Therefore we identify a predeuteronomistic redactor as the person who was responsible for putting it in its present place. In any case, the likelihood is that this story was not attached prior to the original Elijah cycle–Elisha cycle combination.

There is nothing save what we consider a secondary naming of Ahab in I Kings 20:2, 13f., 22:20, plus the redactional notice in 22:38, to connect our not yet named third collection with either the Elijah or the Elisha cycles. We have, of course, the explicit association of Ahab and Elijah in I Kings 21 (LXX 20). Every argument favors the early connection of chap. 21 (MT) with chaps. 17–19, possibly, but not necessarily, prior to the redactional insertion of 19:19-21. Contrariwise, 22:1-2a can be seen as an early redactional link between chaps. 20 (MT) and 22. It is likely a predeuteronomistic redactor who put the Naboth narrative in its present Hebrew position, thereby strengthening the thematic bond between Elijah's prediction of Ahab's death in 21:19 MT and its fulfillment in chap. 22. Since it does not seem likely that the LXX would have had access to a Hebrew *Vorlage* retaining an order predating this redaction, we must agree with Noth[9] that the LXX (unknowingly?) restored the original order through a desire to emphasize the Naboth story's thematic connection with the Elijah cycle.

Thus it seems that our third collection has to have been inserted in an already completed combination comprising most of the Elijah and most of the Elisha stories. We cannot tell for sure whether it had already been added to this combination before the Deuteronomist used it for his history, or whether the latter redactor drew from it as a separate source, inserting it in its present place because it had come to be associated with Ahab.

2. THE ELIJAH CYCLE

It is necessary to suggest how we conceive of the emergence of the separate Elijah and Elisha before it will be possible to deal understandingly with this third collection. We make grateful use of the important recent work of G. Fohrer and O. H. Steck on the Elijah narratives,[10] though our form-critical analysis of the individual narratives within this collection has departed significantly at some points from the results of their studies. Steck has been particularly helpful in making clear the influence of Jehuite ideology in the redactional combinations. Including II Kings 1:2-17a, the original Elijah narratives, as we see them, were all representatives of the supplicatory power subgenre. Belonging to the earliest collection were the legend presently found in I Kings 17:1-16; 18:1-3a, 5-9, 12, 15-18, 41-46 and a second legend of the very same type found in I Kings 18:21-30a, 31-39.[11] Surely it is significant that all three original Elijah stories are of the very same type. It is likely that at least the two stories of I Kings 17–18 are relatively early, reflecting a pioneering stage in the struggle of Yahwism to define its claims over against the aggressive baalism that Jezebel had so newly introduced. The three stories together polemicize against Baal's usurpation of Yahwism's prerogatives.[12] The specific aim in each is to champion Elijah as the man who was authorized to speak and act in Yahweh's name, bringing rain or fire from heaven to prove that Yahweh is sole God in Israel — and that he, Elijah, is his true prophet.

It is possible that prior to the redactional combination of the drought legend and the fire-on-the-altar legend, the first attracted to itself as a narrative embellishment the prophet-legitimation legend of I Kings 17:17-19, 21-24,[13] drawn from the tradition that finds a variant shape in the Elisha legend of II Kings 4:8-37. This expanded drought narrative received still another expansion when the fire-on-the-altar legend came to be inserted. This expansion was the highly tendentious work of a redactor living in the time of Jehu and infused with the vengeful antibaalism that so enthusiastically supported that king's insurrection. The work of this Jehuite redactor may be seen in I Kings 18:3b-4, 10-11, 19-20, 30b, 40; it is he who transferred the fire-on-the-altar legend to the summit of Mt. Carmel. We may further ascertain that this redactor drew from his tradition to compose the unique narrative in 19:1-18, the legend in which a spiritually depleted Elijah returns to the source of theophanous empowerment to receive superlative authorization for destroying her — Jezebel — who had threatened to destroy him and all that he stood for.[14] From the fact that this narrative credits Elijah rather than Elisha with "anointing" both Jehu and Hazael, we may infer that our Jehuite writer was no adherent of the Elisha school. It is he, more than any other, who contributed to the idealization of the Elijah figure, identifying him as a veritable "new Moses."[15]

It is within the circle of those who applauded the accession of Jehu that one must seek also the original author of I Kings 21 (LXX 20). As many critics now agree,[16] vss. 27-29 form the authentic conclusion to this narrative.[17] These verses provide an effective climax to a story of regal self-judgment. By lending his regal authority to the effectuation of Naboth's judicial murder, Ahab succeeds in taking possession of Naboth's vineyard; but his act of taking possession established his own self-judgment (vs. 19a), which is specified in vs. 19b in terms of dogs licking his blood where they licked the blood of Naboth. But, as generally in this subgenre, Yahweh retains the prerogative of redirecting the penalty. As the narrator tells it, Ahab shows a repentance that moves Yahweh to reveal to Elijah a modifying interpretation of his original message: not in Ahab's days, but in the days of his son will Yahweh bring this evil (vs. 29). We discern that our narrator is animated less by hostility toward Ahab (who in the Naboth story actually plays a remarkably passive role) than by vengefulness toward Jezebel.[18] Our narrator knows very well that in historical fact it was Joram's — not Ahab's — blood that the dogs had been licking in Naboth's plot of ground, and to his mind this was Yahweh's real intent, a fulfillment that fully met the demands of divine justice on Jezebel's wickedness. We have further confirmation, therefore, that the historical Ahab did not in his own person experience the fulfillment of Elijah's dire prophecy, in spite of I Kings 22. The Naboth story is valuable testimony that it was not so.[19]

3. THE ELISHA CYCLE

The literary relationships within the expanded Elijah cycle may be schematized approximately as in Table Two. The Elisha cycle, on its part,

TABLE TWO
THE ELIJAH CYCLE

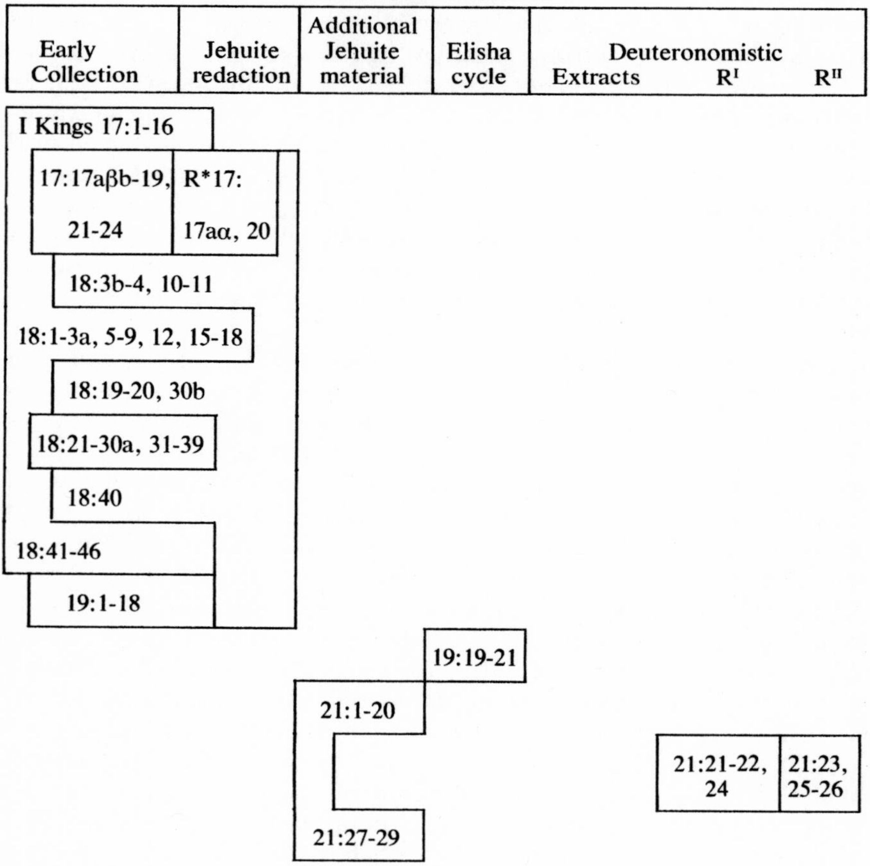

Early Collection	Jehuite redaction	Additional Jehuite material	Elisha cycle	Deuteronomistic Extracts	R^{I}	R^{II}
I Kings 17:1-16						
17:17aβb-19, 21-24	R*17: 17aα, 20					
	18:3b-4, 10-11					
18:1-3a, 5-9, 12, 15-18						
	18:19-20, 30b					
18:21-30a, 31-39						
	18:40					
18:41-46						
	19:1-18					
			19:19-21			
		21:1-20				
					21:21-22, 24	21:23, 25-26
		21:27-29				

TABLE TWO—(CONT.)
THE ELIJAH CYCLE

Early Collection	Jehuite redaction	Additional Jehuite material	Elisha cycle	Deuteronomistic Extracts	R^{I}	R^{II}
					II Kings 1:1	
II Kings 1:2-17a						
				II Kings 1: 17b-18		

*In Tables Two—Four "R" indicates a redactor; "gl" indicates an unassociated gloss.

appears to be the result of several elemental collections attributed to Elisha and developed among his disciples. We have schematized its development in Table Three. At least six separate collections were made by

TABLE THREE
THE ELISHA CYCLE

Early legitimation collection	Later legitimation collection	Early Syrian-war collection	Jehu accession narrative	Later Syrian-war collection	Late Jehuite narrative	Deuteronomistic Extracts	R^{I}	R^{II}
R I Kings 19:19aαא								
19:19aαב b-21								
II Kings 2:1-18								
	2:19-22							
R 2:23a								
2:23b-24								
R 2:35								
						3:1	3:2-3	
					R 3:4-5a			
					3:5b-25a			

Table Three—(Cont.)
The Elisha Cycle

Early legitimation collection	Later legitimation collection	Early Syrian-war collection	Jehu accession narrative	Later Syrian-war collection	Late Jehuite narrative	Deuteronomistic Extracts	R^{I}	R^{II}
					R 3:25b-27			
	4:1-7							
4:8-37								
	R 4:38aαא							
	4:38aαבb-41							
	4:42-44							
5:1-27								
	6:1-7							
		6:8-23						
		R 6:24aα						
		6:24βb-30, 32a, 33						
		R 6:31, 32b						
		7:1-2						
		R 7:3-5						
		7:6-7aαא						
		R 7:7aαבβb-13						
		7:14-17						
		R 7:18-20						
8:1-6								

TABLE THREE—(CONT.)

THE ELISHA CYCLE

Early legitimation collection	Later legitimation collection	Early Syrian-war collection	Jehu accession narrative	Later Syrian-war collection	Late Jehuite narrative	Deuteronomistic Extracts	R^{I}	R^{II}
		R 8:7aα						
		8:7aβb-15						
						8:16-17, 20-26, 28	8:18, 27	8:19
			R 8:29a					
			8:29b, 9:1-7, 10-14a, 16a, 17-25a, 27, 30-36a				9:8b-9, 14b	
						9:28		9:29
			R 9:8a, 15a, 16b, 25b-26, 36b-37					
			10:1-11					
			R 10:12					
			10:13-14					
			10:15-17					
			10:18-27					
			R 10:28					
							10:29-31	
						10:32-36		
						13:1, 3-5, 7-10, 12-13		13:2, 6, 11

TABLE THREE—(CONT.)
THE ELISHA CYCLE

Early legitimation collection	Later legitimation collection	Early Syrian-war collection	Jehu accession narrative	Later Syrian-war collection	Late Jehuite narrative	Deuteronomistic Extracts	R[I]	R[II]
				13:14-19				
				R 13:20a				
				13:20b-21				
								13:22-25

the so-called "sons of the prophets" belonging to Elisha's school.[20] In their probable chronological order, these are: (1) an early legitimation collection; (2) a later legitimation collection; (3) an early Syrian-war collection; (4) the Jehu accession narrative, combining a variety of independent materials; (5) a later Syrian-war collection; (6) a late Jehuite narrative.[21] At the very least, the early legitimation collection had been combined with the completed Elijah cycle prior to the insertion of I Kings 20, 22; and the likelihood is that all, or virtually all (possibly with the exception of II Kings 3), had antecedently been brought together. A word must be said about each of these six collections.

(1) We have seen that I Kings 19:19aαℵ served to introduce the narrative of Elisha's call, vss. 19-21. The legend of that prophet's legitimation, II Kings 2:1-18, followed. The seemingly aimless journey of Elijah and Elisha is indigenous to this story; it is an element that may have influenced the redactional shaping of this entire first collection, including the itinerary notices at II Kings 2:23a, 25, which bring Elisha first to Bethel (incorporating the she-bear narrative) and thence to Mt. Carmel and on to Samaria. Our inference that the narrative of 2:19-22 was not included in this lineup is partly based on the observation that "there" (*šām*) in vs. 23 can hardly refer to "the city" of vs. 19, since Gilgal and Jericho do not fit the description of having foul water or lying in barren land. The redactor's reference to Carmel (ignoring the references to Shunem in 4:8ff.)[22] and Samaria is designed as a combinational transition to the group of stories in which Gehazi is to play a prominent role, 4:8-37; 5:1-27; 8:1-6. These Gehazi stories were once independent since the figure of Gehazi is variously focused within them, yet the redactor's joint introduction indicates that they had already been brought together when the first Elisha collection was added to the Elijah cycle. From the fact that Gehazi speaks in

8:1-6 as if Elisha has already departed this life, we are inclined to conclude that this early legitimation collection was made after the prophet's death. Although "Joash" may have been added secondarily to "the king of Israel" in II Kings 13:14, leaving open the possibility that Elisha may have died prior to that king's accession in 798 B.C., the Deuteronomist's extract in vs. 25, whose preservation accounts for the insertion of vss. 14-19 as illustrative support, is probably historical. This means that the initial Elisha collection was not combined with the Elijah cycle until that time.

However late we are obliged to date this redactional activity, we are very probably dealing with source material of very early derivation. Apart from references to an unnamed king of Syria in II Kings 5,[23] these various call and legitimation legends reflect no significant political or military background whatever, hence they may come from as early a time as the period prior to Jehu and Hazael.

(2) The same is true in principle of a second legitimation collection consisting of II Kings 2:19-22; 4:1-7; 4:38aαבβ-41; 4:42-44; and 6:1-7. There is nothing whatever to date these stories; they too are completely apolitical. They differ essentially from the first collection in sharing a common style, a common elemental structure, and a common theme of wonders worked in the realm of nature. Most of the incidents described in this second collection take place at unnamed or unspecified localities, but the reference to Jordan in 6:2ff. has influenced the person combining these stories to insert his own itinerary notice at 4:38aαא. The fact that the redactor here writes of Elisha returning (*šāb*) to Gilgal is an indication that he was acquainted with the previous collection; he inserted these narratives into the previous collection even though as they now stand they disturb the original redactor's design to locate in Samaria all of what was to follow the Gehazi story in 4:8-37.

(3) II Kings 8:7-15 may have once been anonymous, but is associated with Elisha in its present form. Although 8:1-6 implies that that prophet was already dead, vss. 7ff. proceed as if he were still alive. The redactional introduction, "and Elisha came to Damascus," can hardly be a transition from vss. 1-6, hence we are invited to assume that these words continue from the prophet-authorization narrative of 6:24–7:17,[24] which, in turn, has been redactionally connected to still another narrative of this same subgenre, 6:8-23, by the phrase *wayhî 'aḥ^{a}rê kēn* in vs. 24. These three stories constitute an early Syrian-war collection that was apparently inserted in its present place because of the Samaria locale of 5:1-27; 8:1-6. The Hazael oracle was placed after 8:1-6 because it takes the prophet on to Damascus. Perhaps the two separate narratives of chaps. 6–7 had already been bound together before 8:7ff. was added to them; they assume a military-political situation in which the kings of Israel (unnamed in both stories) are constantly harassed by the Syrians but are still able (with

divine help!) to drive them off, whereas 8:7ff. contains the announcement of a desperate new situation in which Hazael is to menace the very life of his neighbor (cf. vss. 12f.).[25] Though inserted lately into the framework of the previous collections, these three stories themselves probably go back to the time of the Omrides.[26]

(4) Next, a few words about what we have called "the Jehu accession narrative," II Kings 8:29–10:28. Though relatively early in origin, this political document was added at a fairly late stage to the existing Elijah-Elisha collection. The narrator made use of four separate historical reports (10:1-11, 13-14, 15-17, and 18-27), but his most important source was the prophet legend of 8:29b–9:36a.[27] This story, an instrumental fulfillment narrative with a high level of historical factuality, itself reflects an attitude of stern censure toward Jezebel; but the accession historian has intensified this element of censure at 9:8a, 25b-26, and 36b-37[28] with his own pointed polemic. While the prophet legend views the deaths of Joram and Ahaziah as instrumentally inevitable, and hence justifiable, for the accomplishment of the divine judgment on Jezebel, the accession historian gloats in their deaths, demanding the extermination of every last living person with a drop of Ahab's blood in his veins! Eventually this complex composition was added to the Elisha cycle because of that prophet's initial role in its elemental structure.

(5) The Deuteronomist was able to incorporate Judean sources for his account of Joash's reign in II Kings 11–12; then, coming back to Jehu's successors in the northern kingdom, he drew upon the prophet document once more in chap. 13, which contains two legends belonging to a later Syrian-war collection, vss. 14-19 and vss. 20b-21. They reflect a drastically altered situation in which Joash of Israel was at last able to retake from the latter Ben-Hadad the territory lost to his father. An earlier redactor had already combined these two narratives with the transitional formula of vs. 20a, "And Elisha died and they buried him." Because vss. 20b-21 were thus attached to the preceding legend, the Deuteronomist copied them into his narration, though his intent was to adduce vs. 19's prediction of three victories as support for his final datum in vs. 25.

(6) A sixth addition to the Elisha cycle was II Kings 3:4-27. That it did not belong to the early collection seems evident from the redactional itinerary of 2:25, which, as we have seen, prepares for the incorporation of 4:8-37; 5:1-27; and 8:1-6. In chap. 3 Elisha goes neither to Carmel nor to Samaria; he is somewhere out in the eastern desert. Our previous discussion has shown that this narrative combines tradition derived from widely separate sources, viz., I Kings 22 and II Kings 8:29ff.[29] We have designated it as a late Jehuite narrative[30] — meaning that it originated sometime (later rather than earlier) in the period of the Jehuite kings, down through the long reign of Jeroboam II. The core of this narrative is the instrumental fulfillment legend of vss. 5b-25a, expanded by an historical

framework in vss. 4-5a, 25b-27.[31] In this expanded version it assumes the form of a political propaganda piece, comparable in motivation and intent, if not in historicity, to the Jehu narrative.[32]

4. THE OMRIDE WAR CYCLE

Inasmuch as our "third collection" features several different prophets, only one of whom — Micaiah ben Imlah — is named, and contains references to an anonymous Israelite king, identified only secondarily as Ahab, we can propose no more suitable title for this collection than one that reflects their original historical background: "Omride war cycle." Since some of the Elisha narratives likewise reflect the wars of the Omride period, this title is not meant to be exclusive, yet it does have significance in that it is the scene of warfare with Aram under the Omride kings, rather than any association with a particular prophet, that defines their mutual interconnectedness. "Omride war cycle" is more appropriate than the usual designation, "Aramean war cycle," because the narratives included here were developed from an Israelite rather than Syrian perspective.

As we have argued, this collection existed independently until added to the Elijah-Elisha combination at a relatively advanced stage in the development of that combination. Because II Kings 3, the latest addition to the Elisha cycle, is heavily dependent on the tradition of Narrative A in I Kings 22, it may seem probable that the Omride war cycle (without Narrative B) had found its place in the prophet document prior to the addition of II Kings 3. On the other hand, II Kings 3 may simply have known Narrative A in oral form. It is possible that the Omride war cycle was not added until Narrative B had also come into the text.

However the case may be, the Omride war cycle reveals itself to be essentially the work of a predeuteronomistic redactor who merged four separate narratives into a single, cohesive account. The four narratives are: two historical demonstration stories in I Kings 20:1-21, 26-29,[33] a regal self-judgment narrative (Type I) in 20:30b-42,[34] and our superseding oracle legend, Narrative A of I Kings 22. The question immediately arises, to which king of Israel do they pertain? "Ahab" has been redactionally added to "the king of Israel" in 20:2 and 13,[35] while the oracular form of 20:14a (following the climactic oracle of vs. 13) marks this half-verse, containing the proper name "Ahab" without the title, as another very probable addition, made perhaps by the same redactor.[36] Although it is nonetheless possible that the historical Ahab may have been the king of these two stories, there is contrariwise nothing to prove that it could not have been someone else. All that can be said for sure is that the evident seriousness of the Syrian threat implied in all these narratives makes one of the late Omrides very probable. The Jehuites do not come into consideration because the Syrian king is Ben-Hadad, who can hardly be the second king of that name. We have already established that Joram ben Ahab was the historical king of Narrative A in I Kings 22, and the prediction of calamity on the nation at the end of our regal self-judgment oracle (vs. 42, "your people for his people") fits Joram better than Ahab because Hazael, coming to power during Joram's reign, was the first Syrian king to bring serious harm upon the Israelite nation.

The hypothesis that the Ben-Hadad of I Kings 20 may be the second king of that name must be rejected all the more inasmuch as the dire predictions for the Israelite king do not in any way fit the reign of Jehoash, who is credited only with success against Syria (II Kings 13:25; cf. vs. 19). It is, then, the first Syrian king of that name who must be considered, unless there were in fact two Ben-Hadads before Hazael. Although the king who was reigning *ca.* 850 might reasonably be the same king with whom Asa had been allied prior to 886 (I Kings 15:18-20), if that Ben-Hadad is our king, then his father, who in 20:34 is said to have captured certain Israelite cities and to have established commercial booths in Samaria, would have to be the Tab-Rimmon, son of Hezion, mentioned in chap. 15.[37] But, since I Kings 15:20 reports that Ben-Hadad, Tab-Rimmon's son, captured Ijon, Dan, Abel-beth-maacah, and all Chineroth and Naphtali, it is he who would be the most plausible candidate as the "father" mentioned in 20:34. It is this consideration that supports the claim of those who argue that there had to be two Ben-Hadads before Hazael; but since it is unlikely that a father and a son would bear the same name, this is not an attractive solution unless we are to assume the intervening reign of a third, unnamed king, in which case the "father" of 20:34 would actually be the king's grandfather.[38] We have no final answer to this problem. It is necessary to exercise great caution in using prophet legend material of this sort for any kind of historical reconstruction.

The upshot of the preceding discussion is that in all probability Joram is the Israelite king of most — if not all — of these prophet narratives. Nevertheless, each king soon came to be identified as Ahab. A religio-political ideology, blaming Ahab for the apostasies that came to justify the Jehuite revolt, shaped them all toward another, more subtle apologia in support of Jehu, resulting in a politically tendentious document that may once again be compared with II Kings 8:29–10:17. An important difference between the Omride war cycle in its redactional form and the Jehu accession narrative is that the determinative role given Elisha in the latter led to its early inclusion in the Elisha cycle, whereas our Omride war collection remained independent of direct association with either of the two great prophet figures until a relatively late stage of redactional combination.

We may say with some assurance, then, that our Omride war redactor must have been some influential person associated with the Jehuites. He was not the official propagandist of II Kings 9–10, and his temporal remove from the events of 841 is to be measured on the basis of the historical refraction evident in the Micaiah narrative, as well as from this redactor's new identifications in chap. 20. The materials for which he was directly responsible are those that join the several independent narratives with one another and bring the whole collection to a programmatic conclusion in the poignant comment concerning Ahab's final disgrace in 22:38. Our redactor added "Ahab" in 20:2, 13, then wrote 14a; he also inserted 20:20b in preparation for vss. 26ff., 30ff.; he next designed 20:22-26aα as a preparation for the Aphek account,[39] then disposed of a few more thousands of Syrians in vs. 30a — following the fantastic, stereotyped climax at vs. 29 — in order to prepare the scene for Ben-Hadad's flight of vs. 30b, which in the original account was intended to serve as an introductory characterization.[40] We prefer not to ascribe to this redactor responsibility for vs. 43aβ (*sar w^e^zā'ēp*), reserving this for a glossator who already had 21:4 before him;[41] but it is likely that vs. 43b belongs to his handiwork and is not part of the original narrative in vss. 30ff., which concludes with the laconic report in vs. 43aα that the king of Israel went home (*wayyēlek melek yiśrā'el 'al bêtô*). Our redactor inserted vs. 43b *wayyābō' šōm^e^rôn)* to bring his king — now clearly identified as Ahab — back to Samaria in preparation for chap. 22; for, though Narrative A does not begin in Samaria (cf. Narrative B in 22:10), it ends there, and in this redactor's mind this was the place. He now wrote 22:1-2a, mentioning three years as the period of peace in order to allow for an appreciable change of conditions from chap. 20 to chap. 22.[42]

We now see that the Jehuite redactor intended the prophecy of 20:42 to find its fulfillment in chap. 22's account of Ahab's ignominious death. This explains why 22:38 has been added to a narrative in which the narrative's own prediction (22:17) had already been explicitly fulfilled. The report in 22:37 that the king was honorably buried in Samaria — in spite of his tragic death — did not satisfy this redactor, who was familiar with another creation of the Jehuite narrators, the Naboth legend of chap. 21. He did not know it well enough, however, to quote it verbatim. Since he was not sure who the prophet in question might have been, he simply reported: "according to the word of Yahweh" (*'^a^šer dibbēr* is a late insertion in MT; cf. LXX^B^).[43] He did not remember the particulars about Naboth, either; thus he quite understandably assumed that the blood-licking, which in chap. 21 had to take place in Jezreel, must have occurred in Samaria. Since his Ahab had died in battle at Ramoth-Gilead, it had to be the chariot into which he bled, washed at Samaria's pool, that carried Ahab's blood there. Composing 22:35b as preparation, our redactor added his own grisly notice in vs. 38 to the effect that "the harlots washed themselves" (*wᵉhazzōnôt raḥᵃzû*) — evidently in the pool rather than in the chariot — as a final (and in his mind entirely belittling) indignity.

Thus we may schematize the development of our Omride war cycle as in Table Four. Perhaps before this cycle was taken up into the prophet document the variant Micaiah legend — Narrative B of I Kings 22 — was added. Either way, the Micaiah account was in its combined form no later than the end of the eighth century B.C., probably after the fall of the northern kingdom but before the deuteronomistic redaction actually began.

TABLE FOUR
THE OMRIDE WAR CYCLE

Prophet legends	Jehuite redaction	Pre-deuteronomistic additions	Deuteronomistic Extracts	Deuteronomistic R^I	Deuteronomistic R^II
I Kings 20:1-13, 14b-20a, 21					
	20:14a, 20b, 22-26aα				
20:26aβb-29					
	20:30a				
20:30b-43aα		gl 20:43aβ			
	20:43b, 22:1-2a				
22:2b-9, 15-18					
		22:10-12a, 14, 19-25 / R22: 12b-13+			
22:26-35a, 36-37					
	22:35b, 38				
			22:39-42, 44-51	22:43	22:52-53

Here our history of the Micaiah tradition comes to an end. The redactional rearranging that occurred under the auspices of the deuteronomistic school did not alter its present form. This deuteronomistic redaction simply recorded from its prophetic source-document the narrative of "Ahab's" death, adding an extract from official records implying that king's honorable and peaceable departure (vs. 40), apparently without understanding its implications. Since it was the "house of Ahab" that had come to ruin in Jehu's revolt, the Deuteronomist added programmatic, highly formulaic words of dynastic repudiation in I Kings 21:21f., 24, employing the same pattern used with respect to Jeroboam's and Baasha's dynasties (I Kings 14:9ff.; 16:1ff.). Here was his opportunity to insert denunciation into prophetic speech directed toward the father of the ultimate victim. The Deuteronomist found it inappropriate to repeat his invective in the form of an expansion of Micaiah's speech of I Kings 22, however suitable a point of attachment vs. 23 might have seemed to him. Because of 21:27-29, this account of "Ahab's" own death hardly commended itself as a suitable fulfillment of Elijah's words; this could be none other than the story of Joram's death in II Kings 9–10. But because so much narrative material from the prophetic collection had to be passed over before one could read an account of the ultimate downfall of Ahab's house, the Deuteronomist seized upon a new opportunity in II Kings 9:8b-9 to make prophetic denunciation the vehicle of dynastic doom.[44] "Ahab's" death, recorded in I Kings 22, had no ultimate theological significance in the Deuteronomist's eyes because it concerned only Ahab himself, not the fate of dynasties and the course of national history.

5. SUMMARY TO CHAPTERS SIX AND SEVEN

We may now sum up the major results of this chapter and the one preceding:

(1) Ongoing discussion of the chronology of the Omride-Jehuite period has done nothing to alter the options for identifying "Ahab" and "Jehoshaphat" in the Micaiah narratives; if these figures do not represent the actual historical kings bearing these names, they can represent only Joram of Israel and Ahaziah of Judah.

(2) Since no ruler in either of the separate Israelite kingdoms died a natural death, in peace and honor, without being recorded in the Deuteronomist's sources as having "slept with his fathers," and since no ruler in either kingdom who is mentioned as dying in exile or through violence is in fact so recorded, the apparent exception of Ahab in I Kings 22:40 is valuable evidence that he too died in peace and honor, in which case he could not have been the king of Israel who died at Ramoth-Gilead.

(3) The only viable solution to the historical problem identifies Narrative A in I Kings 22 as a free elaboration of events more factually recorded in II Kings 8:28–9:37; since the latter, as a piece of ostensible political propaganda, quickly established itself as the normative account of the Ramoth-Gilead campaign and its aftermath, the variant tradition of I Kings 22 was shifted to Jehoshaphat and Ahab, the latter being typologi-

cally representative as the arch-offender in Jehuite eyes among all the Omride kings.

(4) Three criteria for establishing comparative historicity have been identified: meaninglessness except upon the assumption of historicity; the presence of inimical elements; the absence of idealizing and tendentious elements. Although II Kings 8:29–10:27, the Jehu accession history, is propagandistic and self-congratulatory, it clearly meets the first criterion, while neither version of the Micaiah narrative meets this criterion or the other two. Narrative A in I Kings 22, showing far less ideological structuring than Narrative B, emerged from prophetic circles in the early Jehuite period, while the latter can be best explained as deriving from expatriate Israelite prophets living or working in Judah after the fall of the northern kingdom, prior to the earliest deuteronomistic redaction.

(5) For his account of the Omride and Jehuite periods, the Deuteronomist was able to draw upon a prophet document consisting of all, or virtually all, the prophet legends presently found in I Kings 17–II Kings 10, 13. This document represented the gradual crystallization of this material in three distinct collections: an Elijah cycle, an Elisha cycle, and what we have called an Omride war cycle. The first two began to grow together at an early period, as the rudiments of the Elisha cycle were connected to a virtually completed form of the Elijah cycle. Jehuite ideology has been a significant factor in the redaction of the Elijah narratives, in I Kings 22, and in II Kings 3, extending the polemic of II Kings 8:29–10:27.

(6) The Omride war cycle, consisting of I Kings 20; 22:1-38, restructures four originally independent legends of prophetic activity during the initial phases of the Israel-Syria war. Two "historical demonstration narratives" in 20:1-21 and 20:26-29 feature a prophetic figure cooperating with the institution of the kingship in eliciting the divine intervention on the nation's behalf; these two stories are set against the background of Ahab's or Joram's early victories against Ben-Hadad. A narrative of regal self-judgment in 20:30b-42 reflects the same situation, but presages the reverses that were to come with Hazael's coup in Damascus. A superseding oracle narrative presently found in I Kings 22:2b-37, derived originally from the tradition of Hazael's successes at Ramoth-Gilead and the subsequent death of Joram at the hand of Jehu, expresses disillusionment with the simple theme of guaranteed Israelite victory. The Jehuite redactor who combined these four stories intended to teach that "Ahab" had failed to carry out his responsibility to deliver a telling blow against Syria when the opportunity presented itself, and had therefore fully deserved the calamity he had brought upon himself and his house. To the tragic tale of his defeat, ending in I Kings 22:37, this redactor appended the bitter, mocking words of vs. 38, as though to confirm that Jehu had been more than justified in bringing Ahab's dynasty to its bloody ruin. Narrative B,

one of the very latest additions to the predeuteronomistic prophet document, retained from the Micaiah tradition the theme of prophet versus prophet, modifying the theme of prophet versus king that had entered so heavily into the formation of the prophet legend tradition as a whole. To the writer of Narrative B and the redactor who combined it with Narrative A, the problem of prophet against prophet had become far more vexing than the problem of prophet versus king. Hezekiah was a monarch amenable to prophetic leading; but even in his time prophets could not agree (see especially Micah). Thus the combined Micaiah narrative forebodes the final breakdown of prophetic authority, when kings would feel free to follow prophets of their own choosing.

NOTES TO CHAPTER SEVEN

1. Proceeding from the formal analysis of primitive narrative structures, we have attempted here to reconstruct the entire history of redactional combination, supplementation, and readaptation, up to the point where these primitive materials became part of a sophisticated literary document, the deuteronomistic history book. As will be seen, there is good reason to believe that the entire northern prophetic corpus, from I Kings 17 to II Kings 10 and including II Kings 13, was substantially in its present form prior to the work of the deuteronomistic school. We leave open the question of the redactional insertion of Judahite prophetic traditions within the Isaiah cycle, but are confident that the close affinities among deuteronomistic comments inserted in I Kings 11, 14, 16, 21, II Kings 9 identify the first three mentioned chapters as elements taken up into the original deuteronomistic history.

Walter Dietrich's recent study, *Prophetie und Geschichte* (1972), approaches this problem from the opposite end and arrives at strikingly different results. There is unquestionably much worthwhile discussion in what he offers, especially in his formulaic studies in Part I and his analysis of linguistic patterns in Part III. But his reconstruction of literary history (Part II) and redaction history (Part IV) suffers from the serious handicap of having neglected the internal structural analysis that has engaged us here. The consequence is that he has often made wrong identifications of what is early and what is late, in turn using these erroneous conclusions to bolster a theory that I Kings 13, 14, 17, 20-22, II Kings 1, among other passages, were added by an exilic supplementer (Dtr^P) to an already completed deuteronomistic corpus. Depending heavily on formal and linguistic similarities shared by his Dtr^P and the exilic prophets (cf. pp. 64-83), he argues that the former has been influenced by the latter, but in many instances the reverse could equally be true. Dietrich cannot be absolved of *argumentum in circulo* when he reasons that a number of nonprophetic passages ordinarily taken as early, and containing elements of the formulas in question, must on this account be late. Although he tries to support this contention by a literary analysis that allows the isolation of such material from its context (e.g., II Sam. 17:14; cf. p. 73), his proof is often tenuous. He is at times obliged to resort to sheer conjecture (e.g., on p. 71, where he offers the unsupported statement that such passages as I Sam. 15:10; II Sam. 7:14; I Kings 13:10; 17:2, 8; 21:17 — integral structural elements in early narratives — "*scheinen* [my emphasis] nicht von hohem Alter zu sein"). In any event, the evidence of probability that in some instances might associate a particular expression specifically with the exile period (as "and you have cast me behind your back," I Kings 14:9; cf. Isa. 38:17; Ezek. 14:9) can scarcely bear the strain of proof placed upon it, viz., that the chapter in question has to date from Ezekiel's time rather than Josiah's (or Hezekiah's). The linguistic milieu is too broad, and at the same time too nebulous, to support such a claim. Though a certain element of redactional activity within the deuteronomistic school may indeed have been specifically concerned with prophetic prediction and fulfillment, Dietrich has been unable to demonstrate that it actually resulted in substantive additions to the content of what was already offered in the basic deuteronomistic narrative drawn from its northern Israelite sources. Much more impressive than Dietrich's abortive effort is the sober, rigorous analysis of introductory formulas made by Helga Weippert in *Bib* 53 (1972), 301-339. From it, solid conclusions regarding the final structuring of the deuteronomistic history book can be safely drawn.

2. *Die Quellen des Königsbüches*. The existence of a special "*Nabiquelle*" may be acknowledged without committing oneself to all of Jepsen's predeuteronomistic sources. Most critics, including Noth, assume that the prophet stories existed in oral form as the Deuteronomist made use of them. On the other hand the argument of R. Smend, "Das Wort Jahwes an Elia," *VT* 25 (1975), 523-543, allows for no intermediate redactional activity in I Kings 17–19 between the earliest collection and the work of the Deuteronomist.

3. Surely there existed no special "Ephraimite history" or "acts of Ahab" (Wellhausen and others). The third collection was, like the other collections, a prophetic and not a political document.

4. On the coexistence of separate Elijah and Elisha cycles see especially O. Eissfeldt, "Die Komposition von I Reg 16:29–II Reg 13:25," in F. Maass, ed., *Das ferne und nahe Wort* (Festschrift L. Rost; BZAW 105; Berlin, 1967), pp. 49-58.

5. Cf. A. Rofé, *JBL* 89 (1970), 427-440 (see Chapter Five, n. 22).

6. See above, pp. 57, 82f. It is not concerned with providing biographical data respecting Elijah, but with securing the succession from that prophet to Elisha.

7. It is surprising that Eissfeldt, pp. 57f., should deduce that the adverb *šām* ("there") refers to northern Transjordania. Though that is where Jehu, Hazael, and Elisha were later to be associated with one another (II Kings 8:29ff.), the legend of I Kings 19:1-18 places Elijah at the "mountain of God," without reporting that he actually carried out the divine commission.

8. See above, pp. 61-63, 98f. The chronological disparity between II Kings 1:17b and II Kings 3:1 has led to much ingenious speculation, such as W. Dietrich's argument (*Prophetie und Geschichte*, pp. 125-27) assigning 1:17b to a deuteronomistic redactor later than the person responsible for 3:1. But 1:17b is a final notice for a northern king while 3:1 is the opening notice for a Judahite. Though the two chronologies are in seeming contradiction, their very disparity may be an argument for their originality, while the explanation for their chronological disparity is to be sought in terms of variant methods of calculating reigns, as in the case of II Kings 8:25 versus 9:29 (see S. J. De Vries, "Chronology of the Old Testament," *IDB*, I, following Thiele). A single deuteronomistic redactor may have found the variant Joram synchronisms in his sources, incorporating them without correction at suitable places in his narrative.

9. *Überlieferungsgeschichtliche Studien*, p. 82, n. 6.

10. Fohrer, *Elia;* Steck, *Überlieferung und Zeitgeschichte*. R. Smend's case for

deuteronomistic insertions in the early Elijah cycle (*VT* 25, 532ff.) rests on the circular argument that since emphasis on the word of God is typical of the Deuteronomist, references to the word of God in our material must be deuteronomistic. Smend seems generally hypercritical in isolating literary glosses, offering little if any rationale for their supposed insertion.

11. See above, p. 85 n. 32. Dietrich, pp. 122-25, offers a defective argument identifying I Kings 17 as an early narrative unrelated to chap. 18, later inserted into its present position by Dtr^{P}. His treatment suffers here because it has no conception of formal structure. (Dietrich cites Steck in his bibliography but fails to mention him or use his work in his own text or footnotes.)

12. Cf. L. Bronner, *The Stories of Elijah and Elisha as Polemics Against Baal Worship* (Leiden, 1968).

13. Vss. 17a and 20 are redactional, connecting this story with the preceding. One should not overlook that this story speaks of a "woman," "the mistress of the house" (*hā'iššâ, ba'ᵃlat habbāyit*), whereas in vss. 9f. the woman of Zarepath is designated "widow" (*'iššâ 'almānâ*); cf. vs. 20, *hā'almānâ*.

14. Though no doubt the narrative of 19:1-18 draws from received tradition, this story is composed as a literary continuation from chap. 18. It is the extensive contribution of the Jehuite redactor that has misled critics like Fohrer and Eissfeldt to view all of chaps. 17–19 as a literary unity, overlooking the evidence for primitive subunities within this section.

15. On the idealization of Elijah relative to Elisha, cf. G. von Rad, *Old Testament Theology,* II, pp. 23-25. H. Gese, "Bemerkungen zur Sinaitradition," *ZAW* 79 (1967), 145ff., sees I Kings 19 as a drastic reshaping of the Sinai tradition. From a comparison between I Kings 18:36 and Exod. 14:31 it becomes clear that the Elijah legends do intend to cast Elijah in the figure of Moses; cf. S. J. De Vries, "The Time Word *maḥar* as a Key to Tradition Development," *ZAW* 87 (1975), 78f.; see also G. Seitz, *Redaktionsgeschichtliche Studien zum Deuteronomium*, p. 306; R. P. Carroll, "The Elijah-Elisha Sagas: Some Remarks on Prophetic Succession in Ancient Israel," *VT* 19 (1969), 400-415.

16. E.g., Eissfeldt in Festschrift Rost, p. 50; Steck, *Überlieferung,* pp. 40ff. The arguments of Dietrich, *Prophetie und Geschichte,* pp. 21f., 36, 47, that vss. 27-29 are an exilic addition are weak and tendentious.

17. An early deuteronomistic redactor added vss. 21f., 24 (cf. I Kings 14:10f.; 16:1-4); later deuteronomistic hands added vs. 23 (which is significantly at variance with parallel material in the original legend at II Kings 9:10a and in the work of a Jehuite redactor at II Kings 9:36b-37, both of which use *ḥēleq yizrᵉ'e'l* rather than the Deuteronomist's similar sounding *ḥēl yizrᵉ'e'l*) and vss. 25f.

18. Cf. Steck, *Überlieferung,* pp. 40ff., and our comments in Chapter Five, n. 59. Steck argues that vss. 17-18a, 19-20bα form the tradition core from which the present narrative developed, recording essentially only the (historical) fact that Elijah the Tishbite uttered a deadly oracle against Ahab; the narrative of Jezebel's contrivance (vss. 1-16) together with the reshaping of the fulfillment (vss. 27-29) arose as a polemic against Jezebel and Joram subsequently to Jehu's revolt. The weakness of this analysis lies in the difficulty of supposing that the tradition of a prophetic oracle like this would have been preserved without adding a narrative context. While acknowledging the element of artifice (as well as confusion) in the Jezebel section, we believe that it reflects substantial historical fact; that even though Jezebel may not have taken a dominant role until after Ahab's death and her own elevation to the "office" of queen-mother, she could very well

have had strong influence on internal affairs while Ahab was still reigning. If I Kings 21:1-16 were imaginatively invented with the event of 841 in mind, we would hardly expect the complaint against her to be shifted so dramatically from "harlotries and sorceries" (II Kings 9:22) or killing the prophets (I Kings 18:13; 19:2) to the engineering of judicial murder, as serious as this crime was in itself.

The reason why Elijah appears first only in vs. 17 may be understood from a careful examination of the structure of the entire narrative, which is designed to draw attention to Jezebel's and Ahab's abuse of authority, leading to inevitable judgment; also to the opposing authority of Yahweh, asserting sovereign freedom in reassigning the impact of this judgment. The outline which the narrative itself discloses shows a development from (1) the problem to (2) its illegitimate resolution to (3) the divine retribution, as follows:

- I. The problem of Naboth's reticence
  - 1. The unsuccessful negotiation
    - a. The situation, 1aβb
    - b. Ahab's offer, 2
    - c. Naboth's refusal, 3
  - 2. The prospect of successful intervention
    - a. Ahab's dejection, 4
    - b. Jezebel's resolution
      - (1) Ahab recounts his failure, 5f.
      - (2) Jezebel introduces the prospect of a successful outcome, 7
- II. The problem resolved through the abuse of authority
  - 1. Jezebel engineers Naboth's judicial murder
    - a. Her forged letters, 8-10
    - b. Narrative of compliance, 11-13
    - c. The report to Jezebel, 14
  - 2. Jezebel disposes of her prize
    - a. Her offer to Ahab, 15
    - b. Ahab takes possession, 16
- III. Prophetic judgment on the abuse of authority
  - 1. Elijah the Tishbite condemns Ahab
    - a. The divine instruction
      - (1) The command, 18
      - (2) The accusatory question, 19a
      - (3) The threat, 19b
    - b. The confrontation, 20
  - 2. Reinterpretation: the judgment deferred
    - a. Ahab's contrition, 27
    - b. An oracle of interpretation
      - (1) Narrative introduction, 28
      - (2) Appeal to Elijah as witness of Ahab's contrition, 29a
      - (3) Specification of evil for Ahab's dynasty, 29b

The secondary material appearing in vss. 21-26 represents early and subsequent levels of deuteronomistic interpretation (see below). We can appreciate the substantial unity of the material that remains once the design of its structure is clearly understood. Thus must a refined form criticism abet and correct the insights of a one-sided tradition-critical analysis.

19. Scholars involved in the dispute whether the Naboth incident took place in Jezreel or Samaria (see J. M. Miller, *VT* 17 [1967], 307ff.; Napier, *VT* 9 (1959), 366-378; Jepsen, "Ahabs Busse," Festschrift Galling (1970), pp. 145ff.; P. Welten,

"Naboths Weinberg," *EvT* 33 [1973], 18-32; Seebass, "Der Fall Naboths in 1 Reg. xxi," *VT* 24 [1974], 474-488) have failed to observe that the narrator is himself unclear where the story is supposed to have taken place. Naboth as a Jezreelite is not likely to have possessed a vineyard in Samaria, claiming this as his patriarchal heritage; thus it is often held that the vineyard was actually in Jezreel, the references to Samaria in vss. 1, 18 being explained as glosses added under the influence of 22:38. The palace of vs. 1 would then have to be the royal residence in Jezreel (cf. I Kings 18:46; II Kings 9:17ff.), since the vineyard is described as being beside (*'ēṣel*) it (this location is presupposed in vss. 2ff., 16); yet the palace where the ensuing conversation between Jezebel and Ahab takes place must be in Samaria because she has to send letters to Naboth's own city (evidently Jezreel) and receive word back from there (vss. 8, 14). This confusion cannot be harmonized and should be attributed to the original narrator, who appears to have been composing freely from the uncontrolled tradition at his disposal.

20. While the locution *b^e^nê n^e^bî'îm* is characteristic of the Elisha legends, it is hazardous to infer that I Kings 20:35ff. must on this account belong to the Elisha cycle (cf. Amos 7:14). Elisha's frequent identification as *'îš hā'^e^lōhîm*, another notable characteristic, is shared by narratives from so remote a tradition as that of I Kings 13. R. A. Carlson has drawn attention to a number of stylistic and ideological characteristics of this cycle in his essay, "Elisée — le successeur d'Elie," *VT* 20 (1970), 385-405.

21. This order is intended to suggest the relative order in which the collections were brought together and does not preclude the possibility that the later collections may contain materials older than materials in some of the earlier collections.

22. The reference in 4:8 to Elisha's journey to Shunem introduces the independent narrative. The redactor assumed from vs. 25 that Mt. Carmel was now the prophet's place of residence, hence treated his two side trips to Shunem as temporary forays.

23. From Naaman's bearing and the king of Israel's general anxiety (vs. 7) we are justified in identifying a situation in which Israel was subservient to, and somewhat threatened by, Syria; yet the reference to "raids" (*g^e^dûdîm*) as the most serious Syrian incursion suggests an early date, probably in the time of the Omrides.

24. See above, p. 61. This story has been expanded by pro-Elisha propaganda in 6:31, 32b, by the lepers anecdote in 7:3-5, 7-13, and by a late didactic summary in 7:18-20. Cf. S. J. De Vries, "Temporal Terms. . . ," *VT* 25 (1975), 100-103.

25. See above, pp. 64-65.

26. Because of the probability that these three narratives were originally anonymous (the name "Elisha" has been sporadically added to the title "man of God"), caution is in order with respect to any conclusion about Elisha's dates.

27. See above, pp. 67-69, 102f. Although this legend appeals to Elisha as the ultimate authority behind Jehu's accession, the fact that an anonymous apprentice delivers the operative oracle shows that it did not derive from an established Elisha school. This fact argues for an earlier rather than later origin.

28. Three separate levels of interpretation are reflected in vs. 36. The prophet legend places in Jehu's mouth as his final, interpretive word the declaration, "This is the word of Yahweh" — referring back, of course, to the prediction of the young prophet in vss. 6-10. The accession historian, adding vss. 36b-37 without the identification "Elijah the Tishbite," embellished the original prediction with pathos and bloody detail. Another redactor added the Elijah identification

after this narrative had been added to the Elijah-Elisha combination.

29. See above, p. 102.

30. As has been argued, this is no Judahite document. Though he retained I Kings 22 almost intact, the Chronicler was so little impressed by Jehoshaphat's role in this story that he readily sacrificed it to the baroque contrivance of II Chron. 20 (on its artificial structure, see De Vries, *VT* 25, 103-105).

31. See the textual evidence for this analysis in Chapter Five, n. 49.

32. A careful evaluation of the thesis offered by Bernhardt in *Schalom* (Festschrift Jepsen), pp. 11-22, provides a perspective for understanding the historical background of this narrative. Bernhardt makes five inadequate or inconclusive arguments for dating the war of the three kings against Moab to the reign of Jehoash, *ca.* 800 B.C.: (1) the freedom of Moabite marauders to raid Israelite territory reported in II Kings 13:20f. is commensurate with Moab's assertion of national independence in II Kings 3, hence demands a date later than Elisha's death; (2) Jehoshaphat is secondary in the text of II Kings 3; (3) this narrative has an historical background equivalent to that of II Chron. 20 (but see n. 30 above); (4) an opportunity on the part of the three kings to retake Moab can be understood as taking place only under conditions identical to those obtaining when Adad-nirari III put sufficient pressure on Syria to enable Jehoash to conquer territory previously lost to Hazael (II Kings 13:25); (5) since the stele of Mesha mentions no significant Israelite success against Moab, the attack on Kir-hareseth could hardly have taken place during Mesha's reign (but it was never the habit of oriental rulers to celebrate their defeats!).

While none of these arguments is sufficiently valid to carry Bernhardt's case, there is a sixth consideration that does definitely have a bearing on the problem, and Bernhardt is justified in stressing it. According to II Kings 8:20-22, Edom had been a dependency of Judah and did not succeed in setting up its own king until the reign of Jehoram ben Jehoshaphat (cf. I Kings 22:48 [E 47]). This is clearly in conflict with II Kings 3:9ff., which mentions the Edomite king as a contemporary of Jehoshaphat and Joram ben Ahab. Scholars have pointed to the probability that the king of Edom accompanied his Hebrew counterparts only as a subservient vassal, but even so the emphatic negation of Edomite kingship during Jehoshaphat's reign appearing in presumably trustworthy deuteronomistic source-material at the passages cited would seem to eliminate such an attempt at harmonization (even though the LXX reading at I Kings 16:28+, "Nasib was king," might commend itself as a substitute for the MT in I Kings 22:48b, "a deputy was king" [so many scholars], it must be seen that the LXX reading of "Syria" for "Edom" does not eliminate the internal contradiction of the Greek text, which thereby shows its own tendentiousness).

Thus we must agree that II Kings 3 developed under the conditions prevailing after Jehoshaphat's time (also before the commencement of Judean-Edomite hostilities as reported in II Kings 14:7, 10). This does not incline us to accept Bernhardt's dating of the campaign itself *ca.* 800, mainly because — as Bernhardt fails to observe — vs. 13 identifies Joram as the Israelite king, even though his name elsewhere is textually secondary, and because Jehoshaphat is definitely original. Since for the original narrator neither king was in fact anonymous, how are we to conceive of him cloaking the deeds of two later kings — presumably known to all — in the disguise of an earlier period? Yet this narrator's reference to the king of Edom being essentially coequal with the others tells us that the narrator was indeed living after the reign of Jehoshaphat, anachronistically transferring the circumstances of his own time to the period in which the event actually took place. We have little alternative but to suppose that, in spite of the highly imaginative composition of this story, Joram and Jehoshaphat did in fact carry out a campaign against Moab, forcing the co-operation of Edom as a Judean dependency (significantly, our narrator does not seem to know a name for his Edomite "king"; it is because his historical counterpart was in fact no king but the lieutenant mentioned in I Kings 22:48).

As we have seen, the core of II Kings 3 developed as a late prophet legend (subgenre 10: instrumental fulfillment) strongly influenced by I Kings 22 and II Kings 8:29ff. The anti-Omride bias is already present at the core of this narrative, coming pointedly to expression in Elisha's rebuke in vss. 13f. and in the schematic depiction of Joram's unfaith (vss. 10, 13b). Thus it was first told in a period subsequent to the events narrated, probably not as late as Bernhardt supposes, but sometime after Jehu and Athaliah had seized power. We can explain the framework provided by vss. 4-5a, 25b-27 as a further reworking, designed as a subtle rebuke to the Omrides, who no longer win, as in the original story, but are forced to depart Moab under the curse (*qeṣep*) of a mysterious taboo (cf. Josh. 9:20).

33. See above, pp. 57f.

34. See above, p. 63. The crucial question whether all of vss. 30b-43 belongs to a single, unified narrative is resolved in the affirmative through the observation that the prophetic invective in vs. 42 (*ya'an 'ašer šillaḥtā 'et 'îš ḥermî* . . .) is thematically connected to the climactic element in the first part of the narrative, i.e., the concluding word of vs. 34, *wayešalleḥēhû*, "and he sent him away." The function of the two main thematic elements over against each other may be seen in the following outline:

I. A king's word establishes deliverance
  1. Ben-Hadad treats for negotiation (*ḥesed*)
    a. His predicament, 30b
    b. The entreaty
      (1) The proposal, 31
      (2) The approach, 32a
    c. The identification of affinity
      (1) The king's query (*'aḥî hû'*), 32b
      (2) The servants' response (*'aḥîkā ben-ḥadad*), 33aα
      (3) The invitation, 33aβ
  2. The negotiation of the treaty
    a. Ben-Hadad's approach, 33b
    b. The offer of concessions, 34a
    c. The acceptance, 34b (conclusion: *wayešalleḥēhû*)

II. A king's word establishes judgment
  1. A prophet prepares himself for judgment
    a. The validation of attendant revelation
      (1) A command refused, 35
      (2) The refusal punished, 36
    b. The preparation for a symbolic role, 37
  2. Symbolic judgment on the prophet
    a. His disguise, 38
    b. His address to the king
      (1) The fictitious charge, 39 (key phrase: *napšekā taḥat napšô*)
      (2) The delinquency, 40a
    c. The king's decision, 40b

3. The judgment applied
   a. The prophet's self-disclosure, 41
   b. The oracle
      (1) Invective (*ya'an 'ᵃšer sillaḥtā 'et 'îš ḥermî . . .*), 42a
      (2) Threat (*napšᵉkā taḥat napšô*), 42b
   c. Narrative sequel, 43aα

We see that this narrative has been constructed in such a way as to play off the king's power to open up deliverance by his crucial word in the first part (where the operative phrase is *'aḥî hû'* in vs. 32; cf. 33) over against the king's power in the second part to determine judgment for himself and his people through affirmation of a symbolic word spoken by the prophet (*napšᵉkā taḥat napšô*).

35. A reasonable conclusion from the observation that "the king of Israel" otherwise occurs without "Ahab" in this cycle.

36. RSV, "and Ahab said," in 20:34 is an interpretive insertion. It may be necessary to emend the difficult Heb. text as in BH³mg, but cf. A. S. van der Woude, "I Reg 20, 34," *ZAW* 76 (1964), 189-191.

37. Cf. the stele of "Bar-hadad" dedicated to Melqart, *ANET,* p. 501.

38. On the historical problem as a whole, see A. Malamat's article on "The Aramaeans," in Wiseman, ed., *Peoples of Old Testament Times,* pp. 134-155, summarizing the discussion from two extensive studies in modern Hebrew published by him: "The Wars of Israel and Assyria," in J. Liver, ed., *The Military History of the Land of Israel in Biblical Times* (Jerusalem, 1964), pp. 246ff.; *The Aramaeans in Aram Naharaim and the Rise of their States* (Jerusalem, 1952). Cf. also M. F. Unger, *Israel and the Aramaeans of Damascus* (London, 1957).

39. Significant differences in language and point of view mark these verses as redactional; cf. *YTT,* pp. 231-33.

40. The syntax of vs. 30b, with subject foremost followed by characterizing participle, then by a waw-consecutive imperfect, provides the customary beginning of a new account. The LXX reading, "into (his) house," is more original than MT's "into the city." Even from the redactor's point of view, Ben-Hadad should have been included among *hannôtārîm* who had fled into the city of Aphek.

41. This may be considered evidence that the Omride war cycle must have been taken into the prophet document prior to the deuteronomistic redaction, because the Deuteronomist does not customarily insert isolated glosses of this kind.

42. "Three" is a convenient, schematic number. It is its use rather than any anterior unlikelihood that the Syrians would quickly have reneged on their treaty that identifies 22:1-2a as a purely conventional transition.

43. See above, p. 18. Elsewhere the formula specifies the prophet who spoke; cf. I Kings 15:29; 16:12; II Kings 10:17; 24:2.

44. Dietrich, *Prophetie und Geschichte*, pp. 9-28, while calling attention to the strong similarities among deuteronomistic additions in I Kings 11, 14, 16, 21, II Kings 9, has come far from demonstrating that their characteristic formulas are exilic. He has not proven that the narratives to which these formulas are attached are late insertions into the deuteronomistic corpus (cf. n. 1) though unquestionably they are programmatic within the deuteronomistic work as a whole, like II Kings 17:7-41; 24:3f.

CHAPTER EIGHT

Theological Perspectives

WE BEGAN BY POKING OUR HEAD THROUGH A HOLE — AS IT WERE — AND finding a vast underground cavern to explore. We expressed curiosity at the phenomenon of prophet opposed to prophet, something apparently unique to ancient Israel. Of the two original Old Testament narratives in which this motif is integral to the structure, in I Kings 13 it proved to be thematically instrumental to the prophetic authentication of disputed prophecy, in which prophet against prophet ultimately becomes prophet *for* prophet. Thus I Kings 22 has been left standing alone to develop this motif in terms of the paradoxical counteraction of prophecy by prophecy. In the process of clarifying this distinction, we have made some intriguing discoveries. Although new twists and turns invite us still onward, we have come far enough to grasp something of the depth dimensions of our initial discovery. We are now at the point of looking back, summing up, and estimating the wider significance of all that we have discussed.

1. RESUMÉ

A major lesson of this book has been that the answer to no problem is simple. Our responsibilities for critical understanding have proven to be more varied and complex than we initially suspected. We know now why no investigation of I Kings 22, or of any other biblical passage, on the basis of a narrow, specialized technique can hope to provide definitive answers. This is no task for the textual critic *qua* textual critic, for the literary critic *qua* literary critic, for the form critic *qua* form critic, for the historian *qua* historian, or for the theologian *qua* theologian. The competent exegete must listen to them all — and strive to *be* them all! Only when he brings light to bear from all sides to the object of his study will it stand out in its true proportions.

a. Text criticism

While hesitating to claim that we have achieved final or absolute clarity with respect to the precise reading of the original Hebrew text in I Kings 22:1-38, we must own to some satisfaction at having moved significantly beyond the usual level of nonspecialists. Too generally, text criticism seems to be a haphazard weighing of preferences for one reading over against another. But no choice between the Hebrew or some other reading ought to be made without endeavoring to give some account of the causes that have produced the variants under consideration, and without a firm grasp of the history, ideology, and techniques of the major textual witnesses with their recensional variants. We have gratefully benefited from the new, intensive study of the Greek text of Kings. Since few Septuagint specialists have done much to demonstrate the relevance of their discoveries for the specific problems of exegetical investigation, the present work may serve as an illustration of just how crucial textual study may prove to be in defining the object of study. In the present pericope, very much has revolved upon textual evidence to the effect that I Kings 22:4 originally expressed not Jehoshaphat's subservience to Ahab but Ahab's dependence on Jehoshaphat. Equally decisive in a negative way has been evidence that the original text lacked virtually all the pluses that have arisen within the Hebrew and the Greek textual traditions.

b. Literary and structural criticism

It seems to have become a fashion in some circles to carry out form-critical analysis in isolation from literary criticism.[1] The philosophical bias of structuralism, consciously or unconsciously operative, lies at the basis of such a procedure. Radical structuralists believe that what matters is not the development of new forms within an historical process, but form in itself: any form. The fact is that the structure of pericopes is subject to reshaping in the process of literary development and has communicative significance only in terms of the function of these pericopes within the setting of their respective new historical situations. It is absurd to think that the study of form can ever have meaning outside an understanding of the literary forces that have shaped this form. Of course, "old style" literary criticism, concerned only with the disentangling of documentary strands, is passé; what is needed is a literary criticism that informs and is informed by the analysis of structure, in awareness of the shape of constituent traditional materials worked into the total literary product.

Our examination of the structure of the separate Micaiah narratives has accentuated the significance of the literary inconcinnities that some sharp-sighted critics have previously detected. But our analysis of the Micaiah narratives furnishes an instructive instance of how a narrowly designed form criticism might have gone astray, for without question the combination of the two narratives that now constitutes the text, with or without subsequent redactional and scribal additions, does exhibit an "understandable" structure. Our question is whether the present redactional structure is functional as well as understandable. If not, there remains little presumption of originality since primitive narratives have carefully designed, functional structures. A decisive insight in the present instance has been an awareness brought here from wider investigations, namely, my earlier study of the functions of potent time-designatives, illumining the unique role of *bayyôm hahû'* past and future, which appear at vs. 25 and vs. 35, respectively, and define the point of culmination for each original narrative.

c. *Genre criticism*

Our study has brought us to a definite decision regarding the question whether I Kings 22 is a political history or a prophet narrative. We have come to see that political histories are virtually absent in I Kings 17 to II Kings 10, 13, appearing only as the redactional restructuring of a prophet legend (with anecdotal reports) in the political document presently found in II Kings 9–10. The very fact that this propagandistic composition was preserved within a prophetic collection ought to convince us how very much the prophets were concerned with politics. There was no separation of church and state for them! Here were "spiritual" men willing to mingle in public affairs, eventually putting their own clear mark upon the reporting of them.

Our defense of the genre name "prophet legend" has been fully validated in our ability to identify a meaningful pattern of constituent subgenres. Although our categorization remains provisional and fellow scholars will endeavor to improve it, it clearly opens up a whole new dimension of understanding. Our lengthy discussion of subgenres, including a structural analysis of crucial passages and detailed comparisons of closely related subgenres, has proven to be both necessary and fruitful. We have done much, but not too much — no more than is needed in order to place the early and the late Micaiah narratives firmly within an understandable pattern of structural — and hence ideological and functional — comparison. A firm grasp of their respective places within genre history has shed light on the previous development of prophet legend, allowing us glimpses of its origins and subsequent development, suggesting something of its destiny.

d. *Historical and tradition criticism*

Addressing the most essential chronological and formulaic problems, we have arrived at important negative and positive probabilities — if not always certainties — regarding the origin of the Micaiah story. In view of the care with which we have dealt with the important questions, it should no longer be possible to treat I Kings 22 as a direct source for the political history of Ahab and Jehoshaphat. On the positive side, we may say with assurance that the encounter of a certain Micaiah with a certain king of Israel did in all probability take place; it is the narrative shaping of this event that is imaginative and only peripherally historical. A more significant historical conclusion is the light shed on the theological questions that animated the spiritual life of Israel in the Jehuite period — otherwise darkly obscure. A line of kings who had dared introduce the worship of a foreign god had come to ruin, yet the kings who had replaced them were being forced to endure the ignominy of Syrian oppression. Thus it continued throughout the reign of Hazael, until "Yahweh gave Israel a savior" (II Kings 13:5). Narrative A of I Kings 22 reveals to the informed observer the theologizing judgment that in another place says:

> *The fathers have eaten sour grapes*
> *and the children's teeth are set on edge.*[2]

The Omrides would ever be blamed for Hazael's depredations. I Kings 22 drastically recasts what happened in 841 B.C., providing a more subtle and profound vehicle for interpreting Yahweh's purpose in this paradoxical history than appears in the direct reporting of Jehu's ruthless deed according to II Kings 9–10. Surely there would have been some in Israel already at this time who, like Hosea, believed that Jehu had widely overstepped his bounds, who agreed with their later colleague that Yahweh would surely punish the house of Jehu for the blood of Jezreel (Hos. 1:4), who were moved to complain like Hosea against all who seize power by violence:

> *All of them are hot as an oven,*
> *and they devour their rulers.*
> *All their kings have fallen,*
> *and none of them calls upon me.* (Hos. 7:7)

The Micaiah story survived a century, taking on a new structure and a new ideology in Narrative B. Again, though this version of the legend is remote from its historical origin, it sheds light upon the theological climate of the time when it arose. The Jehuite kings, with all the other kings of northern Israel, have passed into memory and the nation has come to ruin. Narrative B is not content to blame one dynasty for the problems of another. It seeks positive meaning in the final destruction of northern Israel. Even though each of its rulers had had prophets aplenty to guide its public life, its kings had gone astray. Narrative B resists the dualistic temptation of believing that failure can thwart the divine purpose. There is no force, however evil or willful, that can ultimately derail the plan of history. Even kings who misrule and prophets who misguide are instruments under Yahweh's control.

e. Redaction criticism

An analysis of redactional procedures was essential to a final accounting of the place and shape of the variant Micaiah narratives. Ranging far outside I Kings 22, we were able to develop a clarifying hypothesis by discussing the origin, place and function of each separate pericope within the prophet legend collection. In the perspective of this total picture it became apparent why the Micaiah narrative, concerned with Ahab, had been placed in the midst of the Elijah cycle — also concerned with Ahab — without becoming part of it. Narrative B is a late expansion, modifying the original narrative's shape and thereby its message. Narrative A itself represents the culmination of a programmatic arrangement within the Omride war cycle. The redactor who put together the four stories of I Kings 20; 22:1-38 was not content to justify the Jehu insurrection simply on the basis of Jezebel's apostasy, as in II Kings 9–10 or in the redacted form of the Elijah collection. He identified the fact that "Ahab" (like Saul) had neglected a *ḥerem,* this time against Syria, when it was in his power to carry it out (I Kings 20:42), as the basis for his bloody death recorded in I Kings 22. This Omride war redactor was thus returning to a more traditional, and in some ways more profound understanding of why Yahweh rejects his kings. As our review of subgenres has revealed, primitive forms of prophet legend emphatically express the priority of the prophet in designating, empowering and supervising the kingly office, but have little to say regarding the struggle against rival gods. This then was "Ahab's" greatest failure: putting king before prophet. But in the final literary recasting the Deuteronomist ignores this unique insight. He intensifies the polemic against Ahab in I Kings 21, now inserted between the two parts of the original Omride war cycle, re-emphasizing the theme of baalistic apostasy and identifying II Kings 9–10 as the fulfillment of I Kings 21 and the final realization of God's judgment on "Ahab." And so — while the Deuteronomist has to concede that even Jehu did not depart from the sin of Jeroboam (II Kings 10:31), and thus contributed to Israel's ultimate downfall — Jehu's special mark in history would remain his having "wiped out Baal from Israel" (II Kings 10:28).

2. THE TESTS OF TRUE PROPHECY

We return to the question of prophet against prophet. It was destined to become a central problem in most of the pre-exilic canonical prophets. Although it is not mentioned in Amos, it is incipient in Hosea (4:5; 12:10;

cf. 12:13), structural in Micah (2:6-11; 3:5-8),[3] important in Isaiah (8:16-22; 30:8-11), thematic in Jeremiah (23:9-40; 26–29), casually normal in Zephaniah (3:4), prominent in Ezekiel (13:1-16), and wanting only in the strongly cult-oriented books of Nahum and Habakkuk, along with Amos. Thus tension between prophet and prophet would become constant in the period between Israel's (723/22) and Judah's (586) downfall. Who can doubt that it was a symptom of the nation's malaise? Was it also a contributory cause?

The usual polemic sought to account for contrary prophecy by characterizing rivals as (1) deceived ("drunken," "asleep"), (2) corrupt and materialistic,[4] or (3) plain liars. Not always seen by modern interpreters as crucially decisive is the prior question of political orientation. Though no doubt individual prophets may have been susceptible to self-deception regarding their true motives, there is no reason to believe that they were as a whole motivated by self-aggrandizement or the pursuit of personal power in opposing their fellow prophets, so much as by erroneous conceptions of Israel's ultimate well-being and their proper role in working to realize it. In other words, the central conflict was theological. The struggle was rooted in traditional ambiguities regarding a prophet's primary responsibility and allegiance.

This ideological problem can be better understood in an analysis of the two main answers Israel came to give regarding the test of genuine prophecy: (1) that true prophecy is vindicated in fulfillment and (2) that it is guaranteed by its affinities.

a. *True prophecy is vindicated in fulfillment*

God's word was a power that moved forward irresistibly to realization in action. Although in the heathen world one god's word might possibly be counteracted by another's, in Israel only one god was God, and he was sovereign over all nature and history. That a word spoken by this God's authentic and authorized intermediary must inevitably come to fulfillment had been axiomatic from earliest times. This is thematic in all the prophet legends featuring some form of word-fulfillment motif. But there was not originally any effort to correlate word with word. Only gradually did the prophet legends endeavor to develop a principle of intentional supersession — as in I Kings 22, Narrative A — or of intermediate instrumentality — as in the instrumental fulfillment legends. The deuteronomistic history in its turn made the principle of validation through fulfillment thematic in its arrangement and central to its interpretation.

So too Deuteronomy. Evidently the lawbook of chaps. 12–26, representing Deuteronomy's literary core as well as its initial program, was much concerned about identifying authoritative revelation. All its laws are traced typologically to Moses, and through him to the Sinai theophany. But, looking forward, the Deuteronomic laws show awareness of the need for ongoing new revelation. In 17:8-13 the people are commanded to obey the priest and the judge who shall be required to render decisions on controverted matters. In 18:15-22 the people are likewise commanded to heed the words of the prophet who speaks like Moses. Such a prophet is to take the place of diviners, soothsayers, sorcerers, etc. (vss. 9ff.); the problem is, what happens when a prophet speaks "presumptuously" (*yāzîd lᵉdabbēr*) in Yahweh's name, i.e., speaks a word that Yahweh has not commanded? He is, of course, as guilty as if he had spoken in the name of some other god, and hence must bear the penalty of death (vs. 20).[5] But how does one know, in practical terms, whether in fact a prophet is speaking what Yahweh commanded? Deuteronomy knows only the test of fulfillment:

> If the word does not come to pass or come true (*wᵉlō' yihyeh haddābār wᵉlō' yābō'*), that is a word that Yahweh has not spoken; his word is presumptuous (*bᵉzādôn*), so of that prophet it is not necessary for you to be afraid (22).

Still, this criterion has little validity except as the test of time. The parenetic consequence drawn from it ("it is not necessary for you to be afraid of him") has little practical relevance since, while the people wait to see whether a particular prophecy will be fulfilled (and often it is long delayed; cf. Hab. 2:1ff.; Ezek. 12:21ff.), they must remain in anxious uncertainty.[6] They may have to wait all their life to know whether a prophet has spoken for Yahweh — and then it is too late to give him his proper fear.

Alongside this Deuteronomic rule, we find a classical test in the report of Jeremiah's argument with Hananiah.[7] Jeremiah has advised the people and the king to get used to Nebuchadrezzar's yoke, for it must long be borne; but Hananiah says in Yahweh's name that "within two years" the exiles will return and Nebuchadrezzar's yoke will be broken (28:4). To this Jeremiah replies, "Amen, may Yahweh do so!" (vs. 6), thus putting himself on a common basis with Hananiah and all the listening people, affirming his adherence to the highest eschatological ideals of covenant-oriented Yahwists. But he knows that "wishing will not make it so," and that a decisive test must be found. Modifying the rule of test by fulfillment, Jeremiah interjects as a prior qualifying element an oracle's content. The essential theme of traditional prophetism has been — he declares — that of "war," not "peace." This has characterized the message of prophecy "against many countries and great kingdoms"; the unresolved, immediate question is whether it also pertains to Israel/Judah. Here and now, is it to be peace or war? The historical signs are distressingly ambiguous, and each prophet sees them differently. Hence Jeremiah knows that only the presumption of probability is on his side; the final answer must await fulfillment in the future:

> As for the prophet who prophesies peace, when it actually happens the prophet whom Yahweh has truly sent will be known (vs. 9).[8]

This principle of proof by fulfillment remained dominant throughout the classical age of prophetism. Thus Ezek. 33:33: "When this comes — and come it will! — then they will know that a prophet has been among them." True prophecy will be fulfilled; what is fulfilled is true prophecy. The question of course remains, When and how? But the fulfillment of their words of doom ensured the preservation and eventual canonization of the writings of the *Unheilspropheten*. That is why our Bible has a book of Jeremiah but no book of Hananiah. Close inspection may reveal that the canonical prophets did indeed predict certain things that apparently never have been and never will be literally fulfilled, but that is beside the point. It is their essential message, not the form their message may have taken in particular instances, that is validated.

When Israel/Judah came at last to the situation where it could recognize no fulfillment, it inevitably repudiated all prophecy as more nuisance than help (cf. Zech. 13:3f.). This was a clear sign that the people had ceased to look upon history as revelatory, as something in which Yahweh and his people could engage in meaningful participation. It was believed yet that Yahweh superintends and controls history, but from above. He is no longer active in it. Israel, on its part, could only endure history and wait for its end. The death of *Heilsgeschichte* is coterminous with the death of prophecy.

b. *True prophecy is guaranteed by its affinities*

Jeremiah hinted at this second test in his repartee with Hananiah. The qualitative element to which he was pointing had something to do with the character of Yahweh and a prophet's role in mediating its implications for practical understanding. It is in the prophecies of Hosea and Isaiah, along with Micaiah narrative B, that this principle comes clearly to expression.

Once all was simple; Israel dwelt secure among the nations — the little realms around her — confidently possessing the land. In this idyllic context, primitive prophecy strongly supported Israel's rise to nationhood. But as Israel became a state among states, theological ambiguities arose. Before the rising power of great foreign empires Israel was forced increasingly to adjust her vision of unabated optimism. A problem coming to sharper focus was the paradox of repeated foreign success at the expense of Yahweh's chosen and covenanted people. How could Yahweh be (1) sovereign Lord of nature and history, (2) faithful to the well-being of the elected nation, and (3) willing to allow enemies to threaten her national existence?

The institution of the kingship, viewed with misgivings even from its first introduction, never ceased to be a complicating factor. Its constant tendency was to confuse the issue of the nation's well-being by pre-empting it to regal self-aggrandizement. Sensing that it was in their hands to make their own terms with foreign nations, Israel's kings came to look on this as their right and hence responsibility. It became relatively easy to appeal to the people's patriotism; all that was needed was to turn the eschatological promise of land and prosperous peoplehood into a dogma guaranteeing the success of all nationalistic aims. At last it became impossible for the kings, supported by the people, to identify the point where they had begun to trespass on Yahweh's prerogative.

Although the four-hundred-to-one ratio of the Micaiah story suggests that the vast majority of prophets fell into subservience to the political institution, this is obviously a typological schematization, grossly exaggerated for dramatic effect. Yet we receive from the great prophets the impression that many of them did experience painful isolation from the majority of their fellow prophets, as well as from the generality of the people; hence the extreme pathos of those who were the most loyal to Yahwism's authentic principles. Though the prophets of doom dearly loved their people and probably sincerely honored their kings, the nation's willfulness forced them to take a reluctant stand against people and king. They were strengthened only by the assurance of Yahweh's way in history. Since to them Yahweh was no abstract principle or sterile dogma, but supreme power manifested in dynamic personalism, they believed that not even the nation's willfulness could frustrate Yahweh's design. He would not simply bypass it; he intended to use it for the ultimate fulfillment of his purpose, which included the nation's greater well-being in the end, in spite of itself. As Yahweh was sovereign to direct foreign nations, so he was powerful to direct his own people in the midst of their sin and folly. Alas, this would mean judgment and suffering — a thousand times more bitter for the fact that they would have brought it upon themselves — but not without design and purpose!

Thus genuine prophecy was known by its elemental allegiance to the constitutive principles of biblical personalism, by which we mean the interaction of divine and human integrity in purposeful co-operation for the spiritual enrichment of mankind, to the glory of God. Genuine prophecy, subservient to Yahweh's sovereignty, was observant of covenant loyalty, concretized in the demand for radical theonomy in Israel's public life. It was this principle that proved, in the long run, to be the most influential in determining the shape of biblical religion.

It is from this vantage point that one of Israel's very great prophets, Isaiah, condemned the self-willed designs of the leaders and encouraged the people to look only to Yahweh. Paradoxical is Yahweh's design in controlling the nations to his purpose, says Isaiah. Refusing "the waters of Shiloah that flow gently," the people of Israel/Judah "melt in fear before Rezin and the son of Remaliah"; meanwhile a greater force — the giant empire of Assyria just beyond Rezin's borders — is being prepared by Yahweh to "rise over all its channels and go over all its banks," sweeping on into Judah (8:5-8). Thus Assyria is to become the rod of Yahweh's anger, the staff of his fury (10:5). Although "he does not so intend, and his mind does not so think" (vs. 7), Assyria's passion for rapacious devastation will be bent to Yahweh's own judging and saving purpose with respect to his own people — here mysteriously described as "a godless nation," "the people of my wrath" (vs. 6). And in the end Yahweh will consign Assyria itself to a similar fate for vaunting itself against the God who has used it (vss. 12-19).

If Yahweh can so control the awesome instrument of Judah's destruction, how much more will he be able to frustrate the contrivances of Judah's shortsighted rulers! They may make a "covenant with death," but this will be annulled (28:15, 18); they may try to "hide deep from Yahweh their counsel," try to do their deeds in the dark, saying "Who sees us? Who knows us?" but he sees and knows (29:15f.); they may "carry out a plan, but not mine . . . make a league, but not of my spirit," but this will become their shame and humiliation (30:1-5); they may speed on horses, but Yahweh will give them good cause to speed away (30:15-17).

Thus Isaiah warns the nation to give up its restless intriguing, to look instead to Yahweh, who is known through his true prophets, just as in the law of his covenant (8:20). Although the people refuse to accept it, Yahweh's healthful counsel to them is:

> *In returning and rest (bᵉšûbâ wānaḥat) you shall be saved,*
> *in quietness and in trust (bᵉhašqēṭ ûbᵉbiṭḥâ) your strength will come into being.* (30:15)

Yahweh lays in Zion the "sure foundation" that is a trusting faith making covenant justice and righteousness its aim, avoiding the need to be "in haste" — the rush to unprincipled commitments (28:16f.). Rezin of Syria and Pekah of Samaria may conspire against Jerusalem (7:6), but their counsel will not stand, their intent shall not come to pass because each is his own "head," refusing to acknowledge Yahweh's sovereignty in their evil plans (vss. 7-9a). If only Ahaz and Judah will set aside this example, they will cease shaking like the trees of the forest (vs. 2), but "if you will not trust (*'im lō' ta'ᵃmînû*) surely you shall not be secured (*lō' tē'āmēnû*)" (vs. 9b).[9]

True prophecy, like true piety, is guaranteed by its affinities. Isaiah's moving exposition of this theme had its preparation in the Elijah legends — as markedly in I Kings 19:1ff., where Elijah comes to the mountain of God to be reminded that Yahweh still has seven thousand in Israel. Our second Micaiah narrative, arising in the time of Isaiah, offers a paradigmatic structure for this same theme, opposing the court of heaven to the court of kings. So sure is Yahweh's control that his purpose will be fulfilled even in the contrary designs of prophets and kings. Aiming to use and control him, these are, in the end, used and controlled by him.

3. "WHO IS FOR YAHWEH?"

The impact of the foregoing discussion is an intensified awareness that biblical prophetism is not constitutionally "anti"-anything. It is only pro-Yahweh and — in the best and deepest sense — pro-Israel. A true prophet will be anti-people when the people forsake covenant ideals. He will be anti-cult when the cult encourages the people to substitute liturgical punctuality for the practical performance of covenant morality. He is anti-king — against the entire political establishment — whenever the king misuses power to the detriment of the nation's best interest. He is anti-prophet when some prophets become confused about their priorities, supporting ulterior aims over the goal of Israel's deepest calling and commitment.

Our study of the prophet legends has shown that prophet opposes prophet only in extremity and only when a given prophet's (or group of prophets') affinities are clearly and radically out of juncture with Yahwism's elemental ideal of radical obedience to divine direction and control. It is important to note the impressive number of prophet legends that are concerned with identifying, validating, and authorizing a particular prophet for speaking and acting on Yahweh's behalf (subgenres 1, 2, 3, 7, 11). This clearly shows that within the primitive prophetic bands, constant testing and questioning was going on. While it is true that much was made of miraculous signs, at its deepest level of meaning such a narrative as that of I Kings 13 depends on the criterion of radical obedience. While no doubt there would have been an appreciable gap in ideology between the old Bethel prophet and the Judahite man of God, coming to denounce the altar at which the former had lifelong performed his fondest religious duties, the Bethel prophet is ultimately concerned to test whether this bold challenger believes strongly enough in the validity of his alarming oracle to carry out in absolute detail the revelatory demands that accompany it. Thus prophet against prophet was, in fact, a contest between relative levels of adherence to the radical theonomy of Yahwistic faith. Narrative B in I Kings 22, distinguishing between Yahweh's purpose and the king's purpose in the instigation of historical event, includes contrary prophetic advice as the instrumentality toward the paradoxical realization of both. Ultimately this legend too is concerned about Yahweh's priority over all earthly power, so that prophets pre-empted by the king are employed by Yahweh as his unsuspecting agents. They meant good for the king, but in speaking it they instigated evil, and thus fulfilled Yahweh's greater design.

What was the prophet's duty toward the cult? First of all, everything that is said about the Israelite cult must be weighed in awareness that biblical prophetism completely avoids the close identification with the cultic apparatus that is so prominent in Mari prophetism. As we study the prophet legends of Israel, we discover that many, and perhaps all, of the early prophetic schools did have close associations with particular shrines. Samuel seems to be associated with Shiloh, later with Ramah; Nathan with Jerusalem; Ahijah with Shiloh; the prophets of I Kings 13 with Bethel; Elisha with Gilgal; Isaiah with Jerusalem. We also observe that the prophet legends have not yet developed the strong anti-cult invective of Amos, Isaiah, and Jeremiah. But one should note also the peripheral nature of cultic concern in the prophet legends. It is surely significant that the two prophet legends which share with the later Micaiah narrative the theme of prophet against prophet, viz., I Kings 13 and I Kings 18:21ff., are focused on certain cultic features or practices.[10] Yet neither story is to be understood as a cult legend.[11] In I Kings 13 the opposition of establishment prophetism toward a charismatic claim, requiring counterchallenge and testing, is resolved when it becomes certain that it is indeed genuine prophecy that confronts the cult of Bethel.[12] In I Kings 18:21ff. the two rival altars represent two rival deities; Elijah's authority to challenge Baal, along with his altar and his four hundred prophets — and accordingly to demand from wavering Israel a clear decision for operative loyalty — is resolved in a dramatic display of Yahweh's power to answer Elijah's prayer, while the Baal-prophets' prayer remains unanswered.

The Bethel prophets did in fact preserve this inimical element of prophetic denunciation against the shrine with which they were associated, thereby showing that they fully accepted their responsibility to superintend Yahweh's cult in Yahweh's name. Amos 7, also placed at Bethel, shows that certain prophets could at times be seduced into cultic conformity, but it also shows why true prophetism must inevitably oppose the arrogance of such a cultic functionary as would dare to say, "This is the king's sanctuary, this is a royal shrine!" (vs. 13)

It is clear then that the most central conflict was the constant polarity between the spiritual power of prophecy, insisting on Yahweh's absolute priority, and the political establishment — theoretically instrumental but ever prone to forsake its status as servant to Yahweh and the people. The basic conflict is always between covenant integrity and political opportunism. Here is another "eternal triangle": God, people, and king. Ancient Greece sought to involve the gods in its perpetual struggle between autocracy and democracy. In ancient Egypt the people had no chance: god and king were virtually identical. Although in Mesopotamia the king merely represented deity, the priestly mediators of revelation could be counted on to side with the king so long as the king sided with them; thus again the people had no chance. In Israel something refreshingly new appeared: god and people in dynamic interaction, together legitimizing the monarchy and maintaining supervision over it. Saul and David knew that they came from the people, but the others soon forgot it. This was an ideal presupposed in Deut. 17's law for the king (vss. 14-20), which required that the king be chosen by Yahweh and that he be no foreigner but a "brother" to his fellow Israelites.

Recalling our detailed observations in Chapter Six, and particularly those at the end of Chapter Five, we identify as our deepest insight regarding the prophet legend collection as a whole that it represents the constant, overriding concern of the entire prophetic movement in its early phases to counteract the threat of political power, ever used to undermine and subvert the authority of prophetism and with it the cherished traditions of primitive Yahwism:

> Already in the time of Saul, the charismatic designation narrative (subgenre 4) of I Sam. 9:1–10:16a was told to demonstrate that secular leaders are dependent on the prophets for a portion of the divine spirit.
>
> Historical demonstration stories like those of I Kings 20 (subgenre 5) show that victory comes not through the scheming and boasting of kings but by God's design.
>
> The succession oracle narratives (subgenre 6) in II Samuel 7, I Kings 11 and 14, insist that Yahweh through his prophets retains the right to define regal succession.
>
> In most of the prophet-authorization narratives (subgenre 7) some specific regal usurpation is rebuffed by a prophet specially empowered to stand against it.
>
> The regal self-judgment narratives (subgenre 8) employ a prophetic oracle functioning either instrumentally (type I) or interpretively (type II) to show that a king's power may become operative in his own undoing.
>
> The superseding oracle narrative (subgenre 9) demonstrates that Yahweh through his prophets retains the prerogative of altering the terms of his former judgments respecting the holders of regal power; if this pertains even to the kings of foreign lands (II Kings 8), how much more to Israel?
>
> The instrumental fulfillment narrative (subgenre 10) shows that Yahweh brings good or evil for kings, but as instruments to his greater design in history.
>
> The word-controversy narrative (subgenre 11) declares that Yahweh controls deceived and deceiving instruments of revelation, employing even these for the undoing of those who would undo him.

Prophet against prophet was only a symptom. The root cause was king against prophet, requiring prophet to oppose king. Our prophet legends record a dynamic struggle to supervise the kingship. These stories do not yet sense the ultimate failure of this struggle, signaled already in the tendency of prophets to fall out with one another. Their failure would accompany the nation's ruin. Israel was too little — and at the same time too unique — to survive in an imperialistic world, competing as one political institution against other, stronger political institutions.

We have been greatly enriched by our careful study of I Kings 22 and the prophet collection of which it is a part. It has offered us an entree to two dramatic scenes. The early Micaiah narrative shows us a moment of portent and symbolic peril: responding to the threat of the first serious foreign irruption, Israel's king is attempting to domesticate the instruments of transcendental revelation, while the prophet who is initially ready to acquiesce in the king's design is overwhelmed by a revelation which will overwhelm the king. The latter Micaiah narrative shows us a moment of increasing frustration and despair. So systematically has prophecy been institutionalized that one prophet now stands ideologically opposed to his fellow prophet. Their mutual antagonism has the detrimental effect of encouraging those who hold political power to decide as they will, making rash and ill-advised alliances with the confidence that some prophet will always support them. The ultimate tragedy is at hand: but I Kings 22 understands that even the evil that arrogant rulers and misguided prophets may conceive cannot occur without Yahweh's will or outside Yahweh's greater design.

He has shown strength with his arm,
He has scattered the proud in the imagination of their hearts,
He has put down the mighty from their thrones,
and exalted those of low degree;
He has filled the hungry with good things,
and the rich he has sent empty away.

(Luke 1:51-53)

NOTES TO CHAPTER EIGHT

1. This claim would have astounded the pioneers of form criticism. On the proper relationship between literary and form criticism, cf. K. Koch, *Growth of the Biblical Tradition*, pp. 68-78.

2. Jer. 31:29; cf. Ezek. 18:2.

3. So A. S. van der Woude, *Micha; De Prediking van het Oude Testament* (Nijkerk, 1976).

4. So already in Amaziah's threat to Amos, 7:12.

5. The penalty of Hananiah, Jer. 28:16f.

6. Compare the less problematical demand of unquestioning respect for the decisions of judges and priests, 17:8-13. Here is a rule for men to live by — but what happens when even judges and priests are corrupt? Though Deuteronomy naively passes this problem by, it becomes a pressing concern for many of Israel's prophets, from Amos (cf. 5:12) to Malachi (cf. 2:7-9).

7. For a structural analysis of Jer. 27–28, see above, pp. 71f.

8. Cf. Ezek. 13:10. In the sequel, Hananiah's symbolic act oracle (Jer. 28:10f.) provokes a countering symbolic act oracle from Jeremiah (vss. 12-14), leading to Jeremiah's warning (vss. 15f.) that Yahweh has not sent Hananiah (*lō' šᵉlaḥᵃkā YHWH)*, and that accordingly Yahweh intends to remove him (*mᵉšallēḥᵃkā*) from the face of the earth, meaning that he was to die that very year. The striking fulfillment validated not only this particular prediction but Jeremiah's message as a whole.

9. The prophets' condemnation of nationalistic policies has been often been distorted into an argument for the separation of the church from politics. How blind and perverse this interpretation is may be judged from the abundant evidence that the prophets were not only involved in politics but claimed the right to supervise it. An instructive example of the importance of honest exegesis may be seen in Karl Elliger's reply drawn from Isaiah 7 to the attempt of National Socialism to isolate the church from politics (*ZAW* 53 [1935], 3-22; cf. *ZAW* 55 [1937], 291ff.).

10. This may suggest an answer to the question whether the Samaria *gōren* was in some sense a cultic site, like those of Nakon and Araunah.

11. *Contra* Alt and Würthwein; cf. *YTT,* p. 228, n. 288.

12. It is important to see that I Kings 13 depicts establishment prophetism challenging the innovator and being won over in the end, while I Kings 22 has an innovator Micaiah challenging establishment prophetism. Even in the closing scene, where Zedekiah strikes and rebukes him, Micaiah has the final, definitive word.

Indexes

1. Subjects

2. Modern Authors

3. Scripture References

Old Testament passages are as in the Hebrew Bible.

Printed in the United States
22442LVS00006B/221